Warren Bennis

A WARREN BENNIS BOOK

This collection of books is devoted exclusively to new and exemplary contributions to management thought and practice. The books in this series are addressed to thoughtful leaders, executives, and managers of all organizations who are struggling with and committed to responsible change. My hope and goal is to spark new intellectual capital by sharing ideas positioned at an angle to conventional thought—in short, to publish books that disturb the present in the service of a better future.

Books in the Warren Bennis Signature Series

The End of Management and the
Rise of Organizational Democracy

Books by Kenneth Cloke and Joan Goldsmith

Thank God It's Monday: Fourteen Values We Need to Humanize the Way We Work
Irwin/McGraw-Hill, 1997

Resolving Conflict at Work: A Complete Guide for Everyone on the Job
Jossey-Bass, 2000

Resolving Personal and Organizational Conflicts: Stories of Transformation and Forgiveness
Jossey-Bass, 2000

Books by Warren Bennis and Joan Goldsmith

Learning to Lead: A Workbook on Becoming a Leader
Addison-Wesley, 1997

Books by Kenneth Cloke

Mediation: Revenge and the Magic of Forgiveness
Center for Dispute Resolution, 1996

Mediating Dangerously: The Frontiers of Conflict Resolution
Jossey-Bass, 2001

The End of Management and the Rise of Organizational Democracy

Kenneth Cloke

Joan Goldsmith

Foreword by Warren Bennis

JOSSEY-BASS
A Wiley Company
www.josseybass.com

Published by

JOSSEY-BASS
A Wiley Company
989 Market Street
San Francisco, CA 94103-1741

www.josseybass.com

Jossey-Bass books and products are available through most bookstores. To contact Jossey-Bass directly, call (888) 378-2537, fax to (800) 605-2665, or visit our website at www.josseybass.com.

Substantial discounts on bulk quantities of Jossey-Bass books are available to corporations, professional associations, and other organizations. For details and discount information, contact the special sales department at Jossey-Bass.

We at Jossey-Bass strive to use the most environmentally sensitive paper stocks available to us. Our publications are printed on acid-free recycled stock whenever possible, and our paper always meets or exceeds minimum GPO and EPA requirements.

Library of Congress Cataloging-in-Publication Data

Cloke, Kenneth, 1941-
   The end of management and the rise of organizational democracy /
Kenneth Cloke, Joan Goldsmith ; foreword by Warren Bennis.— 1st ed.
        p. cm.
"A Warren Bennis book."
Includes index.
      ISBN 0-7879-5912-X (alk. paper)
   1. Organizational change. 2. Employee empowerment.
3. Self-directed work teams. 4. Management—Employee participation.
5. Democracy. I. Goldsmith, Joan. II. Title.
   HD58.8 .C57 2002
   658—dc21

2001006127

FIRST EDITION
HB Printing   10 9 8 7 6 5 4 3 2 1

Contents

This book is dedicated to our fathers, Dick Cloke and Len Goldsmith, two leaders who continue to inspire us with the human values for which they fought and to which they committed their hearts and minds.

Foreword

A distinct and dramatic change is taking place in the philosophy underlying organizational behavior, calling forth a new concept of humanity. This new concept is based on an expanded knowledge of our complex and shifting needs, replacing an oversimplified, innocent, push-button idea of humanity. This philosophical shift calls for a new concept of organizational values based on humanistic-democratic ideals, which replace the depersonalized, mechanistic value system of bureaucracy. With it comes a new concept of power, based on collaboration and reason, replacing a model based on coercion and threat.

The primary cause of this shift in philosophy stems from managers themselves. There is a vast audience of managers who are wistful for an alternative to mechanistic ideas of authority; they long for more authentic human relationships than most organizational practices today allow. Furthermore, I suspect that the desire for relationships in business has little to do with the profit motive. The real push for these changes stems from the need not only to humanize organizations but to use them as crucibles for personal growth and self-realization.

Another aspect of this shift has to do with humanity's historical quest for self-awareness, for using reason to stretch our potential, spreading to large, complex social systems where there has been a dramatic upsurge in the spirit of inquiry. At new depths and over a wider range of affairs, organizations are opening their operations to self-inquiry and self-analysis, which require changes in how people, who make things, regard themselves. These organizations resemble universities and research institutions, filled with bright, self-absorbed, byline-oriented, interesting, highly individualistic knowledge workers, such as professors, journalists, scientists, and information technologists. It is the capacity of leaders to harvest that human capital that makes them succeed or fail. Bill Gates, architect of Microsoft, heralded this shift from leaders' roles in controlling natural resources to harnessing the power of information. He said, "The only factory asset we have is human imagination." We are moving toward not just a knowledge worker society but toward investor workers—people who bring in ideas that really change the world.

I call this new development *organizational revitalization;* it is a complex social process that involves a deliberate and self-conscious examination of organizational behavior. Never before in history, in any society, has humanity in its organizational context so willingly searched, scrutinized, examined, inspected, or contemplated in order to gain meaning, purpose, and improvement. This book is a practical guide to realizing these changes.

Kenneth Cloke and Joan Goldsmith have done more than provide a practical guide for hungry minds seeking out new ways to understand and change our institutional arrangements. They have taken very seriously Alexis de Tocqueville's challenge when he wrote in the first part of the nineteenth century, "I am tempted to believe that what we call necessary institutions are often no more than institutions accustomed. In matters of social constitution, the field of possibilities is much more extensive than men living in their various societies are ready to imagine."

Cloke and Goldsmith have shown the way in this remarkable book. They are our advance scouts, and for that, I extend a deep bow of respect for their courage and wisdom.

Santa Monica, California   WARREN BENNIS
November 2001

Introduction

*Out of all this has come the first clear recognition of an
inescapable fact: we cannot successfully force people to
work for management's objectives. The ancient conception
that people do the work of the world only if they are forced
to do so by threats or intimidation, or by the camouflaged
authoritarian methods of paternalism, has been suffering
from a lingering fatal illness for a quarter of a century.
I venture to guess that it will be dead in another decade.*
DOUGLAS MCGREGOR

More than a decade has come and gone, and rumors of the demise
of authoritarian, paternalistic management appear to have been
greatly exaggerated. Yet the fault lies not with Douglas McGregor,
whose analysis is clear and sound, but with our failure to recognize
the extent of the illness or imagine in detail what organizations
might look like after it is gone.

This book seeks to fill these gaps. It chronicles the principal
reasons for putting an end to management and the key elements
that are needed to create collaborative, democratic, self-managing
organizations. Its premise is that today's corporations, government
agencies, schools, and nonprofits can dramatically improve by empowering those who work inside them to manage themselves and
take responsibility for their own development and performance.

Through a combination of collaboration, self-management, and
organizational democracy, far-reaching changes can take place. Organizations can consistently operate out of a committed context of
values, ethics, and integrity. Rigid boundaries can be broken down
to form organic, evolving webs of association. Linking leaders can
be identified throughout the organization and selected by the people they are expected to lead, as well as by peers, customers, and
shareholders. Employees can learn to manage themselves in small,

collaborative teams in which responsibility and trust are commensurate with empowerment, and every employee is responsible not to their managers but to themselves, their peers, and their customers. Organizations can implement streamlined, open, collaborative processes that reduce bureaucracy and increase trust, create complex self-correcting systems that foster organizational learning, strategically integrate functions across organizational lines, and change the way they change.

Many organizations are already moving in this direction. Ostentatious titles and multilayered hierarchical positions with military-like status are being replaced with playful, freewheeling roles and self-selected titles such as "Chief Poobah," "International Woman of Mystery," and "Make It Happen Master." "Chief Learning Officers" are modeling life-long learning, encouraging creativity, and supporting authentic learning relationships among staff. "Customer Partners" are assisting internal and external customers in developing strategies and solving problems, nurturing collaborative relationships, increasing the quality of services and products, and developing informal, integrated strategic alliances across organizational lines. Peer coaches, process facilitators, and peer mediators are assisting employees in developing skills, building consensus, designing work processes, guiding strategic planning, and resolving conflicts.

Collaboration, self-management, and organizational democracy fundamentally alter not only the way we work but the nature of work itself. Imagine organizations that behave like organisms, policies that are flexible and value driven, procedures that are instantly customizable and responsive to customer needs, goals that are challenges and contests, feedback that is received as a gift and a compliment, and conflicts that create opportunities for growth and learning. Imagine organizations that treat employees as artists and scientists, see complaints as suggestions for improvement, explore problems as objects of curiosity, and base motivation on love and self-actualization. Imagine work as play, communications as stories and metaphors, differences as welcomed, routines as rituals, and change as exploration and adventure.

These are not wild-eyed utopias or dreams. Each exists in part in some successful organizations today. The details and specifics vary from organization to organization, because the end of management is also the end of uniformity—of prescriptions, blueprints, and one-size-fits-all approaches to organizational operations and design.

About This Book

In Part One, we analyze the increasingly antiquated system of management and reveal the organizational dynamics that perpetuate hierarchy, bureaucracy, and autocracy. In Part Two, we identify the practical mechanisms of organizational transformation and the values, structures, systems, processes, and leadership required to transform existing organizations.

We wrote this book as a tool to help build more collaborative, democratic, self-managing organizations. As a result, Part One critiques the most important systemic failures of management and identifies the root systems and structures that engender them. It ends with a transitional chapter summarizing and analyzing these problems. Our purpose in these chapters is to describe the difficulties, not with poor managers or defective managerial practices, but with the system of management itself, so as to reveal its inescapable destructive tendencies. Part Two then offers a broad range of practical proposals for creating the managerial relationship and designing the values, structures, systems, processes, and skills needed for self-management. These chapters provide a vision of what is possible and a wide range of practical methods to realize it.

We have drawn on over thirty years of practical experience with hundreds of organizations, from Fortune 100 companies to government agencies, schools, and nonprofits, as well as international work in over a dozen countries. Our experiences implementing these ideas and supporting employees in successfully managing themselves, together with years of research into the principles of personal and organizational effectiveness, fill these pages.

Our partnership in writing this book reflects the values we espouse. Each of us took risks drafting sections and revising each other's work in an iterative, recursive process. We had to learn self-management, teamwork, how to give and receive feedback, self-reflect, self-correct, and change. We discussed the ideas with each other before each draft and engaged in lengthy collaborative dialogue and conflict resolution when we got stuck. This book is a result of the processes we advocate and is stronger as a result, as are we.

We believe that the strategies we offer will help create a more collaborative organizational future, more viable social relationships, and more sustainable work environments and that they will broaden the range of human potential. It is our intention that you, the reader, understand your power as the *inventor* of your workplace environment, and therefore of yourself, neither of which is set in stone but can be transformed by understanding, teamwork, and creativity.

We invite you to invent forms of organizational life that are not ceaselessly competitive and destructive of human values. We encourage you to design organizations that are shaped by a context of values, ethics, and integrity and to structure them as living, evolving webs of association, operated by self-managing teams and led by linking leaders located ubiquitously throughout the organization. We invite you to create streamlined collaborated processes, grow through complex self-correcting systems, integrate strategically, and improve the way you grow and change.

What Is at Stake

The implications of self-management, collaboration, and organizational democracy extend far beyond enhanced productivity and employee job satisfaction, although these are important arguments in its favor. Political democracy is not simply a technique for making better decisions; it is also a statement of social values, a method of creating community, a recognition of our essential equality, a promise of fairness, an acknowledgment of the value of dissent, and a freedom to be ourselves. Most important, it is a form of ownership and responsibility for solving problems. So it is with self-management and organizational democracy, whose revolutionary implications extend far beyond efficiency to include human satisfaction, self-actualization, and ecological survival.

The world is facing unprecedented global challenges that are simultaneously ecological, economic, social, political, and organizational. There are growing conflicts within corporations between seizing short-term advantage to maximize shareholder profits and building long-term, sustainable growth—not only for employees within these businesses but society and future generations as well.

It is increasingly apparent that ecological, economic, social, and political collaboration is required to make economic activity sustainable over the long term. Without dramatic organizational changes, our economic system may well turn cancerous, destroying even the planet that fuels its seemingly ceaseless demand for growth and competitive advantage.

We invite you to join us in facing this challenge, exploring why organizations are structured so ineffectively and destructively and considering how we can design collaborative, democratic, self-managing alternatives.

Santa Monica, California   KENNETH CLOKE
November 2001   JOAN GOLDSMITH

Part One

Making a Case for the End of Management

Chapter One

The Revolution of Self-Management and Organizational Democracy

Revolution is not revolt. What carried the Resistance for four years was revolt—the complete, obstinate, and at first nearly blind refusal to accept an order that would bring men to their knees. Revolt begins first in the human heart. But there comes a time when revolt spreads from heart to spirit, when a feeling becomes an idea, when impulse leads to concerted action. This is the moment of revolution.
ALBERT CAMUS

Managers are the dinosaurs of our modern organizational ecology. The Age of Management is finally coming to a close. The need for overseers, surrogate parents, scolds, monitors, functionaries, disciplinarians, bureaucrats, and lone implementers is over, while the need for visionaries, leaders, coordinators, coaches, mentors, facilitators, and conflict resolvers is steadily increasing, pressing itself upon us. Yet revolutions begin, as Camus noted, only when feelings are translated into ideas, when heart fuels spirit, and when ideas and spirit combine to spark concerted action.

Nearly unnoticed, a far-reaching organizational transformation has already begun, based on the idea that management as a system fails to open the heart or free the spirit. This revolution is attempting to turn inflexible, static, autocratic, coercive bureaucracies into agile, evolving, democratic, collaborative, self-managing webs of association. These changes are spreading from innovative Internet

3

start-ups to traditional hierarchical corporations, nonprofit organizations, schools, and government agencies. In a recent conversation with Peter Drucker, a founding theorist of management, we
mentioned that we were writing a book about the end of management. His response was, "It's about time!"

Drucker's comment reflects an increasing urgency in the demand for a new organizational order and the frustration many
employees and leaders on all levels feel with pointless layers of hierarchy, egotistical leadership, autocratic decision making, bureaucratic bungling, wasted time and effort, managerial incompetence,
petty micromanagement, and employee resistance to developing
more mature, responsible, collaborative work relationships.

The days of military command structures in which orders were
announced by CEO-generals and barked by midlevel sergeant-
managers to docile private-employees who blindly obeyed them are
over. The organizational standing army is being replaced by highly
motivated guerrilla units—citizens' militias without rank or insig-
nia in which natural leaders build consensus among equally empowered, responsible, self-managing team members. Autocracy,
hierarchy, bureaucracy, and management are gradually being replaced by democracy, heterarchy, collaboration, and self-managing
teams.

Permanent, stockpiled, one-size-fits-all policies are giving way
to innovative, just-in-time, evolving, made-to-order initiatives. Silos
and competitive departments are being deconstructed into living,
evolving webs of association. Specialized, read-only, jealously
guarded data are being supplanted by highly accessible, interactive,
openly available information that nurtures creative and strategic
thinking. Isolated, reluctant, cynical, immature, apathetic employees are being transformed into connected, motivated, value-
driven, responsible employee-owners.

This is not just wishful thinking but a reality in many organizations, where strategic associations of self-managing employee
teams are collaborating as members of complex, matrixed, high-
performance networks. Greater integrity and responsibility, participatory democracy, collaborative negotiation, consensus decision
making, authentic horizontal relationships, ubiquitous leadership, and team self-management are becoming central to everyday
operations.

These innovations are expanding the capacity of organizations to make rapid decisions, serve customers, communicate effectively, and implement change. Many of these modifications have grown out of rapid-fire innovations in information technology, transportation and communications, automated production, global Internet access, neural net programming, robotics, ubiquitous computing, and nanotechnology, while others have developed out of team building, organizational psychology, communications, process mapping, collaborative negotiation, and conflict resolution.

As this revolution is proceeding, the old order is digging in and resisting change. Bill Gates has commented that the advent of modern technology escalates change to "the speed of thought," but it may be more accurate to say that change takes place at the speed of thought *divided* by the coefficient of opposition produced by managerial hierarchy, bureaucracy, and autocracy, *multiplied* by employee resistance.

The command-and-control relationship between managers and employees generates an institutional blindness that blocks, frustrates, and reduces the speed, extent, and effectiveness of change. Tired, ineffective, bloated hierarchies are vigorously protected by their management, which depends on them for survival. Managers are the linchpins holding these obsolete systems in place.

But the problem is far worse. Many employees actually *prefer* being told what to do by autocratic managers and are willing to accept being treated like children in exchange for irresponsibility and reduced stress. They are willing to blindly obey hierarchical authority and keep silent before their superiors in exchange for job security. It is easier by far to be an unthinking drone who obeys orders from above than a self-managing team member who is responsible for results.

While many employees have grown up in hierarchical organizations and become accustomed to external authority, the dead weight of organizational history, the stultifying, heart-breaking experience of most people's work, and the psychological immaturity that are perpetuated by never learning to think or act for oneself, in concert with others, all need changing. Responsibility is a prerequisite for growing up, and not growing up is not an option.

Management is done by someone designated from above and not by employees who actually do the work. Self-management is done by those who do the work and is not imposed externally or practiced in isolation. It is exercised personally and collaboratively, in teams, and in partnership with leaders who give direction, co-ordinate, and facilitate employees in managing themselves.

Peter Drucker has christened management "an integrated discipline of human values and conduct, or social order and intellectual inquiry" and "a liberal art." Yet in our experience, management as a system rarely lives up to this ideal. Drucker's definition, in our minds, more accurately describes leadership. It is leaders who typically engage in intellectual inquiry and support human values and artistic expression, while managers implement orders and check to make sure specifications are met.

The organizational landscape is littered with examples of great ideas held hostage by bureaucratic managers and antiquated hierarchies. Here are some we have witnessed:

- An Internet start-up company with over $20 million at stake from small investors who believed in its innovative product slowly grinds to a halt as a hierarchical CEO and five bureaucratic managers suppress creativity and slow innovation to a crawl.
- An information systems department in a large multinational corporation restructures to self-managing teams, but assigns managers as heads of teams they had not chosen or been chosen by, causing them to micromanage team members and sabotage improved customer service.
- A public university in a low-income community has its efforts to hire more diverse faculty to reflect the racial and ethnic composition of the student body blocked by midlevel managers afraid of losing their traditional power base and fearful of colleagues who did not resemble themselves.
- A mayor trying to reinvent local government and eliminate traditional turf-based structures in city government is undermined by managers who could not shift to serving constituents directly, leading to increased city council resistance and public suspicion of his motives.
- An innovative nonprofit organization devoted to assisting young artists, with a staff of six, is stifled by five levels of hierarchy, blocking innovation, diffusing responsibility, and preventing change.

These examples of the suffocating, stultifying effects of hierarchical, bureaucratic, autocratic management can be multiplied a thousand-fold. Everyone who has been managed, as opposed to being led, has stories to tell about lost opportunities and wasted efforts that continue being told every day. It is long past time for change. Waste, resistance, and delay become intolerable once we recognize that we have the knowledge and capacity to design organizations not only to operate efficiently, but to enhance human development as well.

Challenges to the Old Order

The ever-extending reach of globalization, continuously rising productivity, growing complexity of information, expanded sensitivity of the environment, and swelling pace of technological innovation are all increasing the demand for alternative organizational practices. The equally speedy rise in employee expectations and competition for closer customer-client-citizen partnerships mean a massive metamorphosis in the way we work.

These challenges create opportunities for systemic improvement not only in organizational structures, products, systems, and processes, but the entire economic, social, political, psychological, and relational framework within which we have thought about and organized our work. In confronting these challenges, we inevitably face the fact that they force us also to transform ourselves as producers. In doing so, we discover that we can consciously improve our human nature and transform the purpose of socially productive work, on which all our social, political, and economic structures are based. While our workplaces and organizations are changing, so is the very landscape or stage on which these changes are taking place.

These recent innovations in technology, organizational thinking, and human capacity are sweeping, deep, and profound. Yet they are being held back, frustrated, and resisted—not so much by individual managers as by the system and the institution of management itself. Management and managerial thinking increasingly are becoming obstacles to the emergence of a future that is straining to be born.

There are countless examples of managerial resistance to innovation. Here is one. In a large entertainment industry organization, the leader of an operations unit came up with a sweeping plan to increase the quality of customer service delivered by his department. He met with middle managers to share his plan and ask them to communicate it to staff who directly interacted with customers. Not only did his direct reports communicate in clumsy, half-hearted, inconsistent ways, they failed to give clear directions or assign responsibilities for results. Staff with direct responsibility for customer service were resentful that they had not been consulted or asked for their ideas beforehand and consequently interpreted his message as a criticism of their work. Because middle managers had no direct relationship with customers, they were unable to lead or participate in problem solving with staff, and everyone went off in separate directions, leading to a decline in customer service.

Six months later, we were asked to help the organization address this failure. In a meeting with the division as a whole, employees were asked to communicate their thoughts about how to solve the problem. At first, they were reluctant to speak in front of their managers, but in the safety of small groups, they put forth several proposals, which they integrated into a single plan to reorganize the entire division. Their plan involved moving every manager into a direct service delivery role and creating a new structure in which the entire staff was organized into self-managing customer-oriented teams.

Their proposal was so bold and convincing that it was clear that nothing would change in customer service if they did not implement it. After a lengthy process of debate, dialogue, and conflict resolution, they overcame the determined resistance of managers who felt they were being demoted, and the proposal was approved by leadership and brought to life by employees. There was no downsizing of managers, who were assigned to new, challenging, and ultimately more satisfying positions working directly with customers and teams.

Because employees participated fully in the process, they felt highly motivated and responsible. Teams were trained in consensus and collaborative processes and were empowered to immediately implement solutions to the problems they faced. Once managers had direct experiences with customers and staff were given adequate trust, authority, and responsibility for producing results, they identified a number of successful ideas for improving customer service. Their solutions began with a simple idea: asking customers what they wanted. This seems like an obvious solution, yet none of the managers had wanted to hear from the customers because they were afraid the messages would make them look bad to their superiors, increase their workload, and reduce their chances of promotion.

The survey revealed that their customers wanted a centralized help desk to respond quickly to complaints. A cross-functional team was organized to design and implement one. Empowered staff were given authority to solve customer problems directly or enlist the services of others and provide "one stop shopping" for customers, who no longer had to wade through layers of bureaucracy to solve their problems. Results included improved customer satisfaction, elevated morale, and substantial savings by removing unnecessary layers of management.

Let's Start with What We Know

The word *management* has many meanings. In one sense, it means simply to administer or handle, as one might manage a business, checkbook, or household. In another, it means to cope or respond to situations, as in "I'm managing well under the circumstances." In another, it means to control or direct others, causing them to submit to someone else's will. It is the desirability of this last meaning that we question.

Our friend Heinz von Foerster, a pioneer in the field of cybernetics, points out that the word *manager* refers to the hands and has the same root as *manacle* or *handcuff.* In this context, managers are the frontline, hands-on enforcers of control, regularity, formality, systems and structures, rules, policies and procedures—each trying to fit round human beings into square organizational holes. There are five basic forms of management:

- Crisis management, oriented simply to survival.
- Administration, oriented to maintaining the status quo.
- Management by objectives or goals, oriented to achieving specific, predetermined results in the near future.
- Strategic management, oriented to vision and achieving long-term organizational advantage.

- Integrated, value-based leadership, oriented to collaborative relationships, strategic integration, process improvement, and self-management based on responsibility and consensus. This is the point at which management turns into leadership.

Each of these forms creates a fundamentally different relationship between managers or leaders and the people they manage or lead. Crisis management and administration merely reinforce the status quo. Although goal-oriented and strategic management focus on the future, they represent the beginning of the end of management and the rise of self-managing organizations. The reasons can be found in what we already know about management based on personal experience.

We all know what it feels like to be told how to do something by someone else, particularly when that person does not do it every day. This is not a problem of ineffective individuals but of management as a system. Whenever someone in a superior position gives us orders, our natural responses are either:

- Blind, robotic obedience, not caring whether it is done well
- Unspoken, passive-aggressive resistance, or what employees sometimes call "public compliance and private defiance"
- Hostility, opposition, and rebellion

Through years of experience, employees learn that it is safer to suppress their innate capacity to solve problems and wait instead for commands from above. They lose their initiative and ability to see how things can be improved. They learn not to care and to accept things the way they are. They justify making mistakes and are allowed to be irresponsible and pass the blame to others for their mistakes. They become mindlessly obedient, fatalistic, intransigent, and hostile. Yet in spite of the obvious limitations created by these responses, managers continue giving orders rather than helping employees learn for themselves what needs to be done and how and when to do it best.

Research confirms this experience. Management researcher Paul C. Nutt wrote in the *Journal of Management Studies* that management actually wastes the time of organizations. Of 376 business managers studied, only 8 percent made decisions by establishing standards and measuring performance against them. Only 16 percent had subordinates participate in decision making. By contrast, 40 percent issued edicts, which resulted in *37 percent* of their decisions never being implemented.

We all know from experience that genuine responsibility and motivation are internal within each individual and grow as a result of training, understanding, leadership, support, and self-discipline. Yet management routinely suppresses the initiative and downplays the creative ideas of employees, imposing external responsibility and infantilizing and humiliating the very people they ought to be leading, supporting, and encouraging to act as adults.

We know that innovation and creative problem solving are stimulated by teamwork, dialogue, experimentation, play, and curiosity and weakened by working in isolation, listening to lectures, performing boring tasks, and engaging in routine and rote memorization. Yet management continues to dictate rigid expectations and requirements to passive employees rather than facilitate their learning or empower their imagination.

Research at the University of California at Berkeley regarding key insights that led to successful scientific discoveries found in interviews with scientists that the main activity that seemed to influence successful results was play. The more these scientists were able to enjoy light, seemingly off-purpose games and activities while engaged in research, the greater were their successes and breakthrough discoveries. Yet play in many organizations is considered immature at best and undisciplined at worst.

We know from experience that organizations can be brought to their knees by working to rule and doing things by the book and that new insights, flexibility, innovation, agility, and imagination lie in the uncontrolled, irregular, informal, unstructured aspects of our endeavors. Many studies of human creativity have shown that it is diminished by rigid instructions, disapproval by peers, and negative reinforcement by authority figures. Yet managers continue to write bureaucratic rules and rigidly enforce them. In the process, they block employee innovation, self-management, growth, and problem solving.

We know that formal, disapproving, disrespectful styles of communication, adversarial styles of negotiation, and avoidant, unilateral approaches to problem solving produce unnecessary conflicts, diminished morale, and reduced productivity. Yet organizations continue to allow autocratic managers to use these styles, delaying work and costing organizations prohibitive sums in salaries, training newly hired employees, lawsuits, and attorneys' fees.

A survey by the American Management Association found that managers on average devote upwards of 25 percent of their work time to resolving employee conflicts. We actually rate this percentage much higher, particularly where management acts autocratically and when subtle, low-level conflicts are included. If we multiply this ratio by the average manager's salary, the enormity of the waste of unresolved conflict becomes immediately apparent.

Researcher Richard C. Whiteley has identified the hidden costs of replacing employees, many of whom leave as a result of conflicts caused by poor management practices. Their replacement has a number of costs, including:

- Lost time invested in training employees who leave
- Lost wages or salaries paid to departing employees while new employees are being trained
- Loss of knowledge possessed by departing employees
- Lost opportunities and clients and customer dissatisfaction while positions remain unfilled
- Lost productivity and morale experienced when employees leave
- Recruiting costs and fees involved in finding replacements
- Time interviewing candidates and training new employees
- Wages or salaries paid to new employees during training and before they know how to do the job
- Supervising new employees until they know how to do the job
- Losses due to mistakes by new employees and disruptions of transition

We know from personal experience that teams perform tasks better, produce higher-quality products, and experience greater satisfaction than individuals working in isolation. Nonetheless, managers persist in assigning tasks to individuals, training single performers rather than teams, providing inadequate support for collaboration, and undermining efforts at teamwork, which they see as threats to their power, prestige, and authority. As a result, organizations experience unfathomable losses in productivity, creativity, quality, and morale.

In a classic study of team effectiveness conducted by Richard L. Moreland of the University of Pittsburgh, the following results were reported:

> Experimenters trained volunteers to assemble transistor radios from 60 separate parts on their own or in three-person groups. About a week later, groups of three attempted to put together a radio. The groups whose members had trained together recalled more about the assembly procedure and produced better-quality radios than groups whose members had trained separately (as is often the case for workplace teams organized to perform specific tasks). Moreover, group training led to greater specialization by each member in distinct assembly tasks, more fluid coordination of the assembly process, and increased trust among group members in one another's knowledge about radio assembly.

We know from experience that managers who are titled "leaders" are often not leaders at all but simply have the authority to order other people around. Real leaders are chosen by their followers out of respect for their abilities and are not necessarily the same as those selected for promotion by upper management. Yet managers continue to be picked by those above and imposed on those below without their consent or approval.

Numerous research studies have shown that natural leadership is present in every group and that natural leaders are rarely synonymous with those who have been designated from above. An interesting study by the Andersen Consulting Group's Institute for Strategic Change found that the cumulative stock price of companies that were perceived as being well led grew *900 percent* over a ten-year period, as compared to only 74 percent in companies that were perceived as lacking in effective leadership. Yet managers continue to be selected from above without input from below, while natural leadership is suppressed or ignored.

We know that work gives increased satisfaction when others find it important or useful. Yet management spends little time showcasing or advertising the work of subordinates, publicly commending it, or even acknowledging their efforts. Often they try to claim credit for it themselves, or publicly advertise themselves as supportive of others while privately promoting themselves. Many managers believe their role is to let those beneath them know where, when, and how they missed the mark and criticize their efforts as inadequate.

Many studies of motivation reveal the power of positive recognition, gratitude, and acknowledgment in achieving results. A recent summary of research in *Scientific American* showed sales improving when customers were positively acknowledged. Self-esteem and self-confidence improved the ability to work creatively, because self-images were based on the perceptions of others. Yet managers continue to give employees disapproving, judgmental feedback that reinforces their impression that they cannot improve.

We know that personal relationships are far more important as motivators than individual wealth and that people skills count for more in making organizations run than technical expertise or the lure of profits and stock options. Yet managers continue to be promoted based on technical qualifications, and to pay more attention to hierarchical authority and financial bottom lines than to the human relationships required to produce them.

Investigations into the tragic accident of the space shuttle *Challenger* revealed that defective O-rings, a key element in lift-off technology, were substandard. Staff reported knowing the parts might not hold up under even mildly adverse weather conditions but were afraid to speak out and reveal their mistakes. Because they were fearful of their managers and reluctant to take responsibility and admit their mistakes, disaster ensued.

We know that democracy produces better results than autocracy and is humanly important, even if it is sometimes less efficient. In politics, democracy not only reduces popular resistance to autocratic government; it creates better decisions in the long run because it relies on a diversity of inputs. Yet management continues, with few exceptions, to manage autocratically, using superior power to achieve results, even against the wishes of an overwhelming majority.

For example, a recent airplane crash was caused in part by the insensitive, autocratic style of a manager who insisted on controlling staff and preventing machinists from performing repairs they deemed essential. The manager ostensibly was trying to save the company money. Yet many managers resist asking employees what they think, or listening to their suggestions or complaints, or allowing them to participate in what they consider to be management decisions.

In short, we know that self-managing employees working in collaborative, democratic, self-managing organizations produce superior results to those produced in organizations that are coercive, autocratic, and managed by others. We pay an unimaginable organizational, not to mention human, social, political, and economic, price for ignoring what we already know.

The Self-Reinforcing System of Management

If these problems were merely the fault of individual managers, we might focus on improving the exceptions and consider how to conduct trainings that would encourage better managerial behaviors. The problem, however, is with the rule rather than the exceptions. Management is a system, and like all systems, it is self-referential, self-perpetuating, self-reinforcing, and self-fulfilling. To change it, we need to understand its systemic complexity and self-reinforcing symmetry.

Management is not merely a role; it is a relationship that consists of two parts: managers who control employees and employees who need to be controlled. The dynamics between these two create the system, justify its continuation, and complete the circle. If we want to break this cycle, both have to be transformed more or less simultaneously. While managers need to relinquish the luxury of prestige, power, and exclusive responsibility, employees need to surrender the luxury of anonymity, powerlessness, and individual irresponsibility.

Mary Parker Follett, a pioneer in democratic management and conflict resolution, wrote in 1925:

> I do not think that power can be delegated because I believe that genuine power is capacity. To confer power on the workers may be an empty gesture. The main problem of the workers is by no means how much control they can wrest from capital or management, often as we hear that stated; that would be merely nominal authority and would slip quickly from their grasp! Their problem is how much power they can grow. The matter of workers' control which

is so often thought of as a matter of how much the manager will be willing to give up, is really as much a matter for the workers, how much they will be able to assume; where the managers come in is that they should give the workers a chance to grow capacity or power for themselves.

When employees are not given opportunities to develop and act responsibly, they are infantilized and stripped of initiative, and lose their capacity for self-management. The inability of employees to insist on responsibly managing themselves creates a justification for managers to do so in their stead.

In one organization that eliminated middle managers and empowered teams to manage product manufacturing, opponents of change included nearly equal numbers of managers who loved giving directions and judging results and employees who loved being told what to do and how to do it. Managers resisted reassignment to teams and could not see the opportunities created by direct participation in the manufacturing process, while employees felt unprotected, insecure, and fearful of making mistakes. The leader who announced these changes without taking time to reduce resistance cancelled the project in frustration and returned to the status quo, causing production to plummet. After considerable financial losses, she returned to her original plan, and with outside help, strategically worked through both sides' resistance.

In most organizations, considerable employee energy is spent ignoring, resisting, or bypassing managers, suffering for their mistakes, or feeling compelled by management to work under conditions that drastically reduce their productivity, motivation, and morale. In the process, these organizations often fail to realize that the problems they face have a common source. They are not isolated but chronic, not temporary but permanent, not occasional but systemic, not *by* management but *of* it.

We dispute the assumption that management is a fact of life that will always be with us. We challenge the premise that the problems created by management are isolated and occasional, have to be tolerated, or are the employee's fault or management's incompetence and can be fixed with more, better, higher levels of management or greater employee compliance. We see the glitches in work life not as isolated problems or the fault of individual managers or outmoded management practices, but as inevitable by-products of the system of management itself. We question the organizational structures, systems, and practices that separate employees from responsibility, decision making, intuition, and ownership.

From Management to Leadership and Self-Management

Traditional corporations rely on multiple layers of management to guarantee that productivity targets will be achieved, bottom lines will be met, and profits will be made for investors. Managers are often directed, explicitly and implicitly, to get employees to work in ways that maximize short-term profits at the expense of health, safety, morale, ecology, and job satisfaction, or even skirt the edges of the law. In doing so, these organizations indirectly support the assumption of many managers that external discipline and formal rules are essential to keep employees in line, thereby requiring managers to become the enforcers, watchdogs, police officers, overseers, and parents of unruly, irresponsible, disobedient children.

Again, our objections are not directed at managers as individuals but at the idea that it is necessary to manage the work of people who are capable, with leadership, support and a team environment, of responsibly managing themselves. All forms of managing other people's work hinder their responsibility, creativity, flexibility, responsiveness, effectiveness, and growth, even in small, subtle ways. They prevent employees from being deeply connected and passionate about their work and keep them in a state of childlike dependence.

Let us be clear. We are not arguing for a new terminology to describe old managerial practices. Some organizations rename managers "team captains," "coordinators," "business analysts," and other innovative titles, but new bottles do not alter old wine. We contest the assumption that a class of people other than leaders, facilitators, coaches, mentors, coordinators, and self-managing team members is needed to make organizations successful. We disagree that managers are essential to the work process, that we need them to get employees to work responsibly, and that it is impossible to solve problems or get anything done without them.

A chief financial officer at a Fortune 100 corporation who re-duced the ranks of middle management and formed self-managing teams learned this important lesson. His CEO passively accepted these changes but did not actively support them, and everyone was skeptical about whether he would succeed. Over a three-year process, he transformed his organization and altered the behaviors of middle managers and employees. Subsequently, he discovered he had prostate cancer. While he was away for two months following an op-eration, he discovered that he could trust the teams to make critical financial and strategic decisions successfully without his daily in-volvement. In his absence, they demonstrated they could improve their effectiveness and experience immense job satisfaction by per-forming without managers standing over them.

Again, let us be clear. Every organization requires administra-tion, coordination, facilitation, and leadership. Administration and coordination can be accomplished through advanced technology, automated processes, and self-managing employee teams. By con-trast, leadership and facilitation cannot by computerized, and the demand for these roles is steadily increasing. The qualities of lead-ership that are required by collaborative, democratic, self-managing organizations go far beyond what most managers are trained to do and include these characteristics:

- Visionary leadership: Inspiring values that are honored not just in the breach but every day—providing direction for the future and articulating big-picture organizational goals
- Principled leadership: Motivating employees to act on the basis of what is best not only for shareholders and executives but for coworkers, society, environment, and themselves
- Empowering leadership: Supporting responsible self-managing teams and helping employees develop the capacity to help themselves
- Facilitative leadership: Eliciting participation and assisting everyone in the organization to work together and act as one
- Collaborative leadership: Building high-performance relation-ships and mutual trust

In self-managing organizations, as managers are increasingly replaced by leaders, facilitators, coordinators, and self-managing team members, a complementary set of cascading transformations happens at the same time. A new synthesis of organizational systems and relationships transforms structures, systems, and processes that support hierarchy into those that support heterarchy, requiring them to shift from notification to consensus, blaming to problem solving, and competition to collaboration.

These changes transmute formal, rigid, tightly structured, linear organizations into informal, agile, loosely structured, creative webs of association, teams, and partnerships. The structures, systems, roles, styles, behaviors, and assumptions that organizations have used successfully for centuries will not allow them to evolve to this next phase of development. To understand why, it is important to briefly review the historical circumstances that created this evolutionary impasse.

Chapter Two

A Brief History
of Management

*This is how one pictures the angel of history. His face
is turned toward the past. Where we perceive a chain of
events, he sees one single catastrophe which keeps piling
wreckage and hurls it in front of his feet. The angel would
like to stay, awaken the dead, and make whole what has
been smashed, but a storm is blowing in from paradise. It
has got caught in its wings with such a violence that the
angel can no longer close them. The storm irresistibly
propels him into the future to which his back is turned,
while the pile of debris before him grows skyward. . . .
The storm is what we call progress.*
WALTER BENJAMIN, in
Benjamin: Philosophy, History, Aesthetics

The study of history is not for those who have chosen to repeat it
but for those who seek to interrupt its retrograde tendencies and
encourage it to spiral around a center of higher human values. Before moving forward into analysis and prescription regarding organizational design, it is useful to look backward, like Benjamin's
angel of history, to locate the strategic decisions, identify the transcendent ideas, and discover how to disarm the capacity of the past
to plot our present and future direction.

When we consider where, when, and why management began,
how it evolved over centuries and shaped the organizations that
house and reproduce it, we will more easily understand how management *as a system* is dysfunctional, and in the process we will learn

how to halt the repetitive behaviors that daily recreate it. By studying the origins of management structures, systems, processes, and roles, we reveal their cryptic hidden meanings and make rational what may otherwise appear confusing, mystical, or unchanging.

History is largely invisible to those who live it. By blindly living it, the strategies and roles that made perfect sense in previous periods get repeated out of habit, fear, or the dead weight of tradition. By making history explicit and presenting it not as fact but as interpretation through the lens of the present, it becomes possible to rethink the way events are understood, organized, and enacted and to make choices.

Through history, we become conscious of our organizational inheritance and able to select what we need or want to create according to our nature and vision of the future. What follows is our selection from the infinite number of facts of the past those that can clarify the roles currently played by management, help us understand how the present came to be, and allow us to imagine an altogether different future.

Slavery and the Birth of Management

Management emerged as a profession as a direct consequence of the rise of slavery. Wherever management appeared, its rise was linked with slavery and the use of compulsory agricultural labor. As the numbers of slaves and indentured servants increased, owners created a privileged class of overseers drawn from the ranks of slaves to control them and to make certain they worked hard or did not run away. Managers were widely used in the first Babylonian Empire and were referenced in Hammurabi's code of laws. Key elements in the modern system of management can be found in early Egypt, Greece, and Rome, where it rapidly became an expedient in the organization of obligatory work.

Managers became increasingly indispensable as slave plantations grew in size, empires expanded, and captured peoples were pressed into military and domestic service. They encouraged the expansion of slavery by disciplining and controlling the workforce, often on behalf of absent owners, and were needed to combat the slaves' lack of motivation to work hard, take responsibility for safeguarding the owner's property, or protect the power and status of slave owners against their far more numerous slaves. Owners had to hire managers because without their vigilant oversight, no one would have chosen to remain a slave or voluntarily submit to arduous labor simply in order to magnify their owner's profit.

Aristotle made reference to the need for men to be managers not only in agriculture to control slaves, but also in households to control women, children, domestic servants, and animals. For Athenian democracy to have eliminated management would have spelled the end of slavery, the loss of slaveholder wealth, power, and status, and reduced time for artistic and philosophical pursuits.

Along with slavery came not only a need for managers but a steady decline in the motivation and loyalty of slaves. Slaves became increasingly alienated, as periodic revolts, such as the one led by Spartacus, reveal. At no time in history have slaves been successfully motivated to work hard for their masters other than through fear, brutality, dreams of upward mobility, or identification with their owners. Yet they rarely identified with the products of their labor or the process of producing it and routinely shunned responsibility for protecting their master's property.

For these reasons, as we read in ancient narratives, slaves were often hated, feared and demeaned by their managers, and vice versa. A slave was considered a thing to be manipulated, a tool to be handled, an ox to be yoked, a disobedient child to be punished. This attitude, though diminished, is alive and well in many organizations today. From this perspective, the very existence of the system of management can be seen as an expression of the continuation of involuntary work and partial enslavement.

From these beginnings, it is clear that the fundamental assumptions on which managerial roles are based were deeply and irremediably flawed from the outset. At its roots, management became inseparable from coercion, inequality, and domination over productivity and skill by ownership and power. Without these, there would be little need for management, and to end the system of management, it is necessary to end these as well.

From Slavery to Serfdom

As the Roman Empire fell into decline, slavery began to evolve into serfdom, which allowed slaves a greater degree of freedom to manage their labor. Serfs, or villeins, were required to work the lord's land but were permitted some independence in exchange for services and products. Instead of being bound to the person of their owner, slaves were bound to the land and the lord who owned it.

Serfs in France, for example, were obligated to perform manual work for their lord, generally three days each week; pay taxes and fees for the use of the lord's land; bequeath to the lord their best work animals; pay a sum if their daughter married outside the manor; perform military service from six to eight years; and tithe a tenth of their income to the church. Prior to the French Revolution, it has been estimated that as much as 81 percent of the average serf's income went to the lord or the church.

No longer obligated to pay for the upkeep of slaves, feudal lords were able to transfer that responsibility to their serfs and reap a higher profit. To enforce these duties, lords appointed managers in the form of stewards, bailiffs, and reeves, backed up by knights, squires, men-at-arms, and watchmen. These feudal managers tracked and enforced the fulfillment of every obligation, supervised work on the lord's lands, collected rents and taxes, enforced obedience, and suppressed rebellion and dissent.

These responsibilities required labor supervisors for field hands and auditor-managers to collect taxes, keep ledgers, and develop accounting methods, leading to the growth of feudal bureaucracy. In addition to bookkeeping, feudal managers had the right to discipline serfs physically and administer punishments and fines.

Managerial roles also steadily increased within military ranks, as fixed armies replaced citizens' militias and people were involuntarily pressed into military service. Sergeant-managers were used to supervise the lower ranks and coerce military obedience from Europe to Asia and the Mayan and Incan civilizations of the new world.

Following the Black Death and loss of over a third of the workforce, serfs were prevented in several European countries from leaving their places of employment under compulsion of law. The Statute of Labourers in England, for example, made it a crime for serfs to leave the land to which they were entailed without their lord's express permission. In this way, managers came to play the role of jailer, while many serfs became prisoners under "manor arrest."

The passage from slavery to serfdom gave workers limited new freedoms and minor rights to direct or control their work. They still had little experience with simple rights such as freedom of speech, religion, and association, equality or electoral franchise, let alone self-management. With the gradual rise of a money economy, due partly to expansion in trade and technological innovations that improved productivity and reduced transportation time, came the demise of feudal tenure, the rise of commercial centers in cities, and the development of a capitalist model of management in the form of the factory system.

The Dickensian Factory

As productivity and craft specialization increased with the rise of feudal city-states, so did internal and external trade and the initially unmanaged tasks of mercantile exchange. These exchanges led slowly but directly from skilled craftsmen who sold their products in local markets, to merchant traders who bought and sold surpluses in distant markets, to capitalists who produced commodities for sale in markets locally and internationally.

Skilled craftsmen and feudal traders did not initially require dedicated managers, but the need for administration, coordination, and oversight increased as their activities expanded and became more integrated and successful. With the rise of capitalism, wage labor, the factory system, and market-oriented production, the scale, complexity, and profitability of work mushroomed, making management cost-effective and essential.

Consider, for example, a craft such as shoemaking. Under feudalism, a single skilled shoemaker worked out of his home to satisfy the needs of a small, relatively stable population, performing other subsistence tasks as well. With increasing population and demand, he was able to concentrate, specialize, and develop his craft. He could travel or send a seller to distant markets in search of higher prices. These traders became professionals, touring local communities and buying items for trade elsewhere. This provided a regular source of demand and increased income for shoemakers, compensating for times when local demand was weak.

For traders, however, trips to and from local shoemakers extended the time required to get their goods to market, increased costs, decreased the ability to compete with shoes produced locally, and reduced profits. Once the shoemaker became dependent on the trader to purchase shoes made for distant consumers, he could not refuse when the trader required that his shoes be delivered to a central location. From there, it was a short step to moving the entire operation to a factory, reducing the costs of production through assembly line organization and machine tools and lowering wages and costs through managerially controlled production.

In the process, skilled craftsmen who owned their tools were reduced to unskilled employees working for a merchant-capitalist who owned the machinery, factories, and raw materials required to mass-produce shoes at competitive prices. The capitalist had a natural interest in intensifying the work process, lengthening the workday, reducing the time required to create craftsmanship quality, and keeping wages and raw materials prices down so as to lower costs, succeed against competitors, and turn a profit for investors. In miniature, this is how industrial capitalism began. With it came a degradation in the lives of employees and a demand for managers to get them to work at maximum efficiency.

Although the factory system of the seventeenth, eighteenth, and nineteenth centuries freed serfs from feudal tenure, it required brutal work even from small children for twelve to sixteen hours a day, six days a week. There were no legal protections against management abuses, and employees had no right to organize collectively to improve their working conditions. Those who did so were spied on, fired, beaten, prevented from finding new jobs, and arrested. For this reason, indentured servants formed a large percentage of those who left Europe for the American colonies seeking new opportunities.

Like the slaves and serfs who preceded them, early factory workers had no right to manage their own labor, have their grievances heard, or keep their jobs if they became sick or pregnant or wanted time off. They were not compensated for workplace injuries or permitted to retire. The legal system forged by feudal aristocrats and factory owners permitted managers, for example under the Statute of Labourers, to terminate employees at will, for "a good reason, a bad reason, or no reason at all." Managers enforced factory discipline, and weeded out potential trouble makers. Alexis de Tocqueville, observing this process during a trip from France to the United States in the early nineteenth century, commented:

When a workman is unceasingly and exclusively engaged in the fabrication of one thing, he ultimately does his work with singular dexterity; but, at the same time, he loses the general faculty of applying his mind to the direction of the work. He every day becomes more adroit and less industrious; so that it may be said of him, that, in proportion as the workman improves, the man is degraded.

In reaction, militant labor battles repeatedly brought production to a standstill. These battles in the late nineteenth and early twentieth centuries were often brutally repressed. In reaction, powerful labor unions were organized to halt strikebreaking, resulting in a new use for managers as substitute workers and strikebreakers. In the United States from Coeur d'Alene to Homestead, Pullman, and the Great Steel Strike of 1919, unions used strikes to win support for workers' rights and reduce the power of owners, while robber baron companies used managers to control, punish, and defeat them. Strikes often succeeded where employers were unable to find strikebreakers who could replace skilled craftsmen, or when managers were unable to perform the complex, multidimensional tasks jealously defended by craft unions. These conditions led to "scientific management" as a way of reducing the power of skilled organized labor.

Taylorism and Scientific Management

Frederick Winslow Taylor, the founder of modern management, was the leading promoter of the idea that managers should design and control the work process scientifically in order to guarantee maximum efficiency. Taylor's central idea, presented in his book *Principles of Scientific Management,* was that time and motion studies could maximize the efficiency of work by eliminating unnecessary or duplicative steps, reducing what he considered laziness and featherbedding by labor.

Taylor advocated creating multiple layers of management to supervise the work process so that productivity targets were met. He believed in controlling the workforce rigidly and the work process in minute detail. His idea was openly and explicitly to stop skilled employees from making decisions about and controlling the work process. Taylorism was a way of reducing the power of organized labor and getting extra work out of employees without increasing their wages.

Taylor argued that "scientific management makes collective bargaining and trade unionism unnecessary" because it substitutes external managerial authority and discipline for employee self-management. He advocated isolating individuals from teams, transferring control over the work process to managers, breaking each task down into a sequence of precisely timed components, and paying workers only for the products they produced.

Taylor recommended that managers specify the precise way each task and body movement was to be executed by each worker. Industrial managers coerced workers into accepting these instructions and trained them by rote and drill to do exactly as they were told. In Taylor's model, managers did all the thinking, planning; and directing; workers did only prescribed hands-on implementing.

Scientific management coincided with a dramatic rise in mass production for an urban consumer market, technical improvements in assembly lines, and an enormous increase in immigration that provided a seemingly unending supply of unskilled, low-paid, nonunionized labor. With increasing prosperity, wages could be lifted, leading many "bread and butter" unions to accept Taylor's ideas in exchange for higher pay. It seemed possible to many to apply the principles of scientific efficiency to every aspect of production.

Taylor's theories justified managerial control over the production process and removed decision making from employees and from owners as well. The increasingly authoritative operational role of management diminished the direct involvement of owners in day-to-day decision making. Managers saw this as an opportunity to solidify their power and adopted Taylor's ideas wholesale. In the process, they affirmed efficiency over collaboration, quantity over quality, and cost controls over customer service.

Taylor's voice did not go unchallenged. Industrial engineer Henry Gantt wrote in the same period advocating that workers be allowed to ignore managerial instructions and improve the work process in their own ways. "Whatever we do," he wrote, "must be in accord with human nature. We cannot drive people; we must direct their development." Gantt believed in rewarding learning with gain-sharing, and argued that autocratic management threatened democracy. Mary Parker Follett also advocated increasing employee self-management:

> The first disadvantage [of giving orders] is that we lose what we might learn from the man actually on the job if we do not invite his co-operation in deciding what the rules of the task shall be. . . . The arbitrary command ignores one of the most fundamental facts of human nature, namely, the wish to govern one's own life. . . . Probably more industrial trouble has been caused by the manner in which orders have been given than in any other way. . . . If a worker is asked to do something in a way which he thinks is not the best way, he will often lose all interest in the result, he will be sure beforehand that his work is going to turn out badly. . . . It is one of the things we should be most careful about—never to interfere with the workers' pride in his work.

Follett was a member of the Taylor Society and agreed that production had to be more efficient, but she disagreed with the strict division of labor, external controls, and managerial supervision of every task.

Managing During the Depression and World War II

The need for managers grew exponentially during the early twentieth century with the growth of international markets, semi-monopolies, Taylor's scientific methods, deskilled assembly lines, improvements in technology, reduced time required for long-distance transportation and communication, and large-scale, integrated industrial factories. Nonetheless, in 1929, the economy collapsed, placing large numbers of employees and managers out of work.

The Great Depression made it clear that private industry and market principles alone could not solve the economic crisis and that government intervention was needed to encourage a more humane, respectful, socially constructive approach to factory management. In order to protect employee rights against the arbitrary power of owners and managers, the system now known as labor-management relations was created. Through the legislative process, government assumed an active role in regulating work life in the interest of fairness to employees and consumers and providing work that private industry was unable to offer.

Through the Works Progress Administration, Social Security Administration, National Labor Relations Board, and similar federal and state agencies, the ancient prerogatives of management to control the workplace were systematically eroded, and objective legal standards were put in their place. For nearly the first time in history, it became illegal to fire employees for organizing a union, grieving over working conditions, or bargaining collectively to improve their pay. Workers' compensation, wage and hour legislation, and similar laws allowed government to intervene in private industry and force managers to meet with employee representatives rather than unilaterally impose their will.

At the end of World War II, the Taft-Hartley Act withdrew government from active support for the rights of labor, yet the practice of curbing harmful managerial practices continued. It became accepted that employees were entitled to elemental standards of dignity and respect, to be free from flagrant forms of harassment and discrimination, and that government was needed to protect employee rights from managerial incursion. Managers were gradually banned from discriminating on the basis of union affiliation, race, sex, color, religion, national origin, sexual orientation, age, and physical disability, and, where union contracts prevailed, were prohibited from disciplining employees without just cause.

As each of these protections was legislated, managerial roles expanded to include supervising and monitoring adherence to governmental regulations. The intervention of government in preventing and reporting on managerial abuses paradoxically encouraged a rapid growth in managerial bureaucracy in order to monitor violations, which still hampers organizations today.

The More Things Change . . .

For most of its history, management directed and controlled work without governmental or employee limits. Indeed, it is possible to see slavery and serfdom merely as extreme early forms of autocratic management, in which employees had no voice whatsoever in the work process and were viewed not as human beings but as alienated forms of individual wealth. Slavery, in this sense, did not die; it continues in modern dress in contemporary organizations wherever managers exercise autocratic power, unequal status, or arbitrary privileges, no matter how scientific the terminology or postmodern the image.

It was not until widespread opposition to fascism following World War II that the authoritarian tradition of management in all its historical guises was powerfully called into question, as the emergence of a powerful new theory of organizational self-management pointed the way toward a different future.

Chapter Three

The Emerging Theory of Self-Management

> *I am sure you remember the plain citizen Jourdain in Moliére's "Bourgeois Gentilhomme" who . . . discovers to his amazement and great delight that wherever he speaks, he speaks prose. He is overwhelmed by this discovery: "I am speaking Prose! I have always spoken Prose! I have spoken Prose throughout my whole life!"*
>
> *[Similarly,] . . . [s]ome of my American friends came running to me with the delight and amazement of having just made a great discovery: "I am living in an Environment! I have always lived in an Environment! I have lived in an Environment throughout my whole life!"*
>
> *However neither M. Jourdain nor my friends have as yet made another discovery and that is when M. Jourdain speaks, may it be prose or poetry, it is he who invents it, and likewise when we perceive our environment, it is we who invent it.*
>
> HEINZ VON FOERSTER, in *The Invented Reality*

We believe there are three additional discoveries waiting to be made. The first is that we *are* our environment. The second is that whatever we perceive, think, invent, and are, we can alter. The third is that whenever we alter what we perceive or think or invent something new, we automatically reinvent ourselves. When we perceive and think of ourselves as capable of self-management, we begin to transform the organizations in which we work, and as we do so, we reinvent ourselves as more capable and competent than we were before.

With minor exceptions, only in the twentieth century did theories of management appear in which employees were recognized as having the innate capacity to manage themselves. Ironically, the turning point came as a result of scientific management. The very time and motion studies pioneered by Taylor revealed that productivity increased dramatically when employees were involved in decision making and highly motivated, creating a connection between employee motivation and the styles and methods of management.

Psychologist Kurt Lewin helped create this breakthrough. Following World War II, Lewin, along with Theodoro Adorno, Erich Fromm, and others, conducted research to understand the authoritarian personality that had flourished under fascism, which correlated with authoritarian management practices. The war against Hitler increased their resolve to develop safeguards against the authoritarian mind-set they found alive and well in organizations even in Allied countries.

Lewin conducted a study of group dynamics that shifted emphasis away from the time-and-motion engineering approach of Taylor and focused instead on human factors, such as motivation, group interactions, and communication styles. Lewin's studies explicitly encouraged industrial democracy and weakened the command-and-control orientation that had flourished under Taylor.

In the 1930s, as part of the same movement, union leader Joe Scanlon created the Scanlon Plan, which advocated that bonuses based on company or plant performance be distributed to all employees. Scanlon found Taylorist micromanagement grossly inefficient, leaving organizations unable to take advantage of employee potential. The idea that "managers should manage and workers should work" fueled adversarial relationships where none were necessary.

Scanlon believed employees should be given full access to information on problems and successes, be asked for their ideas about how best to do the work, be invited to participate in making organizational decisions, and be paid for achieving organizational goals. Subsequent research by Edward Lawler III and others identified several modifications of the Scanlon Plan that could improve its effectiveness, including:

- Creating flexible formulas that reflect real employee behavior
- Paying some bonuses at the beginning and not setting performance levels too high before payment
- Encouraging managers to support employee involvement and adopt more collaborative styles
- Focusing plans not only on labor savings but other costs as well
- Opening communications and emphasizing training to encourage employee trust and understanding
- Encouraging local union leaders to support the plan fully
- Preparing supervisors to have their competencies and decisions challenged by employees

Scanlon's and Lewin's theories reflected the growing strength of the labor movement and social values that had emerged during the New Deal. Lewin found that the best way to advance knowledge was for experts and employees to work together to create the proper relationship among people, tools, and tasks. He maintained that only freely chosen work provided meaning and values that could motivate high performance, that democracy could produce higher achievements and better relationships than authoritarianism, and that people were more committed to solutions they helped design than those that emanated solely from management experts. Lewin's impact on a generation of social scientists in organizational development, educational reform, and social psychology often goes unrecognized, yet many organizational gurus trace their roots to Lewin's ideas of industrial democracy, most notably Douglas McGregor.

The Birth of Theory X and Theory Y

During the 1950s, the industrial psychologists who adopted Lewin's approach continued to focus on human relations issues in management, leading to a human relations revolution. A significant shift took place in redefining management's role when Douglas McGregor, a professor at the Sloan School of Management at MIT, articulated a theory of management that honored everyone's desire to be in charge of their own work lives.

McGregor wrote that classical organizational theory, Theory X, assumes that employees naturally dislike their work, shun responsibility, and are not interested in anything beyond job security and wages, requiring management's role to be authoritarian, top-down, and suppressive. McGregor proposed a new paradigm for management, Theory Y, which assumes that employees want useful work and naturally take pride in what they do. It resulted in an entirely different approach to management. McGregor's theory affirmed the democratic ideals championed during World War II and supported Lewin's more humane approach to work. Table 3.1 makes McGregor's distinction clear.

McGregor's distinctions support the idea that treating people with respect is fundamental to motivating them. He made it clear that self-management is possible when people are given opportunity, skills, authority, and support. This approach requires managers to redefine their roles and to shift from instructing and ordering to educating and requesting, from inducing fear to supporting development and learning, and from monitoring employees to building trust through value-based leadership.

The Flowering of Self-Management Theories

The post-war generation of leading management thinkers, including W. Edwards Deming, Peter Drucker, and Warren Bennis, weighed in heavily against hierarchical, bureaucratic, top-down management in favor of participation, democratic leadership, and self-management. Deming, who assisted Japanese management after World War II and initiated the movement for Total Quality Management, wrote:

> Our prevailing system of management has destroyed our people. People are born with intrinsic motivation, self-esteem, dignity, curiosity to learn, joy in learning. The forces of destruction begin with toddlers—a prize for the best Halloween costume, grades in school, gold stars, and on up through the university. On the job, people, teams, divisions are ranked—reward for the one at the top, punishment at the bottom. MBO [management by objectives], quotas, incentive pay, business plans, put together separately, division by division, cause further loss, unknown and unknowable.

Table 3.1. Theory X and Theory Y: A Comparison.

Traditional (Theory X)	Potential (Theory Y)
1. People are naturally lazy; they prefer to do nothing.	1. People are naturally active; they set goals and enjoy striving.
2. People work mostly for money and status rewards.	2. People seek many satisfactions in work: pride in achievement; enjoyment of process; sense of contribution; pleasure in association; stimulation of new challenges.
3. The main force keeping people productive in their work is fear of being demoted or fired.	3. The main force keeping people productive in their work is desire to achieve their personal and social goals.
4. People remain children grown larger; they are naturally dependent on leaders.	4. People normally mature beyond childhood; they aspire to independence, self-fulfillment, and responsibility.
5. People expect and depend on direction from above; they do not want to think for themselves.	5. People close to the situation see and feel what is needed and are capable of self-direction.
6. People need to be told, shown, and trained in proper methods of work.	6. People who understand and care about what they are doing can devise and improve their own methods of doing work.
7. People need supervisors who will watch them closely enough to praise good work and reprimand errors.	7. People need a sense that they are respected as capable of assuming responsibility and self-correction.
8. People have little concern beyond their immediate, material interests.	8. People seek to give meaning to their lives by identifying with nations, communities, churches, unions, companies, causes.
9. People need specific instruction on what to do and how to do it; larger policy issues are none of their business.	9. People need ever-increasing understanding; they need to grasp the meaning of the activities in which they are engaged.
10. People appreciate being treated with courtesy.	10. People crave genuine respect from their fellow men.

Source: D. McGregor, *The Human Side of Enterprise.*

In the 1980s, Peter Drucker created a profound vision for new organizations and called for the elimination of traditional managerial roles. He thought organizations should be decentralized into autonomous units where decision making was returned to the front lines. In flattened environments, middle management would be replaced by autonomous self-managing teams that worked efficiently without being micromanaged.

In Drucker's view, leaders create vision and direction for organizations much as orchestra leaders conduct individual and group performers, with each performer responsible for setting goals, communicating with other performers, and making their own decisions. Leaders encourage self-discipline and self-management, promote individual responsibility, and build internal and external relationships that make the whole greater than the sum of its parts.

Warren Bennis, a close friend and protégé of McGregor, contributed a critical element to the theory of self-management by distinguishing leadership from management. In his classic work, *On Becoming a Leader* and a later volume coauthored with Joan Goldsmith, *Learning to Lead: A Coursebook on Becoming a Leader,* Bennis subtly contrasted these functions:

Differences Between Managers and Leaders

The manager administers; the leader innovates.

The manager is a copy; the leader is an original.

The manager maintains; the leader develops.

The manager accepts reality; the leader investigates it.

The manager focuses on systems and structure; the leader focuses on people.

The manager relies on control; the leader inspires trust.

The manager has a short range view; the leader has a long range perspective.

The manager asks how and when; the leader asks what and why.

The manager has his/her eye always on the bottom line; the leader has his/her eye on the horizon.

The manager imitates; the leader originates.

The manager accepts the status quo; the leader challenges it.

The manager is the classic good soldier; the leader is his/her
   own person.

The manager does things right; the leader does the right thing.

This distinction between getting other people to do things right
and leading them in the right direction is at the heart of the historical shift we are describing. While individual managers may blur
this distinction in practice, employees know when they are being
directed or managed and when they are being led and supported
in learning how to do it better. While leadership is consensual, management is coercive, and the difference is clearly revealed in what
happens when employees disagree.

In a recent articulation of the role of leadership in "great groups,"
Organizing Genius: The Secrets of Creative Collaboration, Bennis calls for
a new style of leadership that does not tolerate the bureaucratic
stifling of creativity routinely encouraged by middle managers. Organizations are capable of startling innovations, daunting creativity,
and breakthrough contributions when they are led by people who
generate and sustain self-motivated, self-managing teamwork. Bennis
and coauthor Patricia Biederman argue that:

> In a society as complex and technologically sophisticated as ours,
> the most urgent projects require the coordinated contributions of
> many talented people. Whether the task is building a global busi-
> ness or discovering the mysteries of the human brain, one person
> can't hope to accomplish it, however gifted or energetic he or she
> may be. In almost all creative collaboration, roles and relationship
> change according to the dictates of the project. . . . Great Groups
> require a more flexible kind of leader that has more to do with
> facilitating than asserting control. Like cats, the talented can't be
> herded. . . . Great Groups tend to be less bureaucratic than ordi-
> nary ones. Terribly talented people often have little tolerance for
> less talented middle managers.

These contributions by McGregor, Drucker, and Bennis have
been enlarged by others too numerous to reference, many of
whom have offered devastating critiques of hierarchy, bureaucracy,
and autocracy and identified numerous problems with the system
and practice of management. Combined and brought up to date,
these ideas reveal what we believe to be an overarching meta-trend
or direction, indicating a historical end to the age of management.

Why Management Is Ending

Democratic theory makes it clear that management as a system will predictably reinforce hierarchy and bureaucracy, autocracy and injustice, inequality and privilege; that it will block self-actualization, reduce personal freedom, and exhaust ethics and integrity; that it will sap the spirit, deplete the soul, and seek to conquer the very environment that supports it. These defects make democratic, collaborative, self-managing relationships difficult to imagine, articulate or support. As Albert Einstein wrote following the Great Depression:

> Why does this magnificent applied science which saves work and makes life easier bring us so little happiness? The simple answer is because we have not yet learned to make sensible use of it. In war it serves that we may poison and mutilate each other. In peace it makes our lives hurried and uncertain. Instead of freeing us in great measure from spiritually exhausting labor, it has made men into slaves of machinery, who for the most part complete their monotonous long day's work with disgust and must continually tremble for their poor rations.

Deming blamed this outcome on hierarchical management, and the simple fact that organizational power is used to disproportionately reward those at the top and separate them from others, which he traced back to relationships formed in families and schools.

People naturally take pride in crafting products and delivering high-quality services, because doing so contributes to their relationships, sense of self-worth, job satisfaction, and desire to be of service to others. But they do not take pride in being told what to do by people who stand over them and monitor their work in detail, searching for errors; who halfheartedly congratulate them on what they have done well and enthusiastically criticize their inability to meet hierarchically imposed standards, or performance measures they had no voice in creating.

Managerial Relationships Turn in a Circle

If these critiques are correct, what prevents us from redesigning organizations without proscribed hierarchical pathways that require every decision to be checked and rechecked by managers?

How does the system of management keep us from transforming these organizational structures and systems into shapes and forms that reflect and satisfy human needs? Why does the ensemble of these organizational problems seem to go nowhere?

Managerial relationships, as McGregor revealed, are predicated on the assumption that employees are either unwilling or unable to take responsibility for their actions; that they do not really care about their work beyond getting a paycheck; that they are unwilling to think about the big picture; and that they constantly look for excuses, test policies and rules, and need hierarchical structures, controls, and limits for their work to become cost-effective.

Managers who hold these assumptions *automatically and predictably* micromanage their employees. They restrict participation in policymaking and important decisions and institute top-down performance standards that externalize commitment, attitude, and loyalty. They emphasize a formal chain-of-command approach in response to employee complaints and suggestions, design tight personnel rules, limit information given to employees, transfer and reassign people without adequate information, and discipline and retaliate against employees who disagree with their decisions. They restrict strategic planning to upper levels of management, grovel before superiors, hold subordinates up to ridicule, and defend these behaviors against democratic change.

Employees, in response, *automatically and predictably* see these managers as untrustworthy and hypocritical, complain about dual standards, and seek transfers and reassignments rather than solve problems. They view discipline and termination as arbitrary and harassing, engage in gossip and spread rumors, see managers as insensitive, secretive, and manipulative, and accuse them of using organizational power to achieve private ends. They block information from flowing up the organization, allow managers to make mistakes, and blame other employees for failures. They make untenable demands for higher wages and better working conditions, make fun of managers behind their backs, and challenge their decisions. They withhold ideas and suggestions, sabotage decisions afterward, and refuse to work overtime or out of class to solve problems. They avoid responsibility, file technical grievances, form adversarial unions, bring lawsuits, and disregard or resist efforts to bring about change.

In these ways, the dysfunctional relationship between managers and employees turns in a circle and becomes a self-fulfilling prophecy. It is not that one is wrong and the other right. It is that *both* are wrong and right at the same time. In other words, it is not a question of right or wrong. It is a question of systemic dysfunction. Both sides are trapped in a system that reinforces the behaviors in each other that limit both of them.

What is tragic is that neither side understands the automaticity and predictability of the very things that upset them about each other or see that they flow naturally and inevitably from their own systemic behaviors. Both sides feel powerless, trapped, dispirited, and unable to change. They cannot conceive of living under a different paradigm, and easily turn apathetic, cynical, and resistant to change.

This pattern of mutually reinforcing self-destructive behaviors reveals a steady decline in the power and authority of management over the last century, which is now beginning to accelerate. With this decline has come an increase in the demand for new forms of leadership and organization and for employees who are willing to take responsibility for managing themselves. This shift is stimulated by the invention of new technologies and the emergence of new forms of work.

Technological Innovation and the Beginning of a New History

Management theory and practice is only starting to keep pace with the massive shifts in the nature of work sparked by the scientific and technological revolution that began with automation and computerization. These developments include the strategic use of information, ubiquitous computing, neural net programming, robotics, genetic engineering, nanotechnology, Internet and intranet access, linking software, and a host of innovations that were not even in existence ten years ago.

These technological changes dramatically call into question traditional organizational assumptions, including the structures, systems, strategies, styles, and skills that have characterized management for centuries. New entrepreneurial ventures that are springing up in response to breakthrough technologies are sparking organizational mutations that are elevating management by transforming it into leadership, coordination, networking, and strategizing. These changes are forcing management to jettison the ancient, autocratic methods that have defined its theoretical and historical mission.

Rather than building fixed structures with layers of middle management, many innovative organizations function as matrixed webs of association, networks, and fast-forming high-performance teams. Staff on all levels operate simultaneously in multiple roles but rarely as autocrats, bureaucrats, and overseers of other peoples' work. British management professor Charles Handy describes these young entrepreneurial structures as "fleas," as opposed to traditional hierarchies and bureaucracies, which he calls "elephants," that are financially more powerful than most of the world's countries yet responsible to no one. Handy views these new organizations as alchemists creating something out of nothing. They reject traditional managerial structures, which do not permit fast-moving, highly focused work or promote problem solving and troubleshooting.

The most important aspect of these shifts is their paradigm-breaking quality. Throughout most of history and much of theory, management has been focused on controlling rather than freeing labor. Its operative command has been "no" rather than "yes." It has been an enforcer, cop, warden, and strict, controlling parent rather than a liberator and facilitator of self-management.

Self-Management and Organizational Democracy

The most significant trends we see in the theory and history of management are the decline of hierarchical, bureaucratic, autocratic management and the expansion of collaborative self-management and organizational democracy. For the first time in history, it is no longer as profitable to manage in the old as in the new way. Creativity, wisdom, risk taking, invention, motivation, and leadership cannot be forced into existence from above by hierarchical, bureaucratic, or authoritarian management. They must be elicited, facilitated, encouraged, supported, freed, challenged and critiqued by peers in an egalitarian, democratic environment and coordinated by self-managing teams and linking leaders.

One consequence of ubiquitous computing, robotics, and Internet access has been the erosion of traditional administrative and managerial functions, such as scheduling work, coordinating tasks, setting work goals, and delivering strategic information. These administrative tasks are easily handled by computers or employee teams without managerial middlemen. What cannot be automated are leadership, coaching, teamwork, facilitation, vision, intuition, creativity, wisdom, learning, and collaborative relationships.

For this reason, it is both necessary and possible to redesign workplaces and organizations with human beings in mind and to eliminate management as we know it. We now have the ability to create organizations in conformity with values and common sense, based on an enlarged understanding of what is humanly possible. It is now possible to free labor from the constraints of autocratic managerial power.

We are rapidly automating nearly all the administrative, bureaucratic functions of management, directly connecting production orders with distribution centers across departmental and even organizational and international lines, giving teams instant access to vast amounts of strategically important information and using planning and process design models that allow employees to reinvent the way they work.

Throughout its history, management has performed two fundamentally different, even contradictory, organizational functions. On the one hand, it has been a coordinator, organizer, and leader, bringing diverse skills and personalities into a single, more or less harmonious and collaborative effort, resulting in the creation of high-quality products and services. On the other hand, it has been an agent of coercion, enslavement, and exploitation, using its power and status to compel employees to obey orders and work against their will. While the first has declined over time, the second has increased. When we refer to the end of management, we mean the second, not the first. We mean the end of forcing people to work in ways they do not choose. We mean making them responsible for their own work lives.

The ultimate problem with managerial roles is that they produce one-way relationships. They are a story without a listener, a dance without a partner, a song without a melody. In management, as in all top-down relationships, one is assumed to be enough, while the other is always seen as secondary, inferior, and subordinate. The smallest human unit, however, is not one but two, and when one is controlled, managed, or directed, the magic of human interconnection that flows from diverse, equal relationships disappears.

Thus, we arrive at a crossroads, where we discover that we have a unique opportunity to create a new theory of organizations and a new kind of history. This opportunity presents its own challenges and problems, yet it also frees us, for the first time in history, to consciously and intentionally transform the way we work and greatly increase our capacity to make it more humanly satisfying.

To understand more deeply why the system of management cannot be fixed, repaired, or saved, we need to analyze its dysfunction in greater detail.

Chapter Four

Management Reduces Communication, Morale, and Motivation

> *To begin with, always to be doing work that one did*
> *not wish to do, and to do it like a slave, flattering and*
> *fawning, not always necessarily perhaps, but it seemed*
> *necessary and the stakes were too great to run risks; and*
> *then the thought of that one gift which it was death to*
> *hide—a small one but dear to the possessor—perishing*
> *and with it myself, my soul—all this became like a rust*
> *eating away at the bloom of the spring, destroying the tree*
> *at its heart.*
> VIRGINIA WOOLF, *A Room of One's Own*

Hundreds of thousands of change efforts are under way in organizations throughout the world, each seeking to invent new strategies, streamline processes, decrease costs, improve customer service, and increase productivity. Billions of dollars are being spent annually on consultants, workshops, trainings, books, coaches, and conflict resolution, and millions of hours are being devoted to implementing these improvements. Yet all these efforts depend in sensitive ways on the quality of communications, employee morale and motivation, and a supple, sensitive, self-motivated attitude toward quality and customer service. They all require employees who do not pretend to enjoy their work or flatter and fawn, as Virginia Woolf describes, but who actually do.

All too frequently, years of work and millions of dollars in salaries and consulting fees are wiped out by a single thoughtless bureaucratic memo or insensitive authoritarian comment, an unanticipated top-down change in organizational policy, resistance to change brought about by managerial miscommunication and misunderstanding, or lack of genuine employee enthusiasm for implementing the change.

What is missed in these efforts is that the system of management, regardless of the skills and dedication of individual managers, subtly and inevitably obstructs communication, reduces morale, and prevents employees from dedicating their efforts to improving quality, productivity, and customer service. Self-management, on the other hand, subtly and inevitably improves communication, increases morale, and encourages employees to enjoy quality improvement, increased productivity, and customer service. The reasons this is so are worth exploring.

Hierarchical Communications Are a One-Way Street

Fundamentally, organizations are systems that are formed by networks of communication linking people and resources and giving their relationships and interactions meaning, shape, and direction. Most organizational work is accomplished by people stating or listening to messages, posing or answering questions, issuing or following directions, presenting or fulfilling requests, making or meeting commitments, offering or receiving support.

Each of these forms of communication is highly sensitive and capable of being altered by minor, seemingly unimportant differences in understanding, such as those that divide managers from the people they manage. Each is significantly deformed by the presence of hierarchy, bureaucracy, and autocracy and the perceived need to coerce employees into doing what management assumes they will not do voluntarily.

Hierarchies, bureaucracies, and autocracies create unnatural inequalities in power, privilege, and status between managers and employees. These inequalities transform organizational communications into one-way streets that permit management and staff to misconstrue each other's meaning and intent and allow even carefully crafted communications to be chronically miscommunicated. They encourage both sides to ask questions that are closed and pointed as opposed to open and curious, and to ignore answers they do not like. They allow managers to make statements that turn into lectures, requests that feel like demands, questions that seem like interrogations, promises that are contingent on obedience, and offers of support that are hollow or meaningless.

These dynamics result in organizational messages not getting through to their intended targets and a subtle reshaping of the content of organizational communications. Each managerial behavior encourages employees not to listen or to give superficial, insufficiently honest, highly emotional, or disrespectful responses, which result in diminished trust, reduced collaboration, increased conflict, and lack of responsibility for results. If these results occurred in only a fraction of communications, they would still cause enormous unnecessary damage.

Management as a method does everything in its power to reduce undecidable questions to decidable ones and to decide them without having to ask for input or advice from employees who are usually closer to the problem. By doing so, they collapse metaphysical choices into logical decisions and ethics into morality. Worse, they miss important fragments of information that could significantly improve the quality of their decisions.

The ability to make choices is a measure of freedom. Choosing allows us to be ourselves and express who we are. With choice comes responsibility, and with its denial comes irresponsibility and servitude. When we cannot choose, we are enslaved and bound by sometimes subtle, barely invisible chains that appear to be of our own making.

Managerial decisions are, in their essence, acts of power, control, and dominion over shared issues. They are choices made by one group regarding issues that affect others, without their full participation. As such, they produce predictable results in the form of employee resistance, dependency, apathy, and cynicism. They measurably increase hostility and passive-aggressive behavior, and they sap morale. They also reduce creativity, initiative, responsibility, loyalty, and other behaviors that managers typically value.

Self-managerial decisions, on the other hand, are acts of ownership, collaboration, and democracy. They are choices made by everyone affected by an issue, that require their participation. As such, they produce predictable results in the form of responsibility, independence, motivation, and caring. They improve communication and increase morale. And they lead to increased creativity, ownership, loyalty, and other behaviors managers typically value.

A contest was recently conducted on the Internet in which employees were asked to submit quotations from their managers. The following winning submissions illustrate our point. Looking past the humor, the cost of these statements in morale and productivity is obvious:

"What I need is a list of specific unknown problems we will encounter."

"E-mail is not to be used to pass on information or data. It should be used only for company business."

"This project is so important, we can't let things that are more important interfere with it."

"Doing it right is no excuse for not meeting the schedule. No one will believe you solved this problem in one day! We've been working on it for months. Now, go act busy for a few weeks, and I'll let you know when it's time to tell them."

"My sister passed away, and her funeral was scheduled for Monday. When I told my manager, he said she died so that I would have to miss work on the busiest day of the year. He then asked if we could change her burial to Friday. He said, 'That would be better for me.'"

"We know that communication is a problem, but the company is not going to discuss it with the employees."

"One day my manager asked me to submit a status report to him concerning a project I was working on. I asked him if tomorrow would be soon enough. He said, 'If I wanted it tomorrow, I would have waited until tomorrow to ask for it!'"

These ludicrous comments are not exceptional; they occur every day in managerial communications. Indeed, we have become so accustomed to dysfunctional communications that we fail to notice their systemic managerial origins. We greet *Dilbert* cartoons with glee and recognition not because they represent the individual idiocies of isolated managers but because they reveal a system

of idiocies that are increasingly pointless, producing costly outcomes and painful mistakes. We laugh because we have not taken
time to understand why the system is not working and then fix it.

It is not only the absurd quality of individual managerial miscommunications that concerns us, however, but the way these ab-
surdities are produced and go uncorrected, the way they flow
naturally from the system of management itself, the way they represent in miniature the story of the Emperor without clothes, whom
no one would tell because of his superior position in a hierarchy of
power. We have grown so accustomed to mindless, overbearing, of-
ficious managerial behaviors that we are willing to tolerate even
their most illogical and wasteful consequences. Sadly, we all become
complicit in tolerating these consequences when we do not search
for ways of revealing, ridiculing, and correcting them.

Hierarchies and Communication

Jan Carlzon, the legendary chairman of SAS Airlines, who transformed his company into an industry leader by raising quality standards, described the dysfunctional nature of hierarchical managerial
communications:

> The task of [top management] is to control operations by making
> all the decisions necessary to run the company. The sheer number
> of decisions that must be made keeps them occupied with the de-
> cision making process, necessitating that intermediaries convey
> these decisions throughout the company. So a large corps of peo-
> ple in middle management converts top management's decisions
> into instructions, rules, policies and orders for the workers at the
> bottom level to follow. Although these people are called "middle
> management," they are actually not managers at all if by "manager"
> we mean someone who makes his own decisions within a sphere
> of responsibility. In reality, they are just messengers who relay de-
> cisions made higher up in the corporate pyramid.

The inability to make one's own decisions within a sphere of
responsibility, or at a minimum, relay upper management's decisions accurately and transmit information not only down the
hierarchy, but up it as well, are not unique. Rather, they are a predictable consequence of hierarchically managed power, suggesting

a need to redesign the structures and systems that place managers in charge of formal organizational communications.

Kathleen D. Ryan and Daniel K. Oestereich conducted interviews in a number of companies to discover what issues employees felt were "undiscussable," and found "management practices" constituted 49 percent of the total. The main reasons employees gave for not being able to talk about these issues were their fear of repercussions and concern that managers might retaliate. Yet many of these "undiscussable" issues concealed deeper problems that, if addressed, could have increased the success of these organizations.

Communications can be empowering, expanding, and rewarding or demeaning, disillusioning, and distasteful. Consider Figure 4.1, and ask: What will predictably happen to any communication that takes place within this structure?

The arrows in the figure reveal some of the more common distortions created by organizational hierarchies. First, communications moving from the top to the bottom will be subtly altered each time they are transmitted, requiring them to be drastically simplified in order to arrive without distortion. As a result, those at the bottom will be forced to guess about their real meaning and substitute rumors and gossip for genuine information.

Second, there will be too many communications trying to get from the bottom of the organization to the top, and only a few will finally make it. These will have to be compressed and simplified to the point of being practically useless. As a result, the top will predictably be out of touch with the bottom and make critical decisions with inaccurate data, causing those at the bottom to question their judgment. While most information regarding problems emanates from the bottom, most decisions regarding how to solve them emanate from the top. This results in those at the top making incorrect, costly, untimely decisions, and those at the bottom feeling disempowered, distrusted, and disrespected.

Third, communications are unevenly distributed throughout the organization. Any manager can alter the meaning of a communication on its way up or down the hierarchy by blocking or delaying it, treating it as more or less important, or subtly distorting its message. Since vertical departments are often in competition with one another over resources and managers become increasingly competitive over fewer and fewer positions, there is a likelihood of

Figure 4.1. Hierarchies and Communication.

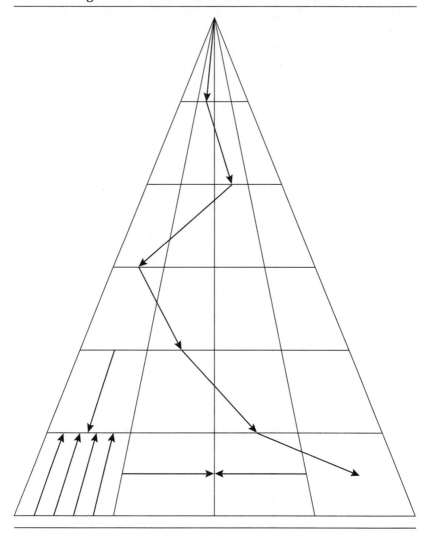

distortion and a motive to mold communications to suit personal and departmental advantage. The relative isolation of parts of the organization encourages rumors and miscommunications to spread.

Fourth, each department and managerial level will predictably reinterpret, or refract, incoming messages to match their own expectations, perceptions, histories, and desires. If a message from below is critical of a department or its manager, there is a greater likelihood that it will be blocked or edited than if its content is favorable. In this way, there is a bias toward passing on good news regarding colleagues and bad news regarding competitors.

Fifth, each of these miscommunications will predictably produce small-scale personal animosities, cross-departmental hostilities, feelings of rejection and disapproval, resistance to change, distrust, unresolved conflict, loss of motivation and morale, and other costly outcomes that continue into the future. On a larger scale, they may lead to paralysis and dysfunctions so severe they can cause the entire organization to fail.

These are only a few of the distortions created by communicating inside a hierarchically managed organization. Because managers guard the gates of communication and relay messages up and down the hierarchy, they restrict access to important information. This, in turn, feeds the gossip and rumor mills that flourish in these organizations, destroying trust and further distorting communications.

Rumors and Gossip

Employees spend a great deal of time and energy circumventing managerial communications and building alternate informal communication networks based on gossip and rumors. Part of the culture of every dysfunctional organization is a rich behind-the-scenes communications network that feeds on hearsay, scuttlebutt, slander, prejudice, and innuendo.

During a break at a workshop we conducted, a supervisor learned from a custodian that a new downsizing initiative affecting his staff was planned for announcement later that day! Executives had ordered the downsizing, and the janitors received word through the informal network before the information reached the supervisors who were expected to implement it. Often the best source of information in organizations is gossip, Although it is often wildly inaccurate, it nonetheless has the virtue of addressing what is actually going on.

Many managers report great frustration at their inability to control the rumor and gossip networks that interlace their organizations. They feel undermined and betrayed by the maliciousness of rumors, confused about the source of comments, disempowered in being able to respond, and isolated from fellow employees. Ironically, it is their own withholding of important information that is largely responsible for spawning these alternate communication systems.

Rumors reflect a fear of the unknown. They stand in for accurate knowledge about the past and realistic expectations about the future. They fill the gaps created by official silence and are a form of retribution by those who feel disempowered, frightened, humiliated, and uncertain against others who are powerful enough to be in the know. They permeate the vacuum created by official pronouncements, bureaucratic slogans, marketing hyperbole, hypocrisy, and retaliation.

Most organizations restrict access to information based on a hierarchical determination of who "needs to know" or whose "eyes only" are entitled to what piece of information. Decisions about who to include and exclude are commonly left to managers, who use access to reward supporters and punish detractors. More frequently, access to information gives management the ability to think strategically and understand the big picture. It lends them an appearance of power over events and an ability to seem all-seeing and all-knowing. In this way, secrecy turns into a self-fulfilling prophecy. Denying access to important information makes employees appear unintelligent, misinformed, and unable to act responsibly, justifying hierarchical and managerial hegemony.

In managerial hierarchies, the ability to monitor or control access to information goes hand in hand with power and status, but it also generates distrust and distorts communication. Organizations, like all other relationships, are distorted and corrupted not only by lies and misrepresentations but by secrets and cover-ups.

Restricting information based on a need to know creates gossip networks that convey most of the information informally anyway and gives accurate information an official, somewhat untrustworthy cast. This dual communication system causes each side to distrust the other's information, either because management disguised or hid important information or because employees distorted what they were partially told or made up facts that seemed to fit.

The distrust created as a result of being either in or out of the know often results in management's being out of the know regarding what is taking place at the base of the organization. Both sides then retreat into a conspiracy of silence, characterized by an unspoken agreement *not* to communicate. They rationalize their actions, solidify their opposition, and lose power as a result, carrying into their next communication stories of abandonment, dishonesty, and betrayal.

The real need to know in organizations extends to all employees, because those who have information at their fingertips feel more powerful and satisfied, make better decisions, and act in ways that increase organizational value. John Case has documented these results in *Open Book Management: The Coming Business Revolution:* "In open-book companies people learn to follow the numbers and help make decisions. They learn to think and act like owners, like business-people, and not the hired hands."

There are countless examples of corporations, nonprofit organizations, and government agencies that have opened their books to employees and benefited enormously in morale and productivity from reductions in secrecy. In one open book manufacturing company in southern California, productivity increased nearly 40 percent as a result of giving employees access to up-to-date information about customers and clients, costs and profits, including what is often considered private information regarding salaries and bonuses.

There are many ways organizations can open their books, including by flattening their organizational structures, entrusting information to teams, building horizontal communication systems, adding information to intranets, rewarding criticism and problem identification, building consensus, and implementing 360-degree evaluations and regular feedback.

In democratic organizations, information barriers are lowered, knowledge is shared, rumors are challenged, individuals confront each other supportively, and there is greater shared responsibility for the success of the organization. Where everyone is considered to have a need to know, less time is spent correcting misinformation, resolving conflicts, and repairing the damage done by gossip and rumors. As managerial roles are eliminated and self-management is implemented, communication, productivity, and morale improve.

The Impact of Management on Morale

As organizations become flattened, agile, and interactive, and as customer service and relationships play increasingly important roles in financial success, employee morale becomes significant for multiple reasons. First, customers can quickly sense how employees feel about working for an organization. They intuitively understand that the quality of service they receive will be better where employees are happy than where they are not.

Second, maintaining customer relationships means more than simply providing a product. It means interacting with customers and anticipating their needs. Employees with poor morale generally do not care enough to nurture relationships, and if an employee's morale drops because of an unresolved conflict with a manager, customers often feel the negative effects as well.

But the problem goes deeper and touches not only the attitudes of employees toward customers but the nature of management. Regardless of the intentions or skills of individual managers, the system of management naturally keeps morale and motivation at a reduced level, simply because someone is telling the person responsible for performing a task how to do it.

While all morale assessments contain a subjective component, they still roughly measure how employees feel about themselves, their managers, the organization, peers, and tasks. In the overwhelming majority of surveys we are familiar with, management is the primary source of poor morale. In a survey we designed and conducted at a large corporation, employees cited the following management behaviors as the source of their poor morale:

• Excessively harsh criticism
• Playing favorites and creating double standards
• Unfair discipline or termination

- Discourteous or disrespectful communication
- Contradictory, inconsistent, or mixed messages
- Secretive decision making and hoarding information
- Unconstructive feedback
- Lack of responsiveness to input or ideas
- Taking credit for other people's ideas
- Cold, aloof, or arrogant behaviors
- Dishonesty, even in small things
- Putting their self-interest before the interests of others
- Inflexibility, despotism, indecisiveness, and abdication
- Avoiding, accommodating, or aggressively engaging in conflicts
- Not walking their talk

Most employees are reluctant to discuss morale-reducing behaviors openly with their managers, primarily because of management's superior power, causing employee morale to decline even further due to a lack of open, honest, authentic, timely communication or genuine efforts at resolution. In nearly all organizational cultures, employees speak more freely with each other than they do with managers, and monitor their communications with managers to make sure they do not risk termination. They do so because in spite of widespread public support for democracy, freedom of speech has yet to be implemented in the workplace, and it is routine for employees to be punished, simply based on the content of what they say.

Many common managerial behaviors silence employees and reduce morale: giving orders, micromanaging, reproving, repeating the company line, listening bureaucratically, ducking difficult issues, hiding behind superiors, refusing responsibility for mistakes, passing the buck, and punishing those perceived as troublemakers. If we added up the damage caused and opportunities wasted by these personally and organizationally destructive behaviors, the figure would be astronomical and far outweigh the salaries of the managers who engaged in them.

The most important thing to recognize is that most poor morale can be cured simply by taking complaints seriously and making employees responsible for fixing the problems they identify—in other words, by self-management. In one organization where we drafted and analyzed the results from an employee morale survey, many people told us they did not complete the survey because the company had never taken their comments seriously or done anything to address their issues.

After tabulating the results, we met with every work group in the organization, accompanied by the human resource manager and chief operating officer, to report directly on what we had been told without hedging or softening their criticisms. We divided each group into small, semianonymous teams, and asked them for more details on what needed fixing and ideas to solve the problems they identified. We encouraged the human resource manager and chief operating officer to begin implementing these suggestions immediately and thanked the group for their courage and honesty. The next morale survey was completed by 100 percent of the employees, and morale increased by over 40 percent. When asked to explain any changes in their morale, they cited the fact that their ideas had been taken seriously by management, and they felt respected and valued as a result.

The Game of Escape

When organizations impose their values and use managers as enforcers, they communicate a deeper value of obedience to external authority and give employees an excuse for making non-value-based, unethical decisions. Managers and employees in hierarchical organizations commonly justify unethical behaviors by citing their duty to be loyal and obey orders, or their desire to please superiors, serve organizational interests, or avoid losing their jobs. These justifications undermine ethics and values as bases for decision making, replacing them with ambition, abdication, and survival, and reducing ethical consistency, organizational integrity, and value-based leadership.

Managers and employees commonly use a variety of rationalizations, covers, and smokescreens to disguise unethical behavior, including hiding behind written policies and procedures, privileged information, and past practices. Managers frequently harass employees who point out these defects or perceive them as critical or negative. In response, employees defend themselves by playing the ever-fascinating, eternally annoying game of escape, in which they try to duck, dodge, hide, and by other ingenious means avoid responsibility and obedience.

By divorcing implementation from responsibility, managed organizations create an environment in which rules can be bent, contorted, misinterpreted, limited, shaded, formally satisfied, rationalized away, or redefined to fall short of their actual violation. This is a natural and inevitable result of enforcing abstract rules, which cannot account for unanticipated contingencies, complexities, human ingenuity, or changes in circumstance. The problem is that as a result, standardized rules always encourage those who conform to try to escape their deadening effects.

This psychological game of escape is played by employees with rules set by management, by managers with rules set by directors, by directors with rules set by governments, and so on. Everyone plays this game, partly out of boredom, or a desire not to be a slave or robot, or a fear of the consequences of acting based on values and integrity and the threat of loss of employment.

Organizations often tolerate this behavior, not only because everyone does it and people admire a skillful escape, but because it is impossible to know in advance whether a rule violation is not actually some new, potentially successful form of behavior. Most significant inventions, discoveries, and innovations violated some rule that said it could not be done. Indeed, every significant social and political change from the American Revolution to the civil rights movement broke somebody's rules.

The problem is: When do rule violations enhance ethical or value-based behavior, and when do they undermine it? Civil disobedience is a good example of rule violations that uphold a higher set of values and challenge unjust laws. During the civil rights movement, demonstrators engaged in civil disobedience in clear violation of segregationist rules. Today we find these acts justifiable, even heroic, because they were done in the name of a higher set of values involving the right to equal treatment under the U.S. Constitution, which had been ignored or suppressed.

This does not mean that every violation of rules should be accorded similar treatment. In the game of escape, for example, employees do not take open, principled stands against injustice but avoid responsibility for changing it.

The Effect of Management on Motivation

While morale is a snapshot that captures people's feelings at a given moment, motivation is an indication of what makes them willing to change or invest their energies in something. Dozens of volumes have been written on motivation, many offering methods management can use to encourage employees to work harder and faster and care more about the quality of their work. Rarely, however, do these texts draw a connection between motivation and the undermining effect of hierarchies of power, bureaucratic mazes, autocratic decision making, and the system of management. Yet we know that when employees feel empowered, are involved in team decision making, and are consulted about issues and outcomes, motivation soars. We know that people do not work nearly as diligently without power, democracy, and shared values as they do with them.

Management motivates employees externally from above, by pushing or pulling them in a given direction. Yet pushing and pulling automatically and inevitably produce varying degrees of resistance that internal forms of motivation do not. By focusing on behaviors and performance, management misses the multidimensional, holistic aspects of work, which are far more important. These are the sources of art, wisdom, innovation, passion, and the highest levels of motivation. These dimensions or aspects of work can be inspired by leaders but cannot be mandated or managed from outside and above.

Motivation is simply an answer to the question, "Why do it?" asked about a particular action. When employees are asked why they are working, the largest percentage of answers are "in order to eat" or "to buy the things I need or want." They see work as instrumental to the satisfaction of their needs rather than as a need in itself. Yet people need meaningful labor and routinely give different answers when asked about their hobbies. Work defines us and fashions our relationships with others. We work for love, for the pleasure of giving, and for self-actualization, which are dependent on egalitarian relationships, personal interaction, participation, cooperation, empowerment, and approval.

Work in hierarchies means working "for" people more powerful than oneself. In this way, the pleasure of working for the love of others or for oneself or for the sheer joy of it is lost or over-shadowed. The inconsistency between outward generosity and inward selfishness reduces employee motivation. Allowing employees to manage themselves in democratically organized teams that are empowered to make decisions regarding important issues is an enormously powerful motivator. Consultation, participation, and empowerment increase self-approval and approval by others. These processes make individuality and self-development priorities, along with social contribution and collaboration.

The essential tenets of organizational democracy and self-management are quite simple:

- Every employee is capable of actively participating in making the decisions that affect his or her work life.
- Everyone is equally entitled to be heard and respected.
- Everyone's opinion counts equally.
- Everyone is a leader in achieving goals.
- Everyone collaborating yields better results.

Regardless of the skills and intentions of individual managers, management as a system undermines these tenets. Simply by exercising hierarchical power, imposing bureaucratic requirements, and engaging in autocratic actions, management reduces morale and eliminates the motivation that arises from love, collaboration, participation in decision making, creativity, and self-management.

Chapter Five

Management Constricts Quality and Customer Service

In organizations where mistakes are not allowed, you
get two types of counterproductive behavior. First, since
mistakes are "bad" if they're committed by the people at the
top, people can pretend that no mistake has been made. So
it doesn't get fixed. Second, if they're committed by people
lower down in the organization, mistakes get concealed.
JOHN CLEESE, *Forbes*, May 16, 1988

In the competitive world of global production, continuous improvement in the quality of products, processes, and relationships is critical. Yet regardless of the commitment of individual managers, the system of management routinely discourages employees from improving quality. The managerial attitude toward errors that John Cleese describes robs organizations of improvements in quality that flow from employee involvement in preventing and correcting mistakes. Reporter Doron Levin described in *The Los Angeles Times* the impact that managers have on quality in an article several years ago about work at Ford:

> Rigid command hierarchies within Ford had discouraged people in every area of the company from showing initiative, from sharing information with one another and from finding creative cooperative solutions to problems.

> Workers, quite simply, were afraid of offending their bosses. A manager's status was measured according to the number of people under his or her supervision. Managers competed fiercely among

themselves for promotions: their subordinates were expected to display loyalty to the chief. To outdo their peers, managers withheld information from rivals and prohibited subordinates from cooperating with members of competitive departments, a practice that inevitably led to design errors, delays and cost overruns.

The blue-collar work force mirrored the office staff. Factory workers had little incentive to offer ideas to improve quality and efficiency. Since the 1930s . . . the Auto Workers union and Ford's management had maintained a tense truce, interrupted by occasional strikes. The union was reluctant to promote closer relations between its members and supervisors, and plant supervisors were disdainful of advice from hourly workers, who often knew simple fixes to complex problems.

The failure of managerial direction described in this report is not unique to Ford, but it is woven into the fabric of managerial roles and functions. Managers are charged with responsibility for overseeing products and services to make certain they meet a predetermined standard or level of quality. Yet the value of these products and services depends on their quality, which depends on the skills, intelligence, experience, learning, morale, and energy of employees.

The True Nature of Quality

Quality is often defined as conformity to a set of standards or requirements. But this begs the question of who sets these standards and requirements, in what amounts, with what consequences, and to what ends. With every increase in the quality of a product or service, there is a financial trade-off, since craftsmanship and distinction have a cost that translates into price. This encourages managers to reduce quality to a set of minimum requirements. The cost of quality can then be measured in terms of profitability for products, fees for services, or votes for government responsiveness. Quality is exchanged with customers for a profit, delivered to clients for a fee, or made available to citizens for a tax. Each is judged by their users in relation to their value, or quality at a given price. This allows organizations, in theory, to compare the costs in wages and materials with market results, client return rates, or ballot box outcomes and decide whether they invested their resources wisely.

Quality is a measure of the usefulness of a product or service, its effectiveness in achieving a given purpose, even its beauty in relation to its cost. Aristotle wrote that "quality is not an act, it is a habit." More than this, it is a state of mind. It is an act of consideration and respect for those who will eventually use the product or service. It is an acknowledgment and commemoration of the integrity, skills, values, and efficiency of its producers or providers. At its highest level, quality is an application of the Golden Rule to work, a recognition that the producer or provider *is* the consumer, client, and citizen; that every product and service is a work of art to be created with pride, polished with love, and received with gratitude. The strongest motivation to produce high-quality products and services is the sheer pleasure of doing so. In this way, quality is an expression of the awareness and intention of the producer. It is a direct, personal relationship among people, products or services, and society, based on functionality, imagination, art, and love. For this reason, quality is an expression of respect for oneself as a creator.

Quality cannot be successfully managed, though it can be facilitated, inspired, and led. The desire to always do better and continuously improve—not only the product but the process of creating it, the relationships involved in producing it, and the level of satisfaction derived from producing it well—cannot be directed or controlled from the outside. Quality means meeting one's own highest standards, along with those of consumers and coworkers. It means discovering what it is possible for human beings to achieve.

As global economic competition increases and costs surge, competitive advantage often lies with seemingly minor improvements in quality, productivity, and costs, or "Better, Cheaper, Faster." The most successful organizations have adopted a method for encouraging employee participation and self-management in relation to quality, such as Total Quality Management, Six Sigma, quality circles, quality teams, and collaborative process that focus on people, in addition to profits and costs.

In most organizations, managers are responsible for quality yet are often seen by employees as agents of a kind of modern inquisition, wheedling, threatening, and controlling their every move and acting as "quality cops." None of these approaches encourages employees to commit to higher levels of quality. Instead, they see managers as punishers for failing to deliver on standards set without their input or as overseers who require them to work harder without extra pay or participation in profits.

Managers' efforts to improve quality are at least one step removed from the actual quality-creating process. When managers are moved out of their intermediate roles as messengers and enforcers; when employees become responsible for improving quality themselves; when the books are opened and teams have direct access to information, colleagues and customers; when they share in the financial rewards; when they are empowered to immediately fix problems, employees are able to satisfy customers, give and accept corrective feedback, and produce higher-quality products, all with increased job satisfaction.

In most organizations, in spite of energetic efforts at quality improvement, managers still define product and service standards and enforce them without employee buy-in. Employee advice is often ignored, and active participation in setting standards is given lip-service or politely discouraged, despite the fact that line employees are far more familiar with work process issues and know better how to resolve them than managers do.

The phrase *quality control* has been called an oxymoron because it contradicts an essential truth: that concern for quality is an attitude that can be encouraged and supported but not controlled or managed. Ownership, enjoyment of work, responsibility, and pride in workmanship are the true generators of quality, but these are attitudes and personal choices that cannot be forced. Rather, they are challenged, elicited, led, inspired, motivated, envisioned, facilitated, jointly created, and empowered.

We were asked to mediate a conflict between two managers at a large electronics firm where billions of dollars in sales were in jeopardy. Esther managed a department that produced a key component before it was passed on to Sam's division for final assembly. Esther's employees were not delivering components on time or with sufficient quality to Sam's team. As a result, Sam and his staff spent weekends and nights trying to cover up for these deficiencies by revising and repairing the materials they were given, resulting in lower-quality products being delivered well past the customer's deadline.

Rather than inform Esther of these difficulties and work with her to solve them, Sam became stressed, compounded the errors, cost the company unnecessary overtime, harbored deep resentments, and sparked conflicts with Esther over issues that had nothing to do with the real problems. In mediation, the real issues emerged. Sam said he had not raised these issues with Esther because he did not want to "get her staff in trouble and have her come down on them." He was afraid his boss would assume he was reluctant to take responsibility and was pushing the blame onto Esther. Everyone paid a huge price, including the company and the customer, and Esther's team was cheated out of recognizing the problem and fixing it.

In mediation, Sam agreed to meet with Esther and go over the problems in detail. Esther agreed not to be so hard on her staff and request their feedback about her style, which was accusatory, hypercritical, and authoritarian. They both agreed to meet with their boss and let him know what the problems were and what they planned to do to solve them. They agreed to facilitate a joint session with their teams to iron out issues and apologize for their inability to communicate with each other.

Quality movement pioneer W. Edwards Deming believed that quality improvement requires a delegation of responsibility to employees organized in teams charged with delivering products that meet standards the team sets for itself. Team members in Deming's model are challenged by leaders to do better, and they are supported and rewarded for doing so. Building responsibility for quality into all job descriptions makes it clear that quality is everyone's responsibility.

Research has shown that when quality becomes the responsibility of employees organized in teams, quality concerns become internalized and are rewarded, work becomes more satisfying, and quality improves, along with rates of productivity. In one Fortune 500 manufacturing firm, a production unit reorganized into self-managed teams. In one year, they applied process improvement techniques and reduced the number of required work processes to manufacture their first-line product from 387 to 4, while increasing quality. This reduction was designed and carried out by self-managing employee teams that reduced the number of mistakes, shoddy output, and failures by nearly 100 percent. Most of the 383 eliminated functions and processes fell into three broad categories:

- Control-oriented or administrative processes that could be eliminated by assigning them to computers or performed by self-managing work teams that were fully responsible for results
- Overlapping or duplicative processes that were intended to ensure quality but increased the number of bottlenecks as well
- Managerial or coordinating functions that could better be performed by team leaders

This example is not unique. Much of managerial work fits easily into these three categories. If it is possible to produce better-quality products and services through a combination of computers, teams, process improvements, and linking leadership, management becomes an unwarranted, superfluous expense. Management unnecessarily lengthens turnover time, removes responsibility for quality from employee teams, and increases the costs of production. We are not suggesting that managers are craven, stupid, or incompetent. They are simply one step removed from the problems they are asked to solve.

Redefining Customer Service

Customer service is increasingly being redefined as customer partnership. But in a genuine partnership, both sides have to be available, authentic, and genuinely interested in solving each other's problems. Barriers to partnership increase when there is a single-minded, self-interested focus on making a sale, or when decisions are rubber-stamped by several layers of managerial hierarchy, each of which is less committed to the sharing that partnership implies.

The reasons are clear. Service and partnership, availability, and authenticity require time, which as everyone knows is money. Every organization needs to balance the amount of time spent serving or partnering with customers with the time required to design and create the service delivered, and not go out of business. In our experience, the quality of service and partnership delivered by fully empowered self-managing teams is significantly greater than that delivered by managers' overseeing groups of narrowly focused, subordinate employees, and at considerably lower costs.

The first genuine act of partnership is looking closely and carefully at who the customer or client actually is. In most cases, this includes not only those who ultimately use the product or service but those who fix or repair it, those who are directly or indirectly affected by it, those who produce or deliver it, those who belong to the team that supports it, those who evaluate its quality and effectiveness, those who work for the organization that produced it, and those in society who benefit or suffer from its effects.

If we recognize that the customer is all of these people, including ourselves, we will be more highly motivated to manage quality and achieve the best results we can. For these reasons, effective customer partnerships mean:

- Assuming the organization is you and the product or service is yours, and making sure the buck stops with you.
- Acting according to the Golden Rule and asking: "What would I want if I were a customer?"
- Making "I" and "we" statements rather than accusations; instead of saying, "It's your fault," asking how you can work together to solve the problem.
- Valuing complaints, thanking people for voicing them, and taking whatever time is necessary to fix the problem.
- Asking for feedback on how you are doing, and acting as though it is true, even if it is not the entire truth.
- Not taking the relationship for granted but following through and checking to make sure it is right.

For customers to feel a genuine sense of partnership, it is necessary that the relationship not be mediated by third parties but engaged in directly and authentically. For this reason, customer partnerships require self-management; they are undermined when managers monitor employees and take responsibility for how they work. This means fully empowering employees to solve problems and inserting customer satisfaction criteria into all job descriptions. It means benchmarking organizations with high customer satisfaction, using process mapping to reduce the steps in customer service, and providing one-stop shopping. It means developing the attitude that you are a customer yourself.

Organizations that are managed hierarchically, bureaucratically, and autocratically reach a limit in their ability to make good on customer partnerships, which require a human touch. For this reason, we question the effectiveness of management as an organizing system, a relationship, and a vehicle for improving quality. We continue to affirm the need for leaders, coordinators, facilitators, and coaches who perform nonhierarchical organizational functions that are needed even in fully self-managing organizations and inspire employees to continue improving the quality of products, processes, and relationships.

Chapter Six

The Double Bind of Managerial Change

What if the whole deal—orientation, knowing where you are, and so on—what if it's all a scam? What if all of it . . . is just the biggest, most truly global, and centuries-oldest piece of brainwashing? Suppose that it's only when you dare to let go that your real life begins? When you're whirling free of the mother ship, when you cut your ropes, slip your chain, step off the map, go absent without leave, scram, vamoose, whatever: suppose it's then, and only then, that you're actually free to act! To lead the life nobody tells you how to live, or when, or why. In which nobody orders you to go forth and die for them, or for god, or comes to get you because you broke one of the rules, or because you're one of those people who are, for reasons which unfortunately you can't be given, simply not allowed. Suppose you've got to go through the feeling of being loose, into the chaos and beyond; you've got to accept the loneliness, the wild panic of losing your moorings, the vertiginous terror of the horizon spinning round and round like the edge of a coin tossed in the air.
SALMAN RUSHDIE, *The Ground Beneath Her Feet*

The problem with management is not simply that it reduces communication, morale, and motivation or that it constricts quality and customer service. It impedes the capacity of organizations to evolve and adapt to rapidly changing conditions. The dead weight of hierarchy, bureaucracy, and autocracy, the inertia of distrust, and the mass of unresolved managerial conflicts drag organizations down—

not only because they have not been addressed but because, regardless of the best intentions of individual managers, management as a system resists change and reinforces the past.

Although many individual managers are forward thinking, creative, and open to feedback, management as a system rewards those who do not take risks—those who bolster the organizational status quo and loyally implement instructions from the top. As a result, managers often resist efforts to improve dysfunctional behaviors, especially when they originate from above or involve power sharing with those below or the elimination of managerial oversight.

Innovation and adaptation are essential for survival in an increasingly complex, fast-paced, unpredictable economic environment. Organizations today cannot afford resistance to change or clinging to the past. They urgently need immediacy, responsiveness, agility, flexibility, and a heightened sensitivity to the subtle emergence of future trends and directions. Yet management methods are dedicated to making sure things are done as they have always been done.

Many organizations seek to overcome this intransigence of middle managers by periodically changing their CEOs. All new executives want to change the organization they direct simply to make it theirs. This is usually done by bringing in new managers at the top, reshuffling their responsibilities, reorganizing the status quo, modifying policies and procedures, or rearranging physical space—all of which gives the *appearance* of change without altering anything fundamental. Nonetheless, the world continues to change, leaving behind organizations that are unable to adapt.

Future trends and directions first become visible through problems, difficulties, conflicts, and dysfunctions, making it essential for organizations to listen nonhierarchically to everyone who has an idea or a problem, whether they are a part of management or not. More important, the pace of change makes it essential that everyone think responsibly and become part of a self-managing team, so that communication and change are not filtered through layers that subtly shift, delay, and distort them.

The Managerial Double Bind

Anthropologist and cybernetician Gregory Bateson developed a number of important ideas regarding social behaviors while studying tribes in New Guinea and Bali. Bateson observed that among the Iatmul of New Guinea, the more men behaved in an exhibitionist and boastful way, the more women became shy and contemplative. Each group's behavior accentuated its opposite in a reciprocal differentiation process Bateson called *schismogenesis,* in which the men competed to outdo each other and the women withdrew in response. Bateson found this dynamic destructive because it created miscommunication, polarized extreme positions, and denied individuals experiences outside these norms.

A similar dynamic can be observed in hierarchical organizations, where managers compete with one another to appear strong, decisive, responsible, and in favor of change, causing employees to retreat and appear weak, indecisive, irresponsible, and hostile to change. In this mutually reinforcing dynamic, the irresponsibility and indecisiveness of employees can be seen both as effects and causes of the responsibility and decisiveness of management. Each creates the other, and both need to change.

Bateson also observed families in which a member had schizophrenia deliver simultaneous contradictory messages to their mentally ill members. He called these mixed signals "double binds," such as being told to "go away" and "stay here" at the same time, paralyzing the recipient. In hierarchical organizations, managers are placed in a double bind when they are simultaneously given double-edged, paradoxical messages and asked to implement both. Harvard Business School professor Rosabeth Moss Kanter calls these mixed messages the "paradoxes of leadership":

- Be visionaries, while avoiding anything that hasn't been thoroughly tested.
- Innovate, while preserving the status quo and maintaining tradition.
- Think strategically and invest in the future, while keeping the numbers up today.
- Continue doing what has always been done, while doing it better, faster, and cheaper.
- Take risks, while not costing the business anything by failing.
- Cut costs and increase productivity, while increasing quality, decreasing expenses, and serving customers, clients, and citizens.

- Produce concrete results, while spending more time communicating with employees, serving on teams, and launching new projects.
- Be loyal to immediate supervisors and those with power, prestige, and status at the top, while supporting direct reports and employees.
- Know all the details, while delegating, resisting micromanagement, and relinquishing implementation to others.
- Discipline and control employees, while empowering and motivating them.
- Become passionately dedicated and fanatically committed, while being flexible, responsible, and able to change direction quickly.
- Speak up, be a leader, and set direction, while being participative, listening well, and cooperating.

These contradictory expectations of managers are passed on to employees through unclear, puzzling, and ambiguous instructions. These double binds have the effect of increasing anxiety, distrust, disengagement, and cynicism, which undermine organizational effectiveness. The result is an organizational environment riddled with schismogenesis, paradox, contradictory communication, and lack of integrity, which lead to role schizophrenia, chronic conflict, dysfunction, and increased resistance to participation, empowerment, collaboration, and change.

In the early 1980s, a visionary senior executive responsible for research and new product development at Polaroid had a powerful new idea. After considerable research in diverse fields such as information technology, biotechnology, and genetic engineering, he proposed that the photographic future belonged to electronic imaging and challenged Polaroid to create new products that would marry instant photographic technology with instant electronic imaging through computers.

The leadership team agreed with his predictions, but middle management did not share his enthusiasm. At that point, Polaroid's stock was riding high, and management believed they would continue being successful if they maintained the status quo. They thought that instant cameras were the only products they could or should manufacture. Their resistance led not only to Polaroid's loss of leadership in digital photography but diminished financial success and eventually bankruptcy.

If It Ain't Broke, Fix It

It is natural and customary for managers to base future plans on what worked in the past. Managers usually have the longest seniority in the organization and are charged with making sure there is continuity in policies and procedures. As a result, they become advocates for precedent, past practice, and "the way it's always been." Managerial thinking tends to value consistency over creativity and implementation over innovation.

Managers and employees often argue, "If it ain't broke, why fix it?" There are at least six good reasons for doing so:

- It may actually be broke, and you haven't noticed.
- The competition is busy trying to fix it.
- When you stop trying to fix it, you stop caring about it.
- It's not about being broke; it's about improving it.
- Unless you consistently try to fix it, you will grow accustomed to dysfunction, and new ways of fixing it will escape your attention.
- Who cares whether it's broke. It's challenging and fun to try to make it better.

In addition, managers naturally resist changes that require the introduction of self-management, flattened hierarchy, or organizational democracy because they correctly perceive that these enhancements will result in a loss of managerial power or prestige. They rationalize their resistance by arguing that employees do not have the skills to succeed in democratic or self-managing organizations, yet they do little to foster or support these skills among employees. Blocked by their own limitations, these managers hide in bureaucratic cul-de-sacs, hoping to avoid or prevent far-reaching changes.

When organizations direct that change be "managed," they imply that it should be directed from above without input or responsibility from below and that employees should be required to move in a predetermined direction even if it is wrong and their resistance is well founded. Managing change is not the same as leading it. It is following orders, even into the abyss.

Whatever the reasons, it is clear that there are multiple organizational rewards for playing it safe and reinforcing the status quo, and few for taking risks and leading change, for both managers and employees. This is why leaders and teams are needed and why employees, whatever their titles, need to do more than "manage" the change process; they need to lead, promote, facilitate, support, and inspire it.

The Organizational Mystique of Immortality

There are many reasons management as a system tends to legitimize the status quo, and leadership tends to transform it. Not only are managers economically vulnerable and dependent on salaries that can be taken away at will but they have a subtle psychological tendency to identify upward toward power and privilege rather than downward toward degradation and drudgery.

In addition, the longer managers remain in an organization, the greater their tendency to identify with it personally and with its mystique or image. If the organization has a long, stable history, an illusion is created of organizationally enhanced identity, as though the managers' personal status, power, and immortality were extended by being connected to the organization.

Veteran managers at Ford, AT&T, IBM, and General Electric; faculty at Harvard, Yale, and Princeton; and civil service staff at the Federal Bureau of Investigation, Central Intelligence Agency, and Internal Revenue Service can easily operate under the illusion that they personally are as powerful, successful, and enduring as the organizations with which they identify. This illusion is also perpetuated by the respect people are accorded on introducing themselves to others as working at prestigious institutions.

This surrogate respect encourages managers to preserve the power and prestige of the organization, protect its past, and avoid anything that might jeopardize its future. It lulls them into complacency and blindness regarding the inevitability of change, and denial regarding the predictable passing of the present. It allows them to forget that even the most impressive displays of organizational power, prestige, and immortality are illusory and that change and death are equally inevitable.

The fantasy that organizational identity extends to individuals generates countless ways of resisting or sidetracking changes perceived as undermining one's image. These include endless mazes of bureaucratic approval with intricate, pointless rules that cannot be changed; arcane policies and procedures that render change meaningless; near-Talmudic job descriptions that tie people in knots; and mind-numbing memos and senseless meetings, each of which produces a semblance of permanence in an otherwise impermanent world.

The mystique of organizational identity, riskiness of change, and job insecurities create a double bind that reduces management's ability to notice subtle shifts in the environment, threats to organizational survival, new ways of serving customer needs, unexpected market niches, alternative delivery systems, improved processes, and increased global competition.

Being a leader means living with the knowledge that identity is personal, change is unpredictable, and job security is nonexistent, which encourages living in the present, being responsible for choices, and committing to the risky process of bringing about a better future. In an interview before his death, Carlos Castaneda, author of the Don Juan chronicles, made an argument for orienting one's life toward the future:

> The difference between me and most people [read: managers]
> is that most people look at their lives as if they're on a train and
> they're sitting in the caboose. They watch the tracks sweep out
> behind them, and they're disappointed. But they adjust. And they
> know exactly what will happen next because of what's happened
> before. They believe their future will be just like their past. . . . But
> me, I look at my life as though I'm sitting in the locomotive. Ahead
> of me, the landscape disappears into the distance. I don't know
> where I'm going, and I have no idea what's going to happen next.
> No matter what went on yesterday, I know that today anything can
> happen. That's what keeps me happy. That's what keeps me alive.

Orienting to the future and being willing to risk the unknown cultivates vitality and regeneration in organizations. Self-managing organizations are better able to respond to leadership and to nurture openness, innovation, authenticity, honesty, common sense, and diversity—not only as ends in themselves but as practical aids in responding to the inherently chaotic, unmanageable nature of work life.

The Managerial Career Track

In hierarchies, career-minded managers are required to navigate progressively narrower career channels and succeed against increasingly competitive managerial opponents. This restrictive career path bolsters the natural desire of managers to maximize their career opportunities and avoid failure by not taking risks. Yet risk taking is a requirement in an organizational environment characterized by constant innovation and sweeping change.

Organizations typically promote employees into managerial positions based on their technical skills or talents. Yet these technical abilities become irrelevant once they are promoted. Instead, they are asked to become masters of an entirely different set of skills, for which they are nearly always undertrained, undersupported, and underqualified—such as:

- Listening actively and responsively
- Responding to difficult behaviors
- Designing group processes
- Engaging in interest-based negotiations
- Facilitating group dialogue over difficult issues
- Leading people in periods of crisis
- Building trust
- Responding to fear, anger, and shame
- Preventing, settling, and resolving conflicts
- Giving and receiving honest and empathetic feedback
- Coaching and mentoring others
- Communicating vision, expectations, confidence, and bad news
- Improving interpersonal relationships
- Inspiring creativity and risk taking
- Modeling integrity and values

Managers rarely receive any training or preparation for these roles, and what training they do receive usually consists of reviews of organizational policies and procedures, general expectations for performance, legal and fiscal responsibilities, and upward reporting requirements. It is rare, for example, that managers receive even cursory training in ways to respond to emotions, resolve conflicts, or inspire commitment to change.

Once employees are promoted into new managerial positions, ready or not, they are measured less by their successes than by their failures. They learn that it is better to do what has always been done than to risk something new and fail. For this reason and because competition increases as one moves up the hierarchical pyramid, politics and playing it safe, rather than courageous leadership and risk taking, become the most important skills in the managerial career game.

As organizations increasingly flatten their hierarchies and form self-managing teams, as team members become increasingly competent in managing themselves, and as managers are transformed into team leaders, coordinators, and facilitators, many of the roles that middle managers have traditionally played evaporate. And as these middle managerial roles disappear, established career tracks for advancement and recognition disappear as well.

Flattened skill-based career paths make it possible for employees to continue to grow and stretch their technical abilities throughout their careers, advance in responsibility, and affect organizational direction without having to climb over the broken ambitions of others. The sources of motivation and morale are no longer located in titles, power, privileges, parking spaces, and salary differentials.

In flattened, team-based organizations, promotion is necessarily lateral, and based on leadership abilities. These environments eliminate ostentatious managerial titles, jealously guarded differences in salaries, rigid protocols regarding status, and petty differences over status-marking furniture. Promotional systems permit those with talent and technical skills to move up the career ladder without having to abandon their experience and technical know-how in exchange for titles or salaries. They allow employees to develop and explore their expertise more deeply, enjoy the freedom to learn, play, mentor, teach, and lead, and provide greater opportunities to express their wisdom and teach others. They permit people to reach similar compensation and status levels as managers without having to move outside their areas of expertise.

Promoting employees into managerial positions that lie outside their competence and skill ultimately reduces morale and generates conflicts. Promoting them within their skills and allowing them to work more creatively benefits both the employee and the organization. For example, we worked with an aerospace manufacturing company in a successful effort to transform a traditional career track. An entire division was being held hostage by a middle manager who was blocking production through a lack of simple communication skills. Although she had outstanding technical abilities and knowledge that was central to manufacturing the product, she blocked effective production with a negative, blaming, divisive communication style.

In a joint problem-solving session, we helped the leadership team design a new career ladder that offered her advancement based on technical skills. She was given an opportunity to keep her salary and status and transfer out of management to a new, high-level position requiring advanced technical skills, which also gave her time to work on special projects of her own design and to mentor and train others.

The leadership team realized that if other staff were given broader technical promotional opportunities, morale would increase and the company would be able to retain more skilled scientific and technical personnel by assigning them to work as master technicians and help others improve their skills. This realization sparked a career redesign process, in which all employees were asked to identify and justify the roles they thought they could play as they advanced within the organization, resulting in a significant increase in ownership, morale, collaboration, and teamwork, and an end to destructive managerial warfare.

The Career Wars

As managers move higher up the career ladder, they are pitted against one another in bitter, costly, meaningless struggles for promotion that are rationalized by the victors as a kind of social Darwinian survival of the fittest. The consequences of even small-scale skirmishes, when added up, are appallingly wasteful. They include petty bickering, childish jealousies, bad-mouthing, character assassination, budget manipulation, and resource hoarding.

For example, we assisted a corporation in which the finance and sales departments were at war. Sales managers, eager for bonuses, were closing contracts for services with customers that made it difficult for finance managers to administer and collect fees. Finance managers gave no input to sales regarding collections on past contracts, current sales of competitors, or advice on timelines and level of services. Finance controlled the technology used to track contracts and measure products sold by the sales teams. The sales force did not have access to this information and had no way of tracing payments or increases and declines in sales. Finance managers felt the sales organization could not be trusted with the financial software, and sales managers felt finance was withholding vital information. These conflicts were aggravated by two competitive managers.

Both sides were then integrated into a single team-based organization, resulting in an overall increase in sales revenue due to greater knowledge and satisfaction among both sets of employees. Finance agreed to provide sales with direct access to computer applications for tracking sales-generated income, graphing sales costs against revenue, and monitoring profitability on major contracts. Sales was able to see the direct result of the deals they negotiated and use this information to negotiate more profitable future agreements. Sales agreed to work with finance to make it easier to interpret the contract, apply it, collect revenues, and audit compliance.

Finance, which had previously guarded its information closely, was relieved of the pressure of constantly criticizing sales for agreeing to financially unsound contracts, while being criticized for hounding customers with whom sales had close relations. Sales, with its detailed knowledge of customers, competition, and past performance, was able to assist finance in collecting more payments sooner with fewer audits.

In the past, finance managers would meet with sales managers monthly to present useless, unintelligible financial reports that were thrown away immediately after the meeting. Now, both groups worked together on customer-oriented teams, and each sales employee received a daily update on the results he or she produced, the payoff for the company, and credit toward future commissions and bonuses. Their motivation increased as a result, with dramatic financial improvements for the company.

Intraorganizational warfare is a natural consequence of the division of organizations into separately managed competitive parts. These battles discourage creativity, risk taking, and innovation throughout organizations, as managers are forced to devote energy to protecting their positions, guarding their turf, undermining their internal competitors, and limiting innovative ideas from below.

Unfortunately, behaviors that stifle innovation are everyday occurrences in hierarchical organizations, and managers are frequently rewarded for engaging in them. As a result, many managers spend much of their time *not* engaged in strategic planning, improving customer service, leading staff, organizing follow-through, or facilitating organizational development. Rather, they become passionately engaged in currying favor with superiors, fighting turf battles, gossiping about enemies, undermining competitors, struggling for control over resources, micromanaging subordinates, suppressing mistakes, countering criticisms, and defending themselves against similar maneuvers by other managers. As a result, precious time, money, and human potential are wasted.

A recent book by Robert Greene, *The Forty-Eight Laws of Power,* describes itself as a modern managerial version of Machiavelli's *The Prince.* Greene advocates a cut-throat approach to managerial competition, citing forty-eight laws for winning over internal competitors. Among the amoral and immoral behaviors he urges are: "Conceal your intentions," "Get others to do the work for you, but always take the credit," "Learn to keep people dependent on you," "Use selective honesty and generosity to disarm your victim," "Pose as a friend, work as a spy," "Crush your enemy totally," "Keep others in suspended terror: cultivate an air of unpredictability," "Do not commit to anyone," "Play on people's need to believe to create a cultlike following," "Control the options: get others to play with the cards you deal," "Discover each man's thumbscrew," "Think as you like but behave like others," "Strike the shepherd and the sheep will scatter," and "Preach the need for change, but never reform too much at once."

The real problem with these and similar suggestions is that they *accurately* describe the ways managers actually succeed in hierarchical organizations. None of these methods has anything to do with leadership, collaboration, integrity, values, or the human purpose of work, which is not to scramble for advantage over the talents and careers of others but to succeed together, based on merit, vision, and partnership.

Transformational Change Requires Teamwork

Leaders who want to improve organizational effectiveness by flattening their hierarchies, eliminating bureaucracy, and building self-managing teams often receive significant support from employees who want to be released from the rigidity of hierarchical structures and allowed to manage their own work processes. It is more often middle management that is asked to give up traditional command-and-control behaviors that resist these transitions.

Often, employees are promoted into managerial positions based on their ability to make decisions quickly rather than their ability to facilitate team decision making. When those promoted to management are asked to adopt an entirely different set of skills, they face problems for which they were not adequately trained and may not be successful without organizational resources or support. Literally caught in the middle, many of these managers resist changes that diminish their power and resent being asked to turn hard-won responsibilities over to self-managing teams.

Several strategies have been adopted to overcome this resistance to self-management. One approach has been to eliminate middle management completely. A more common approach has been to designate managers as team leaders and encourage them to manage in new ways, hoping they will somehow learn to become leaders and evolve a more collaborative style. A third approach has been for teams to select their own leaders by consensus or voting.

Each of these strategies has limitations. Eliminating middle management temporarily increases the amount of conflict, reduces productivity and morale, and sparks departures among those whose jobs are being redefined. Relabeling managers as team leaders without changing their approach sends mixed messages and creates a double bind for employees regarding the organization's commitment to the team process. As a result, organizational inconsistencies and conflicts appear, morale is reduced, and staff feel confused based on the contradictory messages they are receiving.

Team members often feel that if they agree to accept added responsibilities and do the extra work of building self-managing teams, they should not at the same time be hierarchically controlled by former managers using old-style command-and-control techniques in the disguise of team leaders.

The most consistent and effective approach is to allow team members to select their own leaders, using the same basic techniques that are used in political democracies: consensus and voting. In this way, the traditional role of management in controlling the selection of leadership from above is ended. What takes its place are self-management, organizational democracy, empowered leadership, and shared responsibility for outcomes.

Thus, the system of management, regardless of the skills and good intentions of individual managers, naturally and necessarily works externally, trying to fit round employees into square policies and limiting their capacity to lead or manage themselves. Self-management, on the other hand, operates internally on employee motivation, giving them freedom, choices, and responsibility for managing themselves.

It is only when employees have actual experience with the practical difficulties of managing their own work, when they are required to negotiate collaboratively and reach decisions by consensus, when they are organized into highly democratic teams, when they are able to choose their own leaders and follow their direction, that they are able to learn the methods of responsible self-management.

For these reasons, management is increasingly obsolete, costly, and counterproductive. The future belongs to self-management and organizational democracy.

Chapter Seven

Breaking the Hold of Hierarchy, Bureaucracy, and Autocracy

*[The bureaucracy] was permanently organized under the
constitutional government, which was, inevitably, the
friend of all mediocrities, the lover of authentic documents
and accounts, and as meddlesome as a petit bourgeois.
Delighted to see the various ministers constantly at odds
with four hundred petty minds, with their ten or twelve
ambitious and dishonest leaders, the various government
offices hastened to make themselves indispensable by
substituting written work for real work.*
HONORÉ DE BALZAC, *Bureaucracy*

It is difficult to imagine how work in the colossal organizational
structures that command our global economy could be linked and
harmonized without hierarchy, bureaucracy, and autocracy. Yet
most employees know from personal experience that hierarchies
generate inequalities of power and privilege that separate them
from one another based on artificial standards of superiority and
inferiority, that bureaucracies tie creativity and initiative in a knot,
and that autocracies impose their will on subordinates without considering what they think or feel.

What we often fail to recognize is that hierarchy, bureaucracy,
and autocracy cannot function without management and that management cannot function without hierarchy, bureaucracy, and au-

tocracy. Through normal everyday actions, managers and employees create hierarchy, bureaucracy, and autocracy, and these in turn produce the expectations, demands, and assumptions that create and support managers. Together, they form a powerful interlocking system in which each buttresses and depends on the other, resulting in increased stability and making it difficult to change one without fundamentally altering the other. We will not succeed in making organizations more agile, creative, and responsive to customer needs without a deeper understanding of how, regardless of the intentions of individual managers, the system of management automatically and inevitably generates these values, structures, systems, processes, and relationships.

The Sources of Hierarchy

The word *hierarchy* originates in the Greek root *hieros,* meaning holy, implying that those on top have higher, almost sacred powers and that command, status, and power flow from the top. A contrasting word, *heterarchy,* originates in *heteros,* meaning neighbors, implying organizations that are networked, participative, democratic, egalitarian, and self-managing. Heterarchy suggests that peers have equal power that is shared laterally and that important decisions are made at all levels, principally by consensus. Heterarchy means bottom-up, top-down, and sideways.

If we define hierarchy as any form of vertical organization, we miss the point. Anything that is larger, swifter, or stronger than another creates a *natural* hierarchy. But natural hierarchies are based on talent or skill, while *organizational* hierarchies are based on power and status. While the former constantly change and promote creativity, the latter are semipermanent and stifle it. The former apply only to one quality and do not imply a hierarchy of worth; the latter reflect status and power and imply that some are inherently more valuable than others.

A clear example of the differences between natural and organizational hierarchies can be found by contrasting "natural" leaders who are respected regardless of their job titles with managers who are appointed from above and not respected by those beneath them. Natural leadership is a positive contributor to organizational effectiveness; organizational hierarchies hold organizations back and are always, in some measure, resisted by those below.

Organizational hierarchies arise out of the assumption that it is necessary to control the way people work, that if managers do not use their status and power to compel employees to do their work, it will not get done, or done on time, or done well, or done the way someone higher up in the organization believes it ought to be done. This assumption creates a self-fulfilling prophecy, since treating employees as though they were incompetent and irresponsible reduces morale, creates a negative motivation for becoming competent and responsible, and encourages employees to adopt the very behaviors of which they are accused.

Organizational hierarchy, bureaucracy, and autocracy arise when natural leadership points in a different direction, making it necessary to coerce people into obeying managers they would not follow voluntarily. It follows logically that if we want to create organizations that are agile, creative, and responsive to customer needs, we need to reduce organizational hierarchy and support natural hierarchies of leadership and skill that employees easily recognize and follow without being told to do so.

Hierarchies and Organizational Freedom

We hold four fundamental value-based propositions regarding organizational hierarchies. First, human beings are not secondary to organizational life and should not be considered mere "employees" or even "human resources." They are the essence, heart and soul, living energy, ultimate reason for existence, and primary constituent of all organizational endeavors, and the source of all the actions, processes, communications, and relationships that bring them into daily existence.

Second, employees naturally thrive on challenges, and are fully capable of acting responsibly. Irresponsibility is a by-product of the use of coercion and control by organizational hierarchies, together with a lack of teamwork, natural leadership, respectful communication, and equitable compensation, rather than an inherent defect of character or human nature. Irresponsible employees suddenly become quite responsible when they are asked what they think or are placed in charge of something they believe in.

Third, although there are natural hierarchies of ability that arise in every task based on the talent, skill, and capacity of those who perform them, there are no stable, natural, universal hierarchies of worth between people that make one more deserving than another. Even where natural hierarchies exist, they are rarely fixed and unchanging. They flow and shift, allowing some to excel at one task while others excel at another. Organizational hierarchies freeze these qualities and obstruct their natural flow.

Fourth, hierarchies limit the degree of freedom available to employees. This proposition can best be explained by analogy to the idea of a dimension in physics or mathematics, where each dimension is seen to create an added degree of freedom. A point has zero dimensions and allows no freedom of movement. A line permits movement in one direction, for example, up and down. A plane grants an additional degree of freedom, allowing one to move horizontally as well as vertically. A cube creates a third dimension, depth. And a hypercube allows one to move in a fourth spatial dimension.

If we apply this idea to organizations, we can see that hierarchies encourage vertical movement and discourage horizontal movement across departmental lines. If hierarchy represents vertical freedom, cross-functional teams represent horizontal freedom by encouraging employees to work across departmental boundaries. In this sense, teams can be seen to create not merely a more effective way of working but an enlargement of organizational freedom.

The third dimension of organizational freedom, depth, occurs when there is strategic integration, in which teams are linked across professions and disciplines in a single unified strategic direction; when the entire organization operates out of a context of ethics, values, and integrity; and when natural hierarchies of merit replace artificial, fixed hierarchies appointed from above. Beyond this, we believe, lies a fourth hyperdimension consisting of synergy or community.

Organizational hierarchies violate all four of these propositions and promote, sometimes subconsciously, ideas of privilege and entitlement among those at the top, matched by resentment and exploitation among those at the bottom. With privilege comes fear of its loss, together with a desire to defend the existing order and disempower those who might seek to change it.

The Problems with Organizational Hierarchy

The perceived need for organizational hierarchy is reinforced by the failure of managerial relationships and communications, unequal responsibility for results, fear of equality, resistance to change, and a consequent need to command so that others will be forced to obey. In these ways, organizational hierarchy creates an aristocracy of power and privilege that divides those who have from those who have not, an autocracy that keeps them in their place, and a bureaucracy that dampens the fires of initiative and prevents any change that might challenge the systems and structures that support the status quo.

Organizational hierarchies diminish creativity by imposing rigid barriers that reduce flexibility and collaboration between levels, departments, titles, positions, and roles. They allow organizational policy to be set at the top by an elite of owners, board members, and majority shareholders who do not have a detailed understanding of day-to-day problems or perform the work yet are able to dictate organizational policy and direction and receive the greatest financial rewards.

Beneath the owners, board members, and majority shareholders in a typical corporate hierarchy are CEOs, directors, and presidents, who do most of the actual planning, thinking, and decision making and act as titular leaders of the organization. Beneath them are midlevel managers, who are responsible for making sure that plans and orders passed down from above are carried out and that the organization is run efficiently. Beneath them are employees, who perform most of the actual work and obey the orders passed down by middle managers. These hierarchical roles are diagrammed in Figure 7.1, based partly on ideas by our colleague Peter Block.

Organizational hierarchies separate planning from implementation, problems from the ability to solve them, ideas from application, and people from one another. While directors, presidents, and CEOs have considerable power to make things happen, they inevitably and increasingly lose touch with what needs to happen from the perspective of those who perform the work. They lack an organic connection with the demands and possibilities that emerge

Figure 7.1. Organizational Hierarchy.

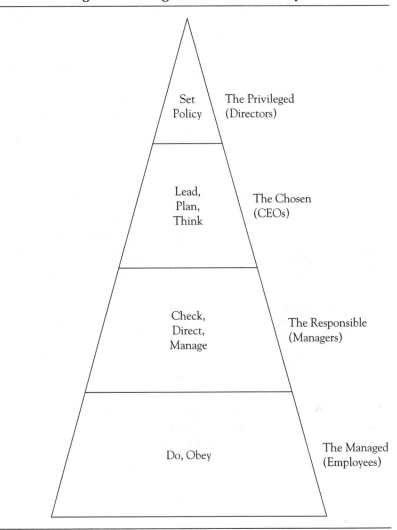

every day from the work process, the subtle, unspoken desires of customers and clients, and the gritty parts of problem solving that lend it creative, social, and human meaning.

The higher one is in the hierarchy, the greater one's income. The average CEO in the United States in 1982 earned 42 times more than the average factory worker. By 1999, that figure had climbed to $475 for every $1 earned by the average worker. This creates enormous social divisions, contradictory values, and loss of morale and places nearly 90 percent of national wealth in the hands of less than 10 percent of the population.

Organizational Hierarchies and Human Values

Organizational hierarchies not only undermine authentic relationships; they encourage managers to act against their own natural instinct that everyone should be equally entitled to respect and free to disagree without censoring themselves or being frightened that they will be fired. Yet hierarchies create these outcomes automatically simply by linking compensation, rewards, advancement, power, and status with hierarchical loyalty and obedience.

While we were conducting an educational program for a large corporation, an employee approached us with an ethical conflict. He knew that a product sold by his division to a long-standing customer would not meet requirements and was bound to fail. He could not decide whether to inform the customer that the product was faulty and risk the wrath of his manager, who had directed him to cover it up and blame customer use for the problem. Long discussions with his manager had been to no avail, and it became clear to him that if he were to play his assigned role, he would fail his customers, coworkers, organization, society, and himself.

After much soul searching, he decided to report the problem to the customer and risk his manager's wrath. His manager told him he had undermined the company, threatened the manager's own position, disobeyed directions, and placed his job in jeopardy. The employee stood by his decision and was eventually rewarded by the customer with a large order for an improved product. There are many other stories like this one, but more often they end with the employee being terminated or downsized.

This disturbing story reveals the ease with which integrity and values can be undermined by managers whose primary concern is their own career advancement or protection of the company's reputation. It reveals the unprincipled nature of hierarchical management's unspoken assignment to cover up mistakes. Trapped in one-dimensional structures that provide little opportunity for creative expression, authentic relationships, ethical dialogue, or regenerative work, people's souls wither and stagnate. Although it is possible to find solace in privilege, status, and power, these are ultimately dissatisfying, empty rewards that do not compensate for unethical behavior.

How Organizational Hierarchies Select Managers

Organizational hierarchies implicitly assume that high-level managers are more capable than those below them, and therefore entitled to select or promote managers without input or participation from below. In most cases, these managers would not be selected by an independent secret ballot election among the employees they are expected to manage or by other managers who are their peers. Yet who is more entitled to participate in deciding whether someone is capable of managing or leading than the people who will be managed or led?

Political democracy was founded on the proposition that the governed have a right to determine who will govern them. Why should organizational governing be treated any differently? Simply because corporations are privately owned does not mean that managers should be appointed from above, since boards of directors and shareholders vote on CEOs, and are subject to numerous legal restrictions designed to protect the rights of those below them. Voting for organizational management already exists. The only question is, Who has the right to nominate and vote?

Organizational hierarchy is a license to select managers based on personal affinity, which has historically been used to exclude candidates based on race, gender, sexual orientation, political views, religious affiliation, and other criteria that have nothing to do with the ability to lead. Managers have been promoted as rewards for obeying orders, playing it safe in office politics, keeping quiet about the mistakes of superiors, allying with the winning side in internal conflicts, flattering the boss, and countless other reasons that are completely unrelated to their abilities or the leadership needs of the organization. While research has identified multiple characteristics of outstanding leaders and criteria for managerial selection, organizational hierarchy allows all of them to be manipulated and disregarded.

Being a manager brings a higher rate of pay, increased status, and power over others. These encourage egotism and a sense of entitlement. In this way, hierarchies both produce and are produced by relationships of domination and subordination. They manufacture and are manufactured by attitudes of superiority and inferiority. Unequal hierarchical relationships create managers who rationalize and perpetuate feelings of powerlessness and inferiority among employees. They legitimize arbitrary authority by generating formally neutral, impersonal organizational processes in which rules are enacted and enforced for the ostensible benefit of everyone, while recreating and reinforcing bureaucratic, hierarchical, and autocratic assumptions. In these closed, self-perpetuating, ego-driven systems, hierarchy supports values and relationships that are antithetical to political, organizational, and social democracy.

The dissonance between life in organizational hierarchies and the democratic ideals that infuse political and social life creates confusing, jarring, depressing experiences for those at the bottom and self-serving, egotistical, isolating experiences for those at the top. The acceptance of unequal, unnatural hierarchical relationships is deeply engrained not only in organizations, but in all our thinking about institutions and the ways they are structured. Galileo's heresy in an earlier time lay not simply in asserting that the earth rotated around the sun, but, by extension, the impact this idea had on whether the laity rotated around the clergy, the family around the father, the serf around the lord, and the subjects around the king. When hierarchy is challenged in one arena, its necessity in others becomes open to question. As we reduce unnatural hierarchy in society, we implicitly challenge its presence at work.

We understand that there are far-reaching consequences to challenging the idea that hierarchical managers are required to run organizations efficiently. We expect that when organizational hierarchies are challenged, they will justify themselves vigorously.

Nevertheless, we find that alternative methods relying on self-management and natural hierarchy produce far less damage, more lasting results, and higher-level organizational values.

The Sources of Bureaucracy

The difficulties with organizational management extend beyond unnatural hierarchy to the entire system of bureaucratic administration. The French novelist Honoré de Balzac defined bureaucracy as "a gigantic power set in motion by dwarfs." While organizational hierarchy is a description of structure, bureaucracy is a description of the systems, processes, and methods that maintain and support that structure. Bureaucratic forms arise automatically in hierarchical organizations.

Like hierarchy, bureaucracy congeals relationships, constricts creativity, and reduces democracy. It is a labyrinth, a closed system that is extraordinarily effective in blocking anything that might alter the status quo, a one-dimensional sieve through which three-dimensional people and ideas are strained. It is an impersonal, faceless, entirely self-referential universe that diminishes authenticity, energy, and responsibility.

The primary characteristics of bureaucracy were first systematically formulated by German sociologist Max Weber, who used the term to describe the formal division of labor inside organizations, their authority structures, the positions and roles of individual members, and the rules that regulate their internal relations. Based on Weber's analysis, we understand the most common and essential elements of bureaucracy to be:

- A precise formal division, separation, and opposition between different kinds of labor that render communication difficult across disciplines
- A hierarchy of titles, offices, power, privileges, and functions leading to class distinctions, entitlement, and privilege
- A fixed set of rules and consequences governing performance that reduce creativity, authenticity, and individuality
- A formal separation of what is personal and private from what is official and public, while informally confusing them

- Overt selection for promotion based on technical skills, degrees, and formal qualifications, as well as covert selection based on favoritism
- Organizational positions and authority that are officially sanctioned yet viewed as the personal, private property of managers
- Goals, measures, rules, and policies that are predetermined by others, disempowering those who actually perform the work
- Structures and processes viewed as primary and superior to values and relationships, relegating human beings to second place
- Avoidance, accommodation, and manipulation of conflict, taking precedence over dialogue, negotiation, and resolution
- Giving facts, reality, details, and evidence great respect, while discounting emotion, art, abstract thinking, and intuition
- Valuing stability, tradition, and experience over change, innovation, and critical insight
- Using secrecy and a need to know and withholding information to maintain or increase personal power
- Gaps separating official from unofficial truth, resulting in the use of rumor and gossip to fill in the blanks
- Overcentralization of functions, leading to inflexibility, reduced innovation, and waste
- Personalized blame, along with impersonalized responsibility

Each of these elements of bureaucratic organization naturally and predictably results in reduced initiative, deterioration of morale, stagnation, chronic miscommunication, widespread distrust, irresponsibility, isolation of leadership, social alienation, rumor and gossip, unresolved conflicts, cynicism and apathy, and a class of managers who are needed to make this complex impersonal system work.

How Bureaucracy Generates Organizational Hierarchy and Management

Each of these elements of bureaucracy generates a need for managers, while managers generate a need for bureaucracy. Indeed, management and bureaucracy can be thought of as flip sides of the same coin, since each supports and reinforces the other. Bureaucracies provide a safe haven where managers can hide from responsibility and avoid being held accountable for errors of judgment or problems they created or failed to solve. In return, managers are able to use bureaucratic rules to stifle self-management and compel employees to follow their direction.

Bureaucracies fragment organizations by developing detailed, overlapping requirements that necessitate managerial oversight, such as forms to make sure money is not wasted and employees do not steal. These forms create a need for managers, both to monitor compliance and, since a great deal of work would come to a halt if employees actually did only what they were supposed to do, to selectively disregard these rules and direct people to do the work.

We worked with a science museum that had an exhibit containing live frogs. In order to feed the frogs, it was necessary to purchase worms each month for little more than a dollar. Despite the regularity of this expense, its obvious necessity, and the minuscule sums involved, each purchase of worms required *five* management signatures, including that of the executive director. The message communicated by this and other bureaucratic processes was that staff were financially irresponsible. This subtle message permeated the organization's culture, reducing motivation to participate in a major strategic planning process.

In theory, the museum needed someone to make certain that employees did not embezzle or waste funds set aside for the frogs, yet self-managing teams could have achieved the same result at a far lower cost. The real problem was that the frogs "belonged" to the museum bureaucracy, not to the people in charge of feeding them. This abstract organizational identity operated in a hierarchical fashion to ensure that worm money was not stolen, while leaving employees feeling irresponsible, distrusted, cynical, and disempowered. The cost in managerial time and poor morale dwarfed any conceivable saving that might have resulted from this policy.

In another example of organizational bureaucracy, an eighty-two-year-old neighbor found her Social Security checks stopped after her husband died. She called the Social Security Administration office to protest and was told that her payments were stopped because she was dead. She replied that she was actually alive or she would not have been able to communicate very effectively over the telephone. Her case officer agreed that she was probably alive, but the check-issuing manager disagreed, and it was taken out of the staff social worker's hands. After six months and dozens of letters, complaints, and calls, she finally received a letter indicating that she had been "resurrected" and her checks were reinstated. She responded: "You have no idea how hard it is to try to prove you are alive when someone with a lot of power says you are dead."

The intrinsic emphasis in bureaucracies on unquestioning conformity and strict enforcement of rules encourages managers to coerce and manipulate employees into obedience. It equally encourages employees to obey rules blindly, resist responsibility for outcomes, and shelve their creativity, reinforcing the need for managers to watch over them. This makes the system self-reinforcing, turning it in a circle. Because bureaucracy mandates conformity to a single standard, it produces apathy, cynicism, and irresponsibility at the bottom and autocracy, privilege, and unilateral action at the top. These dynamics make management even more immune to change, thereby reinforcing the need for bureaucracy.

While exceptions certainly undermine the rule, it is important to question whether the rule is needed in the first place, whether individuals are not already exceptions, and whether we want rules that do not permit exceptions. If the real problem is abuse, why not regulate the abuse or coach the abuser instead of generalizing the rule and punishing the innocent? Whenever there is a problem, bureaucracies respond with broad, generalized solutions based on universal distrust that restrict personal freedom, silence complainers, and force those below to conform to abstract standards of behavior, with no understanding of the social and psychological impact they have on human spirits and emotions.

Yet bureaucratic systems can be broken down and transformed into human-scale interactions. We have seen countless managers recreate themselves as leaders and facilitators, employees reinvent themselves as responsible self-managing team members, and bureaucracies transform into responsive, human-scale organizations. Alternatives to organizational hierarchy are both practical and possible.

Hierarchy and Bureaucracy Result in Autocracy

Organizational hierarchy and bureaucracy force human relationships to conform to patterns that run counter to their natural direction and for this reason generate resistance. In order to overcome that resistance, hierarchies and bureaucracies are driven to exclude those who resist from fully and directly participating in the decision-making process. The result is autocracy.

Autocracy is a natural expression of hierarchical power and an inevitable consequence of bureaucratic formality. It is the self-perpetuation of privilege, the right to deny the rights of others, and the last resort of managerial power. It is the system that gives some the authority to tell others: "Do it because I said so." Because autocracy is a way of organizing and exercising control over others, it is best understood in the context of practical proposals for the democratic redistribution of organizational power, which are considered in detail in the next section.

Democratic organizations require a new theoretical framework for eliminating hierarchy, bureaucracy, and autocracy and a practical redesign for the way we work. The remaining chapters take up this challenge and are a guide to creating collaborative, democratic, self-managing organizations.

Chapter Eight

Where Do We Go from Here?

The difficulty of achieving the simple is infinitely more
complicated than any other task or skill, that is, it is less
difficult to conceive, create, construct and manipulate an
electronic brain than to find in our own the wherewithal to
be happy.
JOSÉ SARAMAGO, *The History of the Siege of Lisbon*

We are at a crossroads in our understanding of organizations and our ability to form work into a vehicle for human happiness. The problems we have identified with management define this crossroads, and with it come demands for the articulation of fresh options. The sweep and magnitude of these options has increased as a result of enormous achievements in science and technology, global communications, and the development of subtle knowledge regarding human potential, group process, organizational learning, problem solving, self-fulfillment, and the significance of play.

As a result of these new understandings, we can now consciously shape our workplaces and organizations to serve human needs, realize our shared values, and increase our happiness. We can cease being victims of hide-bound hierarchies and slaves to bureaucratic thinking. We can create fresh alternatives, design adaptable structures, and select the strategies, processes, roles, and relationships we need to fulfill ourselves as human beings.

In doing so, we face a number of foundational questions. What are the core values that ought to inform our choices? How should our workplaces be structured? In what direction are our organizations naturally evolving? Which processes work most effectively?

How can work be structured to support human relationships and value-based behaviors? What do we really want organizations to do? How can they be designed to be more effective in doing it?

The Evolution of Organizations

We believe the shift from organizational hierarchy, bureaucracy, and autocracy to heterarchy, democracy, and collaborative self-management is part of a larger historical transformation in the satisfaction of human needs and the social nature of work designed to meet those needs. To interpret these dramatic changes, we need to understand in greater detail how work has evolved over time.

According to psychologist Abraham Maslow, we all try to satisfy our needs and do so in an ordered, progressive way. After successfully satisfying one level of need, we move on to satisfy those that remain, and our priorities, goals, and ways of behaving are organized around whatever has to be done to satisfy that need. Maslow posited that there is a hierarchy of needs, consisting of seven primary categories, in the following order of importance:

1. *Physiological needs*—for water, food, warmth, shelter, sex, sleep, health, cleanliness
2. *Safety needs*—for security, stability, economics, dependency, protection, structure, order, law, limits, freedom from fear, anxiety, chaos
3. *Belongingness and love needs*—for partnership, family, friends, neighbors, neighborhood, group affiliation, country, intimacy, affection
4. *Esteem needs*—for self-respect, self-esteem, esteem of others, strength, achievement, adequacy, mastery and competence, confidence, independence, reputation, prestige, status, fame, dominance, recognition, attention, importance, dignity, appreciation, understanding
5. *Self-actualization needs*—for challenge, fulfillment of personal abilities and talents, and expressions of what a person is or must be
6. *Need to know and understand*—for curiosity, knowledge, understanding
7. *Aesthetic needs*—for beauty, order, symmetry, system, structure

Human behaviors change dramatically as each stage is reached, since a strategy that succeeds in satisfying one need will not necessarily be successful in satisfying another. We can now extend Maslow's theory and suggest that organizations that were created to satisfy lower-level needs become expressions of those needs and must change their structures, systems, and strategies in order to evolve and satisfy higher needs.

Each stage in the satisfaction of needs represents a fresh strategy, with a new set of tasks, a new form and process of work, and a new set of organizational relationships for accomplishing that work. Each new stage represents and gives rise to a new form of freedom for those who are able to reach it. There is both a *freedom from* the tyranny of earlier, demeaning stages of work and a *freedom to* explore the meaning and consequences of new ways of working that give rise to unique understandings of what it means to be human. Our challenge is to create organizations that allow us to evolve to higher levels of freedom and fulfillment.

Evolution in the Forms of Work

Over the past several thousand years, human work has progressed through a number of distinct stages. Roughly, we have moved from prehistoric hunting and gathering to subsistence farming, slavery, feudalism, mercantilism, industrial capitalism, and the beginnings of a new stage characterized by greater cooperation, the massive use of computers, scientific and technological innovation, and the internationalization of production and distribution.

We have merged and combined these stages and consolidated them with Maslow's psychological framework to redefine the evolution of work:

1. *Work as survival.* Human labor, reflecting Maslow's primary category, begins in efforts to secure adequate food, shelter, and clothing to guarantee personal, family, and clan survival. Work consists of scraping, squeezing, and prodding nature to yield its rough treasures. In the process, work tends to be seen as humbling and necessary yet natural and satisfying.

2. *Work as social status.* With the rise of privileged elites and slavery, work is seen as demeaning and evidence of an inferior sta-

tus. Under feudalism, work was similarly tied to status, compulsory, and fixed for life.

3. *Work as craft.* The artistic work of feudal craftsmen reshapes nature and turns it into objects that serve practical needs yet also provide human satisfaction. In the process, work is seen as a creative act that has both a practical and an artistic purpose and consists of shaping objects of beauty and utility out of simple natural elements.

4. *Work as commodity.* Work is now transformed into a commodity: employees sell their ability to work to a capitalist, who uses it to manufacture objects to sell at a profit. In the process, work is seen as alienating, oppressive, and instrumental to the achievement of someone else's satisfaction. Workers are separated from their machines and from the products, wealth, and pleasure that result from their labors.

5. *Work as information.* With the development of information and analysis, the worker finds, generates, and directs information in order to enhance organizational knowledge or awareness; work thus becomes a manifestation of practical curiosity and learning. In the process, work is seen as a method of learning and improving. This is the most rapidly growing form of work today.

6. *Work as social contribution.* Work is seen as a form of social responsibility, the creation of a sense of community, a contribution to society, and the social networks that increase our capacity to live more fruitful lives. In the process, work is seen as relational and a gift to the human family.

7. *Work as self-actualization.* When work becomes a form of self-actualization, people use it to create and shape their lives and natures. In the process, work is seen as a path to spiritual and personal satisfaction, as adding meaning to life, and as a source of growth and self-transformation.

8. *Work as art.* The highest form of human labor is work as art, in which work consists of shifting the perceptions and shapes of the world in ways that give pleasure and move beyond craft and utility to unleash the human imagination. In the process, work is seen as elegant and beautiful and an end in itself.

Each of these descriptions of the forms of work combines a psychological perspective with a historical or evolutionary framework in an integrated synthesis. These approaches are not mutually exclusive; rather, they overlap and reinforce each other to create interesting and unusual patterns. The last forms, for example, reveal a common theme of social and individual development that link them in a conjoint purpose. More important, each form reflects attitudes or states of mind that are available to everyone at all times, regardless of the historical period or the kind of work being done. Each represents possibilities that can be furthered or frustrated by the way work is engaged and structured.

It is clear that the need for management is greatest when work is a talisman of social status or sold as a commodity. Lamentably, traditional management blocks achievement of the last four stages. Although it is possible to manage work as information or social contribution, it is rarely necessary to do so, and is in many cases counterproductive. As we have indicated, it is impossible to manage work as self-actualization or work as art without undermining the purpose and obstructing the ability to satisfy these needs. Yet this dynamic becomes even more pernicious. Managers try to confine the work experiences to earlier forms of development in order to maintain not only power, status, and privileges but the very meaning of their stunted work lives.

The Functions of Work

There is a different way to understand the nature of work, which is to see it and the organizations that actively coordinate it from a functional rather than a psychological, evolutionary, or synthesized perspective. In this view, work can be seen as being made up of four separate yet interrelated and inseparable aspects or functions, each culminating in four entirely different products.

First, *work as activity* results in a product or service that is visible and tangible. This aspect constitutes its most obvious goal and purpose. Second, *work as process* is largely invisible and intangible and results in the creation of a way of doing things. Most organizations focus on activities and products, yet processes are far more powerful and lasting. Third, *work as relationship* is similarly invisible and intangible yet connects us to each other, to nature, coworkers, and consumers. This aspect results in social connection, intimacy, and learning. Our relationships are far more powerful and lasting than either the activities or process that express them, yet organizations pay even less attention to relational qualities.

Finally comes *work as self-actualization,* as a creator of integrity, self-esteem, values, and character, through which we define who we are and are able to feel satisfied with ourselves and our work lives. Who we are is vastly more powerful than either what we do or how we do it, even than the relationships we create while doing it, yet organizations devote the least amount of attention to the ways we manufacture ourselves.

Once we recognize that work is not simply an activity designed to create products and services, but a producer of processes and relationships—not only with coworkers but with nature, society, family, values, responsibility, and possibility—and that it defines who we are and gives us the freedom to develop and expand, we can consciously begin to plan the way we organize our work lives so as to maximize our freedom, happiness, and fulfillment.

Management as a system is best at organizing activities and processes, but it has difficulty with relationships, attitudes, values, and self-actualization. This is partly because it is imposed from above and partly because, by definition, we cannot actualize ourselves or be who we are when someone in authority is telling us whom we ought to be.

Every aspect of our work lives can fuel the creative activity of practical, artistic imagination. It can become poetry and art. In truth, the least of what we create at work are products and services. Our greatest creations are ourselves, our relationships, our culture, our society, our happiness, our freedom, our capacity, our future. Our task is quite simply to design workplaces and organizations with this fundamental truth in mind.

The Next Organizational Revolution

In our view, over the past several centuries there has been a slow but continuous, even increasing, movement of polities and societies in the direction of democracy. By democracy, we mean self-government: in Lincoln's classic words, government of, by, and for the people. In a democracy, people of all races and genders, regardless of wealth or ownership of property, participate in selecting their political leaders. There is no compelling reason they should not also be able to participate in selecting their organizational leaders, nor is there any reason they would be less successful in doing so than a handful of majority shareholders or directors.

The next great democratic revolution will transform our workplaces, our corporations, nonprofits, schools, and government agencies into organizations of, by, and for both the people who work in them and the people they serve, without distinctions based on race, gender, social class, condition of ownership, or position in organizational hierarchy. If majority rule and minority rights work for government and society, why not for organizations as well? In practice, this means striving to reach consensus not by silencing dissent or forcing minorities to comply but inviting their input, hearing their experiences, and meeting their interests. It means creating a space that is free and inviolable, in which dissent and difference are encouraged and celebrated.

A common theme runs through complaints about autocratic managers and bureaucratic organizations, from which suggestions regarding how work should be organized can be derived. Nearly every organization on some level understands that employees want their work to be self-managing, value based, and human dimensioned; to consist of weblike associations, teams, networks, alliances, and associations; and to be led by ubiquitous, relationship-oriented, democratically selected, linking leaders. They want processes that are streamlined and collaborative; communications that are open, honest, and trustworthy; self-correcting systems that encourage genuine feedback, learning, and conflict resolution; that are strategically integrated; and to change the way they change.

In collaborative, democratic, self-managing organizations, people no longer work at fixed locations or perform routine, predictable tasks; they respond as needed to problems when and as they arise. Managers no longer assign tasks or monitor compliance. Instead, teams discover problems, assign tasks, and take responsibility for completion. Individuals interact through networks of association that are fueled by communication, commitment, consensus building, and collaboration. Organizational boundaries no longer block the flow of information or work between siloed departments, so that the potential for alliances, associations, partnerships, teams, and networks becomes potentially limitless. Well-defined chains of command give way to people having access to everyone at all times on all levels. Managers no longer operate as captains of industry or power brokers, but as leaders, coordinators, connectors, facilitators, mentors, coaches, and mediators who bridge, network, and link people, and activate group energies to generate new configurations and possibilities.

Seven Strategies for Organizational Transformation

We have identified seven key strategies for transforming organizational hierarchies, bureaucracies, and autocracies into collaborative, self-managing democracies. In succeeding chapters, we develop each of these strategies, and reveal their practical possibilities.

Strategy 1: Shape a Context of Values, Ethics, and Integrity

To support self-management, we require a context of values, ethics, and integrity that is explicit, shared, and embodied in real behaviors that reverberate throughout the organization. Values shape and direct work within the organization and establish its relationship with the outside world. Creating identity, behavior, and culture from a context of shared values and integrity provides a powerful driving force for innovation within the organization that affects each self-managing structure, system, strategy, process, and relationship and integrates them into a sustainable framework.

Strategy 2: Form Living, Evolving Webs of Association

Self-managing organizations are flexible and renewable. They constantly shift and evolve into shapes and structures that are highly responsive to environmental conditions, revealing changing problems and improved strategies for solving them. These structures spring from seeing organizations as living, evolving organisms and webs of association, in which individuals, partners, teams, networks, and alliances design their own roles, communications, systems, processes, and relationships. Each node of activity in a web of association manages itself and links with others in response to rapidly changing conditions, problems, and opportunities. Webs of association constantly evolve in purpose, size, shape, structure, process, and direction. They are self-managing, self-directing, and self-referential and operate continually in a learning mode.

Strategy 3: Develop Ubiquitous, Linking Leadership

A key to success in self-managing organizations is the ability of leaders to link individuals, teams, and webs of association, stimulate energy and commitment, solve problems, build supportive alliances, and learn from experience. Leaders help teams evolve, expand, develop, and stabilize. Organizational opportunities require the development of leadership skills ubiquitously, that is, throughout the organization: character skills that build integrity, relational skills that form interconnections between people, mediation skills that turn conflicts into opportunities, wisdom skills that increase understanding, elicitive skills that motivate people to act, and action skills that marshal forces to achieve results. Leaders in democratic organizations are freely and voluntarily selected by employees who, together with clients, customers, and shareholders, select all organizational leaders including CEOs, and actively assist in making the decisions that affect their lives.

Strategy 4: Build Innovative Self-Managing Teams

At the heart of webs of association are small, flexible, self-managing teams of widely varying sizes, functions, purposes, forms, and life cycles. Teams are responsible for defining and achieving goals, solving problems, and seizing opportunities. The best teams are self-selecting, self-directing, self-managing, and self-sustaining. Their processes include hiring and firing fellow team members, electing leaders, defining roles and tasks, and redesigning organizational parameters from scratch. Networks of teams link up with each other through leadership, information systems, and collaborative processes, which permeate boundaries to build mutual support.

Strategy 5: Implement Streamlined, Open, Collaborative Processes

A rich variety of collaborative group processes are used to support shared values, build teams and webs of association, and develop ubiquitous, linking leadership in a diverse organizational environment. Customer partnerships are streamlined, individual and team responsibility are promoted, and countless organizational processes are reworked. Communications, meetings, negotiations, and decision making are redesigned to encourage diversity, collaboration, self-management, and democracy. While unimportant decisions can be announced, consulted on, or delegated and others have to be voted on, the most important require consensus or unanimity. An essential element in self-management is understanding which decision-making approach to use for what purpose and how to design processes that encourage collaborative relationships.

Strategy 6: Create Complex, Self-Correcting Systems

Systems for self-correction and self-improvement encourage employees and organizations to learn and continue increasing their capacities. The more complex and multidimensional organizational tasks and relationships are, the more complex and multidimensional the self-correcting systems needed to keep them on course. These systems include feedback and evaluation, motivation and rewards, discipline and correction, negotiation and conflict resolution, and methods for creating learning organizations and professional communities. Using these devices and techniques, collaborative, self-managing, self-correcting organizations can turn mistakes, problems, conflicts, glitches, and errors into opportunities for improvement.

Strategy 7: Integrate Strategically, and Change the Way We Change

As organizations implement these strategies, each is simultaneously integrated into a single unified whole, and the methods and change processes used to bring them into existence are transformed. It is not possible to eliminate hierarchy using hierarchical change processes. Democratic changes create multiple opportunities for strategic integration, which adds a third dimension of organizational freedom, based on depth. Changing the way we change means turning every employee into a self-conscious change agent, an organizational revolutionary.

The End of Blueprints

We have reached the end not only of management but of managerial approaches to organizational change, including the use of blueprints, models, detailed instructions, mandates, uniform answers, universal solutions, taboos, categorical imperatives, and management gurus. As we progress beyond hierarchical, bureaucratic, autocratic organizational principles, a critical design principle is introduced: that solutions be customized to fit problems and people rather than generalized as one-size-fits-all recommendations. Universal solutions are no longer applicable. Rather, we are now able to use an array of exciting possibilities to inform our choices and allow individuals and teams to invent and jerry-rig the solutions they need.

It is clear from examining organizational change efforts that pilot projects adapted to local conditions nearly always succeed, while universal models dictated by others based on generalized experiences fail. The reason is that leadership, creativity, motivation, and responsibility rise to a challenge and retreat before a repetition. If it has already been done and cannot be improved, it feels less exciting than pioneering a brand-new approach. Importing solutions that work in one environment to solve problems in another can produce false starts and roadblocks and often end in failure. This approach to organizational change also alters the role of management consultants, eliminating the need for external experts who stamp out cookie-cutter solutions based on generalized principles.

Democratic organizational changes cannot be prescribed or directed by others. We apply this caution to the suggestions we make in this book. If we attempt to do otherwise, we will violate the philosophy we propound in these pages and undermine the values that form the basis for organizational democracy.

The chapters that follow offer suggestions rather than conclusions and admonitions. We do not have The Solution, rather we offer a range of alternative solutions to be explored in multiple ways. Thus, different answers can be given to the same question, and unique solutions can be found for each problem. It is too soon in this evolving process to fix on a single correct answer. Worse, it is antithetical to the values of democracy and self-management. As difficult as it may seem, there are an infinite number of correct answers to many questions, and these can be discovered only by exploring with each other the infinite space within.

Part Two

A Practical Guide to Organizational Democracy

Chapter Nine

Shape a Context of Values, Ethics, and Integrity

*I want to talk chiefly about a "philosophy of
management." I believe that good leadership in
industry depends more than any other single thing
on the manager's . . . convictions and on his beliefs
about people. Are people inherently honest; can they
be taught to be honest? Will people naturally seek
responsibility under certain conditions; or do you have
to fight with them to get them to accept responsibility?
Will people in general break rules no matter what the rules
are: or is it possible that people will live up to the rules
voluntarily? Convictions about matters like these make
up the philosophy that lies behind the manager's job.*
DOUGLAS MCGREGOR

It is rare that we take time to reflect on our philosophy of management or consciously try to improve the values, ethics, and integrity that lend meaning to our lives. Yet without philosophical
questioning, psychological self-examination, and ethical reflection,
we easily slip into rationalizing our actions and justifying everything
we have done, from minor ethical lapses to outright evil. For this
reason, as Socrates proclaimed, "the unexamined life is not worth
living."

For the most part, organizations do not encourage managers
or employees to live ethically examined lives. They do little to encourage philosophical inquiry, psychological self-observation, or
ethical awareness. Perhaps this is because, if they did, they would

be compelled to alter many of their operations, systems, styles, and processes, starting with the simplest, most basic actions. Even a cursory consideration of ethics leads us to the realization that every act, every goal, every process expresses values and has ethical overtones. Affirming values, ethics, and integrity, especially when they run counter to economic self-interest, encourages organizational integrity. Failing to do so encourages organizational corruption.

Creating Ethical Capital

Organizations are not simply financial centers, producers of products and services, repositories of memos and reports, and designers of business strategies. They are also social centers, producers of values and ethics, repositories of integrity and culture, and designers of processes and relationships. In most organizations, close attention is paid to achieving ends, goals, objectives, and targets, while less is paid to the values implications and ethical significance of these goals and the means used to achieve them.

Many successful organizations are engaged in courageous efforts to clarify or make their values explicit, to "walk their talk." The process of identifying, elaborating, and acting on the basis of values, ethics, and integrity plays a critical role in the development of the capacity and motivation of individual employees and the energy and effectiveness of organizational relationships as a whole.

Every organizational system, structure, behavior, and attitude carries an underlying value or ethic that for the most part, remains unconscious, unacknowledged, and unexplored. At the heart of every organization lies a set of values and ethics that defines its identity, culture, and mission and affects every aspect of what it does, whether people are aware of and agree with them or not. Often these values surface when there is conflict, or when someone quits or is fired or has failed. Yet they are always in the background, waiting to emerge.

When organizations are value driven, clear about ethics, and grounded in integrity, employees feel they are able to choose consciously, define publicly, and live by their highest values. When organizations ignore values, ethics, and integrity and operate on the basis of laws, rules, and regulations, they reduce their values to conformity and the narrow self-interest of not getting caught. Everyone makes sure they operate above the floor of prohibition so they will not be fired. Few aim to reach the ceiling.

Organizations can promote adherence to rule-driven values or to value-driven rules. They can impose uniform rules and standards on employees through more or less coercive methods, allowing them to bypass personal responsibility and involvement in ethical decision making and merely do what the law or organizational rules and policies require. Or they can encourage employees to develop their own values and ethics in dialogue with one another, agree on high personal standards, and strive always to act ethically with each other.

Each of these contrasting approaches to values itself represents a deeper set of values. Many organizations, by failing to choose between these approaches, generate confusion as to whether their primary value is obedience to law and authority or encouraging employees to define and live up to their values and reach consensus on the ones by which they choose to live.

What Are Values?

Values are essentially priorities. They are choices that are present in everything we do and do not do, everything we resist and are willing to tolerate. When taken seriously, they are based on real alternatives and a genuine consideration of consequences. They are openly and publicly expressed, acted on repeatedly, and upheld, especially when they run counter to personal self-interest.

Values are builders of integrity and responsibility, authors of optimism and self-esteem, and definers of who we are. They become manifest and alive through action, even the action of sincere declaration. The simple act of opening a dialogue regarding ethics, values, and integrity automatically calls attention to the ways people act in contradiction to their values, places a value on having values, and prompts self-correction.

We find it useful to identify three levels or orders of values. First is the recognition that something is important or valuable to us, such as respect or honesty. Second is the perception that there is a value in having values, which consists of promoting dialogue and conversation about them. Third is the experience of acting on the basis of our values, transforming them into an integral, inseparable aspect of who we are.

The first level of values in organizations consists largely of *declarations* of values that are corrective or defensive in purpose. Their aim is to advertise a value orientation or protect the organization from unethical behaviors. The second level of values consists largely of *understanding* the importance of values, which is developmental or transformational in purpose. Its aim is to encourage growth, learning, change, improvement, and evolution in the ways people work. The third consists largely of value-based *behaviors,* which are integrative or transcendent in purpose. Its aim is for values to become part of our character and organizational culture, so that they flow naturally from who we *are* rather than from what we declare or understand.

By encouraging employees to engage in dialogue over values on all three levels, organizations create a context of values, ethics, and integrity, or what might be called a bottom line of integrity. They create ethical capital by encouraging people to implement their values in everyday work life. In doing so, it is necessary to move from declarations to understanding to behaviors based on values and to integrate them into personal character and organizational culture.

The Bottom Line of Integrity

Unfortunately, much of what transpires in modern organizations in relation to values, ethics, and integrity consists of rationalization and gloss rather than reflection and dialogue. As Aristotle discerned centuries ago, the test of ethics occurs when they run counter to our self-interests rather than when they serve them. Financial self-interest and organizational power are classic examples of self-serving values that often lead to ethical rationalization.

In hierarchical organizations, managers are asked to conform employee behaviors to operational requirements so as to produce results that satisfy customer, client, or citizen expectations and thereby ensure the financial success of the organization. In the process, they make countless decisions that reveal how far they are willing to go in promoting what the organization defines as success. Most managers act as though there is a single organizational value or standard to which every employee should be held, which is financial success and the fiscal bottom line.

When the fiscal bottom line becomes the sole recognized value, ethics begin to deteriorate. Occasionally, these lapses lead to devastating results, as when corporate management fails to re-call defective tires for sport utility vehicles or notify the National Aeronautics and Space Administration of defects in O-rings for the space shuttle solely to maximize profitability. While apparently minor ethical lapses can cause serious damage, there are countless cases in which no visible damage results—yet in a way, these cases pose more serious problems. They reveal that the suppression of truth is routine in most organizations and easily rationalized by the goal of financial gain.

A simple example is advertising, in which a positive spin is placed on a company's product or service in order to encourage consumers to purchase it rather than a similar item produced by a competitor. At a trivial level, there is a subtle dishonesty in not communicating the negative aspects of the product or divulging anything that might result in the consumer's deciding not to pur-chase it, or using sexually exploitative advertising, all of which de-value honesty. At a more serious level, these same justifications are used to rationalize misleading ads for cancer-causing cigarettes, foods containing lead, and hazardous baby toys.

The problem is not that everyone is trying to be financially suc-cessful, but that they have adopted the financial bottom line as a solitary standard and reduced human life to a question of prof-itability. It is easy to forget that there are other important bottom lines besides financial ones, including the bottom line of values, ethics, and integrity, which, it can be argued, is at least as impor-tant to organizational profitability as financial achievement. A bottom-line commitment to values, ethics, and integrity contributes enormously to the development of collaboration, diversity, cre-ativity, participation, responsibility, morale, and unity. When these are valued, the financial bottom line improves as well.

Nonetheless, the primary reason for organizations to develop values, ethics, and integrity is not to increase profits but to create more satisfying work lives so people can feel proud of what they do and how they do it. The goal is for everyone to act with values, ethics, and integrity not because they are told or expected to do so or because they think it will be effective, but because it is right, because they feel better about themselves, because doing so is an expression of who they are or want to be.

Communicating About Values

At a deep level, everyone communicates their values by what they say and do and by who they are and what is important to them. Often the most meaningful communications regarding values occur through behaviors rather than words. When we attempt to define values, we create definitions rather than values. This prompted philosopher Ludwig Wittgenstein to write that "values cannot be articulated," by which he meant that they cannot be clearly or completely defined and need to be lived rather than espoused. When we articulate values, it is easy to slip into preaching, moralizing, and imposing our values on others. While morality and rules can be preached and imposed on others, values and integrity are personal, subjective, open to change, and defeated by coercion and exhortation.

When morals are preached and externally imposed or when they remain unexamined, they easily become contradictory and hypocritical. Hierarchical organizations allow and encourage managers to preach one thing below while practicing another above.

To minimize hypocrisy and duplicity in organizations, it is necessary to shift from external morality to internal values, from preaching and enforcing compliance to dialogue and reaching consensus. Ultimately, everyone needs to identify for themselves the areas where their walk does not match their talk. Instead of being frightened by this discussion, organizations can use it to bring daily practices into conformity with expressed values and integrity.

Most organizations want employees to take risks, think outside the box, push the envelope, be creative problem solvers, and act responsibly. Yet each of these values is contradicted by a second set of contradictory value messages that are communicated verbally and behaviorally. These include being cautious, not making mistakes, not rocking the boat, being a team player, going with the flow, and doing what one is told. When organizations declare that they value risk taking while at the same time punishing mistakes, they act hypocritically, creating cognitive dissonance, confusion, cynicism, and circumspection.

In truth, no one can dictate or manage the values, ethics, or integrity of another. Everyone has to become personally responsible for doing what is right. Yet managers are routinely asked to behave like moral watchdogs and act as police, prosecutor, judge, and jailer, all in one. As they do so, their own behaviors are subject to careful scrutiny by employees, ridiculed in private, and pronounced hypocritical.

Inconsistencies inevitably arise between the values and behaviors of different managers in the same organization or a single manager in response to different employees. In addition, the contradiction between personal responsibility for living one's values and trying to impose them on others communicates a deeper value: that obedience to those in power matters more than integrity. In the process, a subtle level of permission is given to behave unethically.

Values are communicated at every level of human interaction: interpersonally, organizationally, culturally, psychologically, socially, politically, and economically. They are communicated obliquely and in silence, by what we say as well as what we do. Values are communicated in organizations by:

- What we reward, as when those who cause the greatest difficulties receive the most attention
- What we punish, as when we punish collaboration by calling it cheating
- What we say, as when we deny responsibility for what we have done
- What we do not say, as when we keep silent about problems or do not tell the truth
- What we do, as when we become angry at people who criticize us
- What we do not do, as when we do not raise or discuss problems with those above us
- Congruence or hypocrisy, as when our words do not match our deeds, or we act differently in public than in private

In organizations that are hypocritical, lack integrity, or prefer profitability over values, conflicts inevitably appear—not only at the level of values but over seemingly trivial, confusing, superficial issues. The difficulty with these arguments is that they go nowhere precisely because they are not focused on what is really at issue: the values differences that underlie the conflict.

Discussing and exploring value-based conflicts can be highly productive, particularly when values are not really contradictory but complementary and are polar opposites connected by a common axis. Many organizational conflicts originate in the assumption that there is a single correct answer for ethical or values questions, yet it is often the case that there is more than one correct answer. Moreover, the attempt to impose a single correct answer often increases cynicism and apathy and encourages the universal game of escape. On the other hand, pretending that all values are equal fails to address the underlying differences among them or to result in learning or change. Allowing values conflicts to emerge and be discussed encourages people to think for themselves and commit to their values, which is a higher value.

Organizations are strengthened by diversity and the ability to maintain complex, multifaceted, seemingly divergent values. Value conflicts that result in the acceptance of diverse values are worth the temporary awkwardness that occurs when people try to reconcile their differences. At the same time, if a substantial minority of people are clearly not in agreement with a given value, it should not be imposed on them but can remain a subject for ongoing debate and dialogue.

The Paradox of Values

Most values conflicts are not clear-cut. Indeed, it is usually in the gray areas that ethical and values controversies arise. This suggests that whenever clear, consistent, easy answers arise in values disagreements, we are probably not addressing the right questions. Whenever a dilemma, paradox, or contradiction appears regarding ethics and values, it means there probably is not, and cannot be, a single correct answer. Instead, it is likely that there are two correct answers. As physicist Niels Bohr wrote, "A great truth is a truth whose opposite is also a great truth."

Consider, for example, the value of teamwork, which nearly everyone acknowledges is an important value in organizations. Yet individual performance is also an important value, and it becomes clear on closer inspection that these are actually complementary values rather than one being true and the other false. No one believes teams should completely replace individuals. Individual efforts are an important element in what makes teams effective. Indeed, teamwork requires and makes possible a higher level of individuality, which reaches its fullest expression through teamwork, and vice versa. In this case, the presence of two synergistically correct answers is not a pious sentiment but a reality.

This complementarity between teamwork and individuality suggests not only that values, ethics, and integrity cannot be managed, but that any effort to manage values will quickly become counterproductive. We need to stop trying to manage values through coerced uniformity and instead encourage employees to take responsibility for defining and implementing their own values in concert with others. The pressure is then taken off managers to act as police, parents, overseers, judges, and disciplinarians.

All values involve choices, and every choice contains a subjective element, no matter how much it is made to appear objective by being framed in the language of neutrality. In response to the idea that employees need to develop their own values, many managers ask, "What if everyone did that?" But they also need to ask, "What if nobody did that?" Permitting people to hold different values enhances diversity, autonomy, creativity, flexibility, and a respect for individuality that typical managerial solutions do not. It also clearly embodies the value of having values.

Value Relativity, Subjectivity, and Development

A value that represents something we want or need and have been denied ceases to be a value once we secure or achieve it. Once we complete what we value, we are able to move on to higher values. This means that part of what makes something a value is our lack of 100 percent implementation. Values therefore are what we have to *struggle* for, what we cannot take for granted, what we need in order to survive and grow, what does not come easily to us, what we have to try to live up to, what we have achieved and need to protect, what is just beyond our reach or capacity.

A value is determined by its importance to us at a given moment relative to other needs and by its latent capacity for stimulating growth or learning. This means that our relationship to values is developmental. We grow as our values are conceived, committed to, struggled, and sacrificed for; then secured, institutionalized, generalized, taken for granted, and forgotten because they have become integral parts of who we are, allowing us to move on to higher values.

Values are attributions of meaning or significance to things that otherwise appear ordinary. If we value education, it is because we have been or could be denied it and therefore attach importance to it. This means that values are metaphors, symbols, or signs that are defined not by their object but by their relation to something outside ourselves that is important or has meaning for us. Therefore, values are a relationship with ourselves, measured by what we value externally in terms of ourselves.

Yet if we define values as fluctuating and circumstantial, it becomes possible for them to serve opportunistic ends and give rise to two opposing dangers. When no actions appear better or worse than others, there is a danger of moral relativism, which rests on complicity and condonation and gives permission to engage in ethically reprehensible actions. For example, we might say that we value every culture's history and traditions, yet how do we respond to cultures that justify the rape, genital mutilation, and disenfranchisement of women?

Another equal and opposite danger is moral imperialism, which rests on intolerance and arrogance and justifies one group in dominating others through a pretense of moral superiority, appointing itself the arbiter of other people's cultures and traditions. For example, consider the ways Western European religion and morality were used to justify the slaughter of indigenous peoples who were considered inferior because they lacked Western technology, education, religion, or morality.

Each of these dangers can be seen to violate a deeper, more fundamental value: respect for others. There are subtle expressions of both these dangers that allow no easy answers to the questions they present. Every person and organization has to walk a fine line between moral relativism and moral imperialism in order to avoid either excusing or disrespecting divergent value systems.

Having said this, it is nonetheless clear that certain values increase values, ethics, and integrity while others diminish them. For example, valuing coercion or imposing values on others diminishes their capacity to express or form values of their own. According to Abraham Maslow's hierarchy of needs, it is clear that we uphold vastly different values when survival is at stake than when we contend with abundance. Thus, values are not absolute but vary with time, place, and circumstance. What is important or valuable to us at one level of need inevitably evolves as we move to another.

For this reason, there can be no final, complete, or permanent set of values for all people, all times, and all places. Yet while values vary with circumstance, within any given circumstance, they may become absolute. For example, a relatively minor dishonesty regarding a product defect may seem insignificant, but in the context of being told to a customer who is about to use it becomes absolute and inexcusable.

Values are fundamentally a relationship over time between ourselves and the external world, between our own growth and development and the satisfaction of individual, social, and organizational hierarchies of needs. Our task is not to state or declare values for all times, but to develop them in ways that are challenging and evolving over time, not only in *what* we value but *why* and *how* we value, so as to increase our individual, social, and organizational capacity to live by values without having to remember to do so.

Most organizations develop their capacity to embrace and demonstrate high-level values by moving from having no expressed values, to having quasi-values to which they give lip-service, to espousing real values, to living their values in ways that inform everything they do. This evolutionary, developmental process is central to creating a context of values, ethics, and integrity.

Organizational values can be open or hidden, negative or positive, relative or absolute, conditional or unconditional, individual or social, imposed or voluntary, and need not be developed in a linear, uniform way. It is possible, for example, for someone to be honest and withdrawn, collaborative and competitive, relaxed and disciplined, flexible and strong simultaneously, so long as it is clear that there is a deeper value on which these contradictory behaviors developmentally depend.

Only by consciously participating in a values development process can organizations evolve to a place where they reward employees for acting on their values and view values development as a collective opportunity for improvement. The primary goal of each individual and organization is to develop their own values as unconditional expressions of who they are, that do not depend on what others chose to be or do. We encourage recognition of the importance of values by posing the following questions:

Significance	What is the meaning or significance of values? What makes them important?
Universalizability	What would happen if everyone did what I (or they) do?
Leadership	What would happen if no one did what I (or they) do?
Reciprocity	How would I feel if the same standard were applied to me?
Publicity	How would I feel if my action or inaction was made public?
Defensibility	How easy would it be to justify the action to others?
Responsibility	Am I willing to take responsibility for the action or inaction, no matter what the outcome?
Intuition	Does the action or inaction intuitively feel right or wrong to me?
Legacy	Am I willing for my children or future generations to live with the consequences of my action or inaction?

Thinking About Values

Most organizations aspire to become more efficient, produce higher-quality products, protect the environment, maintain excellent customer service, satisfy employees' needs, and act according to the highest human and social values. Their problems do not usually lie with espousing these values, but with developing them as clear, noncontradictory statements, agreeing to them by consensus, communicating them consistently, leaving them open to learning and improvement, translating them into genuinely committed actions, and making them unconditional, integrated elements of their self-definition.

Values often appear difficult to comprehend, articulate, agree on, and actualize. Yet the search for values raises a number of rich, complex questions that are essential for ethical growth. Here are some questions suggesting dilemmas for individuals and organizations to consider in clarifying their values:

- *Why do we not act according to our values?* What motivates us to act in ways that lack integrity? Why do we have to struggle to maintain them? If we stop struggling, are they still values?
- *What is the value of admitting that we do not always act according to our values?* What values do we affirm when we acknowledge that acting according to our values is a struggle? What is the effect on moralizing or preaching to others about how they ought to behave? How do we acknowledge our common struggle to live up to our highest expectations in ways that encourage our mutual development?
- *What is the strategic importance of the reasons we give for not living up to our values?* What is the value of clearly articulating a value to which we are not conforming and the reasons we are unable to do so? How can we use value lapses to encourage self-awareness and integrity? Can the reasons we do not live up to our values help us set more powerful goals and strategic directions as individuals, teams, organizations, and societies?
- *How can we teach values without preaching or moralizing or turning them into dogmas?* Where and how do we learn our values? What would a values-oriented education look like? Which values are learned through experience, dialogue, and contemplation? How can organizations structure experiences, or review them once they have occurred, so as to encourage values-based learning?
- *What do we do when values clash or pull us in opposite directions?* What determines the outcome of a clash of organizational values? What are the mechanisms by which we choose one value over another? How do we identify priority values when we are pulled in

opposite directions by competing choices? How do we rationalize our choices?

- *What do we do when values are changing?* What do we do when important new values appear in the workplace, such as valuing racial, cultural, and gender diversity? Are there better ways of teaching new values than through blame, punishment, and loss of career?

- *What do we do when behaviors do not match values?* How do we know if someone is not acting according to their values? How do we avoid imposing values yet at the same time offer honest feedback about how behaviors are out of sync with declared values and personal integrity? How do we shift the context of conversation about values from threat to opportunity and learning?

- *How can we continuously improve our values?* How can organizations clarify their values priorities? How can they articulate levels of improvement in relation to the same value? How can they learn to accept new challenges and continuously improve rather than rest on their laurels?

- *How can we create a culture of values?* How can we alter organizational cultures to encourage values and ethics and build awareness and acceptance? How can we improve motivation, acknowledgment, and support for values-based behaviors? How can we institutionalize values without violating what made them values in the first place?

The point of these questions is less to prompt answers than to encourage dialogue and a search for answers that will enhance the integrity of each person and organization. Their purpose is to reveal an essential truth: that organizational integrity is increased by a shared process of grappling with open-ended, value-oriented questions that reveal the complex, paradoxical nature of values formation and implementation.

Values Lie at the Heart of Organizations

Values, ethics, and integrity play a defining role in every aspect of organizational life. An inadequate commitment to values encourages autocratic, hierarchical, bureaucratic organizational structures that diminish people's capacity for values development, while a strong commitment to values encourages democratic, collaborative, self-managing organizations that improve values and keep them human.

In *The Art of Japanese Management,* Richard Pascal and Tony Athos present the 7 S Model for analyzing organizations, created with Tom Peters and Bob Waterman. Each of the seven elements they define begins with the letter *S,* and in Figure 9.1, we added a word in brackets indicating a typical value within that element, making it clear that shared values link and shape every aspect of organizational life.

Using the 7 S model, we can guide values-based change and build consensus regarding future direction by focusing actions and initiatives on shared values. A shared value of teamwork, for

Figure 9.1. Values and the 7 S Model of Organization.

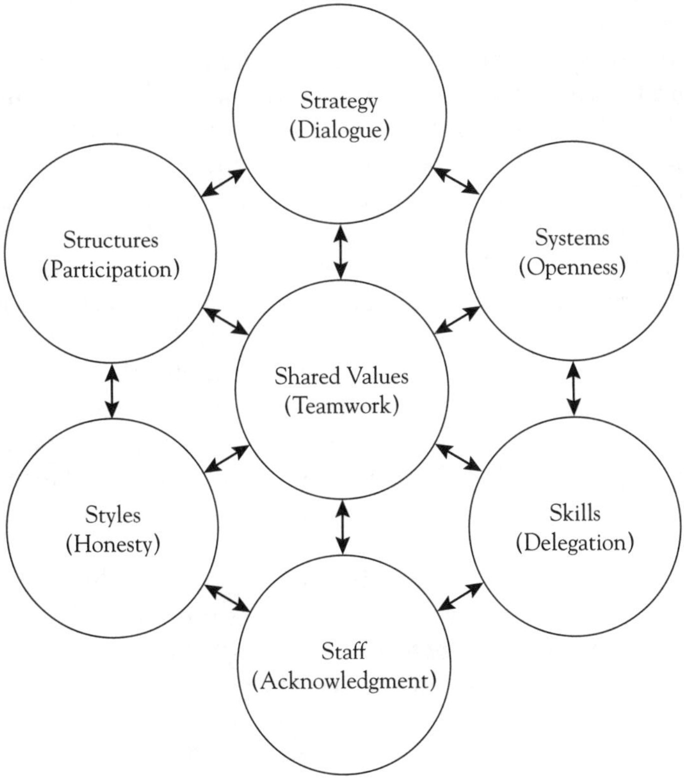

example, subtly reshapes every element in the model, lending coherence and meaning to the organization as a whole, in the following ways:

1. *Shared values* reflect both espoused and true values—those to which lip-service is given and those that are acted on every day. Team values may be unspoken yet form the heart of organizational culture.
2. *Strategy* is the *how* of realizing shared values. It includes plans for designing the future overall direction of the organization. The strategy guides team action and is created by the employees who will implement it.
3. *Systems* are the methods or procedures by which the internal and external business of the organization is conducted. Systems are effective when they encourage team values, increase communication and collaboration, and lead to ethical solutions.
4. *Structures* are reflected in organizational charts, the arrangement of work, and administration. Organizations have formal and informal structures that may or may not resemble one another. Team structures reflect team values when they are flat, interactive, and heterarchical in design.
5. *Skills* comprise the human resources available to the organization. A skill profile of each person includes his or her values, collaborative abilities, and talent in resolving team conflicts.
6. *Staff* includes the numbers, nature, and varieties of personnel. Values are reflected in racial, gender, and other forms of diversity, teamwork, job satisfaction, and motivation.
7. *Style* is expressed in organizational culture and approaches to leadership, negotiation, conflict, and interpersonal relationships. In support of team values, these are collaborative and team centered, and function bottom up, top down, and sideways.

In our experience, identifying shared values at the beginning of a change process powerfully redefines the other elements of the model. Many managers initiate change processes by formulating a strategy, rearranging structures, or adjusting systems, and ignoring what they think of as the "soft" S's, hoping they will simply fall into place. More effective, longer-lasting, further-reaching changes start by asking all employees to reach consensus on shared values and jointly identifying the other *S* elements that are needed to support them.

Twelve Steps to Organizational Integrity Through Shared Values

Organizations can increase their integrity, coherence, and integration and improve their performance by reaching consensus on shared values. They can bolster value-based relationships by recognizing and encouraging the behaviors that uphold their values and discouraging and eliminating those that undermine them. They can communicate and publicize their values and encourage individual and team responsibility for implementing them. They can develop methods for monitoring values compliance, identify and discuss potential conflicts of interest, and give timely, honest, empathetic feedback to people whose behaviors do not match their values. Most important, they can accomplish all of these goals without moralizing, preaching, excusing, or imposing their values on others.

Once employees participate in identifying their shared values, they can expand and reconfigure the other elements in their organization and align them with their shared values. The brief twelve-step values-development process that follows encourages employees to discover, declare, monitor, evaluate, and continually improve their values:

1. Open a conversation about the importance of values among *all* employees—what they are and what happens when people do not act with integrity. Ask them to cite examples from their personal lives and organizational experiences. Conduct a values dialogue, identifying difficult issues and opening them for discussion.
2. Conduct a values audit involving employees in a detailed assessment of the values reflected in their organizational culture and behaviors.
3. Strive for consensus at every step. Start by reaching consensus on the value of having values, or the meaning of consensus, and ways of reaching it.

4. Brainstorm values in small, randomly selected groups, and ask each group to present its proposed values to each other and discuss their disagreements.

5. Draft a single combined statement of proposed values using volunteers from each small group.

6. Review and discuss the draft, asking small groups to propose additions and revisions and receive large group feedback.

7. Prepare a final draft to present for final consensus.

8. Specify the concrete behaviors that support and undermine each value. Then reach consensus on behaviors the group wants to encourage and discourage and the methods they will use to reinforce positive, value-based behaviors and discourage those that are negative and undermining.

9. Brainstorm ways of motivating, acknowledging, and rewarding value-based behaviors on the part of both individuals and teams, including performance evaluation, financial compensation, coaching, and feedback.

10. Extend the process to constituent and collateral groups. Use the values as a starting point, or ask these groups to develop their own values, then meet to discuss commonalities and differences and reach a new consensus.

11. Publicly communicate the values and search for ways of integrating them into the organization's culture and behaviors. Promote positive dialogue over values differences.

12. Review values and behaviors on a regular basis and search for ways of continuously improving them. Celebrate successes and analyze failures for possible improvements.

It is critical that the entire process be open and participatory, that anyone with the courage to withhold consensus be celebrated for making it possible for the group to achieve a better outcome, and that disagreements be used to spark an ongoing values dialogue and development process.

Creating a Values Dialogue

It is useful to see the development of shared values as part of a larger ongoing values dialogue in which organizational citizens participate regularly as leaders, facilitators, and coaches. This dialogue can be shaped by a values audit, consisting of a number of questions that prompt consensus and respectful disagreement toward a common end—for example:

- What do you value most in your work life? In your personal life?
- What values do you most respect in others? In yourself?
- Have your values changed over time? How?
- What do you see as your organization's core values?
- What kind of organization do you want to work for?
- On a scale of 1 to 10, 10 being highest, how would you rank your organization in terms of values, ethics, and integrity? What do you base your rating on?
- What are some examples of organizational behaviors that are not based on values? What was not value based about them?
- Who in the organization most lives up to or exemplifies values?
- Which values are expressed in the culture of the organization? Which are not?
- What systems are needed to support value-based behaviors?
- How would you rate leadership's commitment to values? Employees' commitment?
- What are some things you would not do, even if it were in your self-interest? What are some things the organization would not condone?
- If your opponent or competitor used a tactic you considered unethical, how would you decide whether to use it yourself?
- What do you see as the long-term consequences of individuals and organizations acting on the basis of values, ethics, and integrity?

Example of a Values Development Process

We worked with a highly innovative organization as it developed a shared values process that resulted in a sharp decline in negative behaviors. We began with a values audit that revealed a number of values clashes, negative behaviors, and hostile attitudes. We then facilitated an open dialogue in which all employees discussed and reflected on these behaviors. We read a list of their negative behaviors back to them and asked whether anyone thought these behaviors were useful or professional, whether they belonged in a successful organizational environment, whether they enjoyed having them happen, and whether they wanted to continue engaging in them. The response was an overwhelming no to each question. We used the twelve-step process described above to craft the following statement of consensus-based values:

Shared Values

We, the [executives, team leaders, and team members of the organization] pledge, in our speech and actions, to uphold the following values, and invite others to remind us of them when we forget so they will become part of our everyday behavior. We commit to:

1. Put the interests of our customers, creation of quality products, and organizational learning first, and work to make our company a true learning community
2. Respect differences and diversity in race, gender, sexual orientation, and culture, and in opinion and personality as well
3. Listen actively and respectfully to what others are saying, without yelling, blaming, intimidating, or gossiping about those we disagree with
4. Communicate directly, openly, and honestly, and tell the truth
5. Take initiative and encourage teamwork, inclusion, participation, consensus, and risk taking
6. Talk directly to the people with whom we are having problems, focus on issues and interests rather than positions and personalities, and acknowledge work well done
7. Take responsibility for our speech and actions, follow the rules, and be responsible for our behavior
8. Model the behavior we expect from others, and take pride in our work

If the group had stopped here, they would have had a wonderful statement of values that could have been posted on a wall and ignored in practice. We asked if they wanted this to happen, and the answer again was a clear no. We then asked the group to identify and reach consensus on the behaviors that either supported or undermined these values. Afterward, everyone agreed to do their best to engage in value-supporting behaviors and avoid those that undermined their values. We asked whether it was acceptable for them to give each other feedback if they failed to do so. At this point, the group exploded, and several people said they did not want to create "values cops" who would go around correcting other people's behavior, while others felt that eliminating feedback would undermine any possibility of really changing their behaviors.

After considerable discussion, they agreed that feedback was essential for their values to become real, and that the feedback delivery process needed to reflect their values. They agreed that people who gave feedback should first request permission, then give it in a manner consistent with their values, respecting everyone's right to make their own values choices and recognizing their right not to be treated in ways that contravened the organization's shared values.

The group went further and formed volunteer teams to deepen their understanding of each value, monitor cultural compliance, and report back each month, indicating how well they had done living up to one of their values and how they might do better in the future. They decided to communicate their values to their external customers, clients, and suppliers and enter into a joint values development process with internal customers. In an assessment a year later, nearly all of the negative behaviors that had crippled the organization had disappeared, and productivity had risen dramatically.

Developing an Organizational Culture That Supports Values

In completing a shared values process, it is important to find ways of integrating value-based behaviors into organizational culture so they can be implemented without having to be articulated. Writing in the *Harvard Business Review,* Richard Pascale, Mark Millemann, and Linda Gioja found that organizations are rarely successful implementing significant changes that run counter to their culture or shared values. They found that the cultural elements most responsible for obstructing or supporting organizational change were those related to the following issues:

• *Power and vision.* Do organizational values empower employees to be self-directed in solving their problems and changing the organization? Is there a clear, compelling vision for the future owned by people at all levels of the organization?

- *Identity and relationships.* Does the organization value team identity and relationships? Do people within the organization identify with their teams, departments, professions, or the organization as a whole?
- *Communication, negotiation, and conflict.* Does the organization value conflicts for the learning opportunities they provide? What behaviors do people engage in when they experience conflict? Do they avoid it, sweep it under the rug, or discuss it openly? How are conflicts resolved? Is mediation valued? Do people communicate openly? Do they negotiate collaboratively?
- *Learning and assessment.* Does the organization value learning? How do people respond to new information that does not fit preconceived ideas? Do organizational values support honest, empathetic, peer-based, learning-oriented feedback and assessment?

Each of these aspects of organizational culture can expand or constrict the capacity for change. To alter organizational culture so that it supports values, ethics, and integrity, these questions need to be addressed together and the values that support change consistently applied over time.

Keeping Values Alive

Every organization, parent, leader, political group, and concerned individual would like to know how to preserve values and pass them on to future generations. Countless efforts have been made to transmit values, yet most of the successes have been achieved in form rather than in content. Many of these efforts failed as a result of:

- Adapting values to particular needs or circumstance and losing their universal quality
- Institutionalizing values and dissipating their spirit
- Ritualizing values and confusing the ritual with the reasons for it
- Idealizing values and making them remote from everyday life

- Freezing values into dogmas and losing their paradoxical, personal, existential, indeterminate nature
- Coercing people into adopting values and stimulating their passive or active resistance

Over time, rituals easily turn into traditions, teachings into dogmas, ceremonies into formalities, and values into moral strictures. Even when values are successfully passed on to future generations, they are often redefined to mean something different from what was intended. As William Morris wrote, "Men fight and lost the battle, and the thing that they fought for comes about in spite of their defeat, and when it comes it turns out not to be what they meant, and other men have to fight for what they meant under a different name."

In the rapidly changing world of organizations, the values for which people sacrifice, struggle, and stand can quickly disappear as changing leadership or new conditions demand a fresh focus or different priorities. Some of the clearest examples of the difficulty of keeping values alive come from intense, highly value-driven events, such as the revolutions that took place in the United States, France, Russia, and China. In the aftermath of these efforts at overthrowing antiquated sets of values, it is possible to discern patterns in values degeneration that offer useful lessons for organizations.

In many cases, values were given lip-service rather than being lived, and were not extended or followed to their logical conclusion. For example, during the American Revolution, universal principles of life, liberty, and the pursuit of happiness were not extended to slaves or women. Instead, the right to vote was restricted to white male property owners, automatically establishing racial privilege, gender discrimination, and property ownership as higher values than political and social democracy. Similarly, organizations today that give only lip-service to employee participation in decision making reduce their effectiveness, generate cynicism, and establish hierarchy as a higher value than teamwork.

Limiting the implementation of values ultimately leads to their waning influence and the eventual emergence of renewed efforts to implement them. In the United States, we are still trying to implement the broad values earlier generations fought to revolutionize, and although we have made substantial progress, there will be no end to this process until life, liberty, and the pursuit of happiness are realized for everyone and become an integral part of who we are, allowing us to evolve to a higher set of values. Similarly, organizational efforts to implement the self-managing ideas of Lewin and McGregor will wane and return until they are fully implemented.

The American Revolution may seem a distant example, yet organizations confront similar issues in every change process. It is common for managers to win gains by sacrificing important values, to permit exceptions and variations in the implementation of changes, to fail to live up to their values or follow them to their logical conclusions, to let outmoded values undermine success. Even the most far-reaching revolutions find it difficult to create value systems that endure and leaders who are able to live up to them fully. As a result, new revolutions are required, and every new set of values has to win adherence repeatedly.

For these reasons, values cannot be fully transmitted or kept alive, only communicated and lived. Organizations that operate out of a context of shared values can try to keep them alive through employee orientation programs, personal conversations, group dialogues, retreats, 360-degree feedback, and support for people who raise values problems. They can implement them through mentoring, coaching, peer counseling, collaborative processes, consensus, organizational learning, conflict resolution, regular values assessments, and personal behavior. As long as opportunities exist to periodically reassess organizational values, make improvements, and assess whether behaviors are congruent with expressed values, the value of having values can be kept alive.

If we want to keep important personal and organizational values alive, we need to develop methods of implementation that more deeply express the higher value of having values and do not undermine them. In our view, these higher or deeper meta-values include the following:

- Recognizing that the way we create values is an essential part of implementing them, and if we value equality, we need to integrate it into processes and daily relationships, as well as into long-term outcomes

- Accepting values conflicts as opportunities for growth and change and invitations to engage in dialogue and participate in value-based relationships
- Striving for both diversity and unity in the expression of values and rejecting reliance on superiority and inferiority, correctness and heresy
- Seeing the values development process as inherently collaborative, social, and developmental
- Acknowledging that values improve over time as we pay attention to them and accept our lack of perfection
- Refusing to leave anyone behind

Together, these meta-values require a shift from management, hierarchy, bureaucracy, and autocracy to self-management, heterarchy, collaboration, and democracy. The success of self-management will be measured by the extent to which values are embraced and implemented in the daily life of organizational citizens. This means encouraging people to develop their own values and participate in defining those they share and want to live by. When they do so, they automatically affirm the value of self-management, not only by what they say but how they say it and what they do when their values and self-interests conflict.

Chapter Ten

Form Living, Evolving Webs of Association

> *In a real sense all life is inter-related. All men are caught*
> *in an inescapable network of mutuality, tied in a single*
> *garment of destiny. Whatever affects one directly affects all*
> *indirectly. I can never be what I ought to be until you are*
> *what you ought to be, and you can never be what you*
> *ought to be until I am what I ought to be. This is the*
> *inter-related structure of reality.*
> MARTIN LUTHER KING JR., *Strength to Love*

When we open the process of organizational redesign by creating a context of values, ethics, and integrity, we implicitly recognize that values are not abstractions but functional principles of organizational design. Using shared values as guiding principles, we can design the scaffolding and structures that reflect and implement them.

By doing so, we implicitly recognize that organizations are human environments, in which people performing a variety of different roles interact and depend on each other ecologically, much like organisms, in order to survive. For them to flourish, be creative, act responsibly, think strategically, negotiate collaboratively, and manage themselves, they require living, evolving structures that actively encourage the behaviors that support these functions. Organizational structures deeply and inevitably affect the way people behave, think, and act. They fundamentally transform the rules of the game, disrupt expectations, and redefine how people succeed and fail. And when organizations flatten hierarchies and create self-managing organizational democracies, more effective and advanced ways of working immediately appear beneath the surface.

However, there is considerable risk in questioning the traditional, safe, predictable structures of organizations, especially for those who hold managerial positions inside these structures or hope to be promoted into them. When we flatten hierarchical structures, managers lose power, authority, prestige, financial gain, and the safety of known terrain. And when we create self-managing organizational democracies, there is a danger that with managers no longer in control, operations will stumble or spin out of control.

Changing the Managerial Paradigm

Science philosopher Thomas Kuhn wrote in *The Structure of Scientific Revolution* that paradigms do not change on their own; they are stimulated to change by an accumulation of problems, dysfunctions, conflicts, and anomalies that do not fit within the old paradigm. Anomaly appears only against the background provided by the paradigm. The more precise and far-reaching the paradigm is, the more sensitive an indicator it provides of anomaly and hence of an occasion for paradigm change.

The anomaly in this case is the enormous success of collaboration, teamwork, and democracy, as contrasted with the hierarchical, bureaucratic, autocratic paradigm of management. For centuries, we have designed organizations to satisfy human needs, yet the structures they have created increasingly deny, diminish, and contradict these very human needs.

To make these changes understandable, we need a new paradigm of organizational design, a different way of envisioning organizational structure. We need a new mental model to reshape our perceptions and opinions regarding organizational interactions—one that expands our awareness of what works and what is possible, increases our ability to define problems, improves our coping techniques and skills, and allows us to predict what will succeed and what will not.

As we move along Maslow's hierarchy of needs, the stages of organizational history, or the evolution of work, we increasingly discover that one-dimensional, hierarchical, bureaucratic, autocratic organizations cannot successfully satisfy higher-level human needs and that new organizations are required that are multi-dimensional, heterarchical, democratic, and self-managing. This creates a tension that can be resolved only through the emergence of a new paradigm in which hierarchy is the anomaly and collaboration, democracy, and self-management are the norm.

Any shift from a managerial to a self-managerial paradigm will have profound implications for every part of our lives. It will be far-reaching and affect not only organizational structures but the way we work, how we think about the way we work, the words we use to describe work, and who we are at work and away from it.

In the emerging self-managing paradigm, organizations are transformed into communities and hierarchical pyramids into heterarchical webs of association. Managers are transformed into leaders, groups into teams, and customer service into customer partnerships. Notification gives way to participation. Uniformity becomes less valuable than diversity. Old-style coercion surrenders to consensus, and alienation to self-fulfillment. To understand the contrast between these two paradigms, consider Table 10.1.

Clearly something fundamental is shifting in our notion of what work is and what organizations are supposed to do. These changes are driving us to design new structures that are capable of reflecting and encouraging these behaviors and are congruent with our highest values, ethics, and integrity. Together, they point toward self-management, collaboration, and democracy.

Rethinking Organizations

To design innovative organizational structures, we have to return to basics and ask, What are organizations? The first answer to this apparently simple question may come as a shock. Fundamentally, organizations do not exist. Unlike people, tables, and glasses of water, one cannot put one's finger on an organization. There *is* no Xerox, Microsoft, Mobil, Harvard University, U.S. Congress, or any other organization *except in our minds*. These entities have no existence apart from the people whose values, ideas, skills, processes, and relationships make them real. While there are objects such as offices, mission statements, and products, organizations are mental and emotional constructs, created through assumptions, relationships, words, and actions. Without the people who populate them, they do

Table 10.1. The Changing Paradigm.

Managed Organizations	Self-Managed Organizations
Context of self-interest	Context of values, ethics, and integrity
Departmental silos	Strategic integration
Dependence	Interdependence
Hierarchical power	Team empowerment
Obedience	Questioning
Competitive processes	Collaborative processes
Leaders named from above	Leaders chosen from below
Control orientation	Learning orientation
Rigid and reactive	Agile and proactive
Managers think; employees do	Employees think and do
Resistant to change	Dedicated to improvement
Self-serving, secret communication	Honest, open communication
Profit motivation	Creative motivation
Blaming others	Solving problems
Fixed roles and responsibilities	Changing roles and responsibilities
Conflict avoidance	Conflict engagement
Top-down evaluation	360-degree evaluation
Focus on discipline	Focus on improvement
Hiring by managers	Hiring by teams
Unilateral decisions	Consensus decisions
Covert expectations	Negotiated expectations
Individual rewards	Team and individual rewards

not exist. They are, quite simply, the emperor's new clothes. Yet the clothes are permitted to dominate the emperor and the emperor's employees as well.

The organizational structures we imagine, like a broom in the hands of a sorcerer's apprentice, take on a life of their own and recreate their creators as mere appendages. Who is in charge here: the structure or the people? Who is in control: the bureaucracy or the people whose work it is intended to support and integrate?

Because organizations are created in our minds, they can be recreated, reshaped, and transformed by the people whose ideas bring them into daily existence. Since organizations are assemblages of ideas and actions, conversations and processes, roles and relationships, they can be redesigned to encourage democracy and self-management rather than autocracy and domination.

In the new organizational paradigm, the fundamental unit of structure is not the isolated individual but the collaborative self-managing team. The primary focus is not on personal skills but on relationships between associated individuals in support of a common purpose. In this view of organizations, we are required to abandon the assumption underlying hierarchical structures that managers are needed to control isolated individuals who would otherwise act in uncoordinated ways and disregard the interests of the group; to reject the idea that individuals have to compete adversarially for success, are solely responsible for group actions, and should be rewarded only on the basis of individual skills and behaviors.

Encouraging Democracy and Collaboration Through Webs of Association

This new paradigm of organizational structure encourages the formation of democratic, collaborative, self-managing teams and links them in living, evolving structures we call webs of association. Webs are informal, interactive hubs of self-management, collaborative relationships, and democratic decision making. They are free-floating partnerships in a context of shared values, oriented to fulfilling team tasks and consensus-driven goals.

Webs place responsibility and decision-making power where the problems are, to encourage immediate, direct, one-stop customer service, collaborative group process, and informal problem solving. They require a new, non-Euclidean, multidimensional, curved geometry to describe their interactions (shown in Figure 10.1), as opposed to the static, linear, flat, pyramidal relationships depicted on traditional organizational charts.

While Figure 10.1 appears static and two-dimensional, webs are constantly moving, informal, four-dimensional, nonlinear, curved structures. As we indicated earlier, physical dimensions represent degrees of freedom, and it is clear from organizational charts and actual relationships that hierarchical structures encourage only vertical freedom. Cross-functional teams allow employees to exercise horizontal freedom and work across vertical silos. Creating a context of values, ethics, and integrity and strategically integrating expertise adds depth and a third dimension of freedom by encouraging employees to lead by values and participate in defining organizational strategy. Synergy and community add a fourth degree of freedom by linking these elements in a single, undifferentiated whole.

Round human processes do not fit into square hierarchical holes. Relationships do not obey the laws of formal logic. Time does not stand still. Flexible policies do not result in predictable outcomes. Rather, they are evolving, chaotic, multidimensional, and sensitively dependent on inherently unknowable initial conditions. Old-style organizational charts cannot capture these facets of organizational life. Rather, they force organizational thinking into static, linear, vertical channels. Whereas pyramidal organizational charts reflect classical Euclidean, Newtonian, cause-and-effect paradigms of power, webs of association reflect paradigms of relativity, quantum mechanics, evolution, energy fields, chaos, string theory, and complexity, which are relativistic, relational, self-organizing, uncertain, nonlocal, evolving, and multidimensional.

Instead of thinking of organizations as objects, pyramids, entities, or particles, we find it useful to see them as living, evolving, wavelike, circular, egalitarian alliances and social systems that are defined by the character of their human participants and the quality of their communications, values, cultures, processes, and relationships. Webs are formed by and at the same time give form to who people *are* in relation to each other.

While hierarchies erect internal boundaries and proprietary walls, webs of association blur and dismantle them to increase

Figure 10.1. Webs of Association.

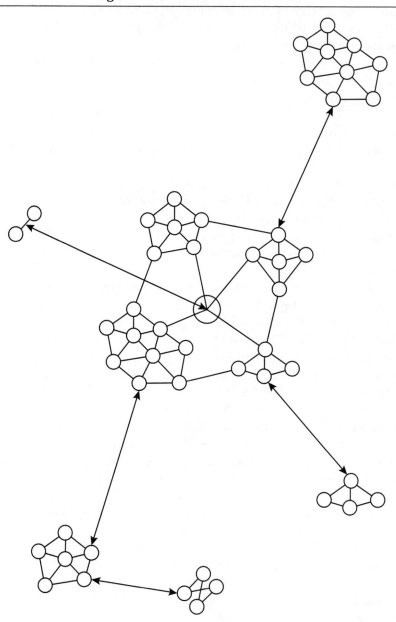

collaboration. Webs invite internal and external links through hubs or nodes where individuals and teams are combined in varying degrees of partnership and teamwork. Their capacity to link people across organizational boundaries creates opportunities for strategic alliances that span geography, mission, structure, and specialization. Linkages can take the form of brief connections, long-term coalitions, or permanent mergers. They can focus on achieving productive goals, maximizing resources, minimizing costs, or addressing common everyday problems. The open structure of webs allows them to link and unlink directly and flexibly with others, without saddling the organization with fixed alliances, delays, inefficient processes, and unnecessary costs.

Webs of association have existed in the shadows as an informal element in organizational structures for years. Every hierarchy and bureaucracy inevitably conceals a half-hidden, shadowy alter-ego of unofficial alliances and informal collaborations in order to function.

Organizations as Organisms

In the new paradigm, organizations are seen as organisms—living entities that are dependent on yet greater than the sums of their parts. They are multilayered and subtle, with more taking place below the surface than above it. They exist less in space than in the spaces between, less outside than within, less in action than in interaction. This makes interrelatedness a key element in the success of webs. Nurturing and caring for the people who make them up becomes a requirement for organizational effectiveness. If one person feels disrespected or mistreated, just as if one part of an organism were in pain, the entire organization becomes less effective, and it ultimately does not matter *whose* end of the boat is sinking.

Like organisms, webs of association consist of small, apparently disconnected systems that fit together like parts of a living network, using complex feedback to coordinate internal collaboration. Organizations begin to function as living organisms when they permit each part to communicate freely with all the others and encourage their interactions to be dynamic, local, and evolving rather than static, distant, and stable.

Like organisms, webs support complexity in relationships, feedback, culture, and communication. Webs act synergistically, forming feedback loops that allow organizations to adapt in complex, rapidly changing environments. Through these loops, organizations naturally and automatically combine into webs of association. Through these combinations, energy is produced and allowed to flow freely and synergistically throughout the organization; indeed, these streams of human energy *are* the organization.

Organizational energy is transmitted through relationships, processes, and communications by way of interlocking requests and promises, commitments and interactions. Because webs are social systems and are team based and democratic, they are able to create energy through direct access to information, teamwork, and the challenge of self-management. In this way, webs automatically make organizations more positive, open, collaborative, and empowering. Because they are living, evolving, organic wholes, they allow employees to continually redefine themselves and their relationships by exponentially increasing the number and quality of organizational interactions and relationships.

By restructuring organizations as organisms, we expand the range of possibilities for how they might function and are able to rearrange them in ways that augment human growth and learning. With webs, we can turn barriers into challenges, problems into objects of curiosity, differences into strengths, complaints into suggestions for improvement, conflicts into opportunities for learning, feedback and failure into occasions for personal growth, and work into play.

Webs as Communities

Unlike hierarchical organizations, webs require confederations, coalitions, and alliances. There are no tops or bottoms, no higher or lower in weblike structures. There are only interacting nodes of responsibility, hubs of creativity, centers of action, and meridians of energy, information, communication, and empowerment. Webs are floating, living, evolving coalitions dedicated to solving problems, generating products, serving customers, and supporting individual and team development. They are circles whose center is everywhere and circumference is nowhere.

Webs of association use both centralization and decentralization, self-managing teams and empowered individuals. They differ from hierarchies in their expanded ability to combine flexibility, humanity, creativity, and customer partnership with planning, efficiency, coordination, and social values. Hierarchies pronounce rules from above based on the values of owners, directors, and managers and make them semipermanent. Heterarchies elicit rules by consensus based on the values of the team, and they allow policies and procedures to evolve with changing circumstances. Hierarchies suppress criticism, problems, and conflicts, which are seen as challenges to authority. Heterarchies encourage criticism, problems, and conflicts, which are seen as suggestions and requests for improvement.

In hierarchies, a single CEO has most of the decision-making power, and the chain of command extends from the top down. In heterarchies, team members and colleagues make decisions for themselves and one another horizontally. Heinz von Foerster cites an interesting example from World War II when hierarchical command gave way to heterarchical authority, producing success even under battle conditions which often favor hierarchy:

> [In] the battle of the Midway Islands . . . the American flagship went down in the first few minutes, and its fleet was left to organize itself, i.e., to switch from a hierarchy to a heterarchy. What happened now was that the skipper of each vessel, small or big, took command over the entire fleet whenever he realized that he, because of his position at that moment, knew best what to do. The result, as we all know, was the destruction of the Japanese fleet, and the turning point . . . of the war in the Pacific.

Missing a fixed organizational hierarchy, a floating, natural one took its place. Access to information, the ability to make quick, clear decisions, and authority to act replaced a rigid command structure as the source of power. While each leader had no reporting obligation or need to follow directions, he had the authority and responsibility to choose appropriate action based on a common goal. The same idea can be applied fractally on smaller and larger scales.

Playwright Henrik Ibsen wrote, "A community is like a ship; everyone ought to be prepared to take the helm." In organizations, this means that those closest to the problem need to be able to assess the situation and make decisions and be encouraged and supported in doing so by the structures of flattened, collaborative, self-managing webs of association, which allow them to create an additional dimension or degree of organizational freedom based on synergy and community.

Webs Promote Organizational Communities

The word *community* refers not just to a group of people who live close to one another but to a perception of connectedness, a method of living together, and a synergy in which wholes become greater than the sums of their parts. Community implies intimacy, a connection of souls that is indivisible yet interdependent. It is a living, evolving link between people that is consensual, fluid, accepting, informal, egalitarian, creative, democratic, caring, and celebratory. In community, we create ourselves through connection with others and understand others as extensions of ourselves.

Creating community means encouraging diversity and constructively resolving cross-cultural conflicts. Community occurs when what binds people is stronger than what separates them, when differences and conflicts are overcome, creating a larger whole. Communities that are based on conformity or self-similarity have greater internal consistency but little adaptability. They easily reach agreement, but as easily slip into mindless homogeneity and the social enforcement of civility or conformity. Diverse communities experience more open conflicts, but resolution processes lead to greater acceptance, richness, and depth as common goals are realized.

Webs of association generate community by encouraging agreement on shared values, ethics, and integrity; by jointly creating visions, goals, barriers, and strategies for overcoming them; and by sharing histories, stories, metaphors, rituals, ceremonies, and cultural associations. In webs, organizational culture fosters a sense of community through collaboration and democracy, equality and participation.

Webs, like other diverse communities, are maintained through dialogue; they focus on common concerns, identification of shared needs, and conflict resolution. Like other communities, they encourage self-reliance, problem solving, united action, and sharing of important experiences. They produce a togetherness of spirit, perception, intellect, and emotion.

It is clear that whatever shows us our common face and reveals our essential connectedness creates and sustains community. And it is equally clear that whatever creates community helps us know ourselves, realize our potential, and make sense of our lives. By acting together, communities of interest are converted into communities of reflective practice. In this sense, webs represent a more human way of working and an increased opportunity for leading more satisfying work lives.

Webs Are Boundaryless

The natural structure of webs of association is open and fluid. Because each node in a web can link up with other nodes at any time, the potential for access, interaction, synergy, and variety of connection is nearly infinite. Because the boundaries of webs are permeable, strategic alliances, opportunistic links, and working relationships with suppliers, customers, and competitors become vital sources of growth and improvement.

Webs link diverse vertical functions through computer interface, replace rigid horizontal departments with cross-functional teams, introduce depth through participation in shared values and strategic integration, and connect people through synergy and community. Webs reach beyond external boundaries to connect the operating systems of suppliers and customers, and dismantle internal boundaries through dialogue, democracy and collaborative interaction. Webs increasingly create movable, temporary, ubiquitous work spaces and merge past and future into the present.

Innovative, fast-paced technology is driving many of these changes. Computer applications create connections that allow organizations to receive, fill, and bill orders, engage in just-in-time manufacturing, promote on-line sales, automate billing and payments, connect disparate professions and skills, and eliminate traditional external boundaries, often with a single keystroke. Internally, self-managing teams can have open on-line access to strategic financial information, performance tracking, project management, scheduling and communications. Employees are no longer restricted by departments, protected turf, and competitive in-house units and are matrixed to multiple teams and diverse internal and external cultures based on changing demands, skills, customer needs, and growth opportunities.

Webs Are Centralized and Decentralized

Technology is not only reducing the need for hierarchical organizational structures; it is rapidly decentralizing virtually every organizational decision. Evolving organizations struggle over whether to centralize or decentralize their functions, activities, and responsibilities. A more useful question, however, is which functions or operations should be housed in centralized nodes and coordinated by a central part of the structure and which ought to be decentralized in diverse nodes and teams.

Centralization generates uniformity, consistency, continuity, and clear standards. But it also produces bureaucracy, hierarchy, autocracy, resistance to change, conformity, and complacency, all of which undermine flexibility and limit the flow of creative energy. Decentralization encourages diversity, creativity, risk taking, and responsiveness, which help organizations remain supple, innovative, and agile. But it also spawns anarchy, duplication, turf building, poor delivery, and a failure of follow-through.

An organic, evolutionary approach rejects either-or choices between centralization and decentralization and seeks to avoid both managerial domination through consolidation and consistency and localized anarchy through variation and flexibility. By creatively combining centralization and decentralization, organizations can produce transformational syntheses that combine employee self-management with linking, empowering leadership. The interaction between these two strategies allows organizations to continually restructure themselves, move closer to customers, clients, and citizens, and become more values based, productive, and human, as revealed in Figure 10.2.

Organizations can avoid fruitless debates by considering not whether but which decisions, services, and functions ought to be centralized, which decentralized, and how to balance and counterbalance each decision so as to achieve a transformational synthesis that combines the benefits of each in new ways.

For example, it is important for us to centralize the questions we ask and allow others to decentralize the answers they give. If the questions are decentralized, the answers will not fit together or form a coherent whole; if the answers are centralized, all the richness, variety, and opportunity for synergy that occur only when

Figure 10.2. The Dialectic of Direction.

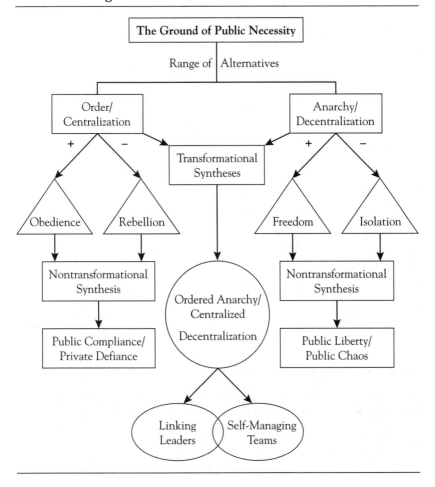

we combine unity and diversity, commonality and individuality will disappear.

Similarly, it is important to centralize regular functions that require a high degree of skill and do not represent the core competencies of any single work unit. Ashkenas, Ulrich, Jick, and Kerr in *The Boundaryless Organization* developed a useful template to describe this process, which we have adapted in Figure 10.3 to indicate which functions to centralize and which to decentralize and where they ought to be located within the organization.

Figure 10.3. Placement of Functions.

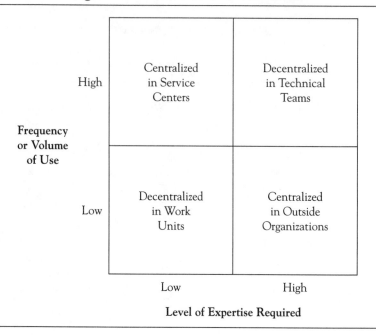

Forming Webs of Association

As organizations increasingly free themselves from hierarchical structures, behaviors, and thought patterns, webs form naturally in response to the challenges of work, linking leadership, and a deep desire for community, interaction, and synergistic relationships. Here are four strategies for moving this process forward and building web-based organizations:

1. Replace Bureaucracies and Fixed Departments with Self-Managing Teams and Nodes

Teams are the basic units of self-managing organizations; nodes are the points of convergence and connection between and among individuals, teams, and partnerships, representing their energetic core. In living organisms, nodes are groups of specialized cells or organs that work together to form systems, such as the nervous system. In organizations, nodes are the places where people connect with goals.

Nodes have easy on- and off-ramps and hot links to other teams, individuals, and organizations. While every employee in a web of association has a home team, they may create a node within that team that takes responsibility for achieving a particular goal, or work on an ad hoc basis in other teams across the organization.

For example, an employee may belong to a sales team that is part of a node organized to serve a particular customer or geographical location, assist another team that is part of a node developing new products, bring specialized knowledge to another team that belongs to a node engaged in strategic planning, and participate occasionally on another team that mediates conflicts or is responsible for improving communication within the organization. The employee can move freely among and between these nodes, negotiate time commitments and responsibilities with each team, and provide ground-level, integrative, horizontal links between different functions.

Nodes are fast forming, inclusive, self-managing, easy to enter and leave, hyperconnected, and ubiquitous throughout the organization. They are linked to organizational goals and objectives, customer desires, personal needs, employee skills, quality improvement, geographical location, ad hoc issues, collaborative processes, and special projects. These may be long lasting or short term, crossfunctional or specialized, virtual or actual, homogeneous or diverse.

Rather than hierarchies with fixed, unchanging, bureaucratic departments, nodes are living, evolving, organic centers of energy, talent, and relationship that are defined by explicit, shared, fluid purposes. They are energy fields, centers that draw diverse individuals, teams, and networks into coordinated activity and distribution centers for incoming work.

Nodes are defined by the values, goals, needs, interests, problems, and timelines of a group or project. They operate in a context of shared values, using consensus decision making, personal choice, and collaboratively negotiated agreements. They are sustained by ubiquitous, linking leaders who facilitate and coordinate the flow of information and energy between them.

For example, the highly successful Mondragon cooperatives in the Basque region in Spain began not with productive activities or tasks but with identification of shared values and development of individual and team relationships. Teams of employee-owners worked together for months on values and improving their skills in teamwork and collaboration without producing a single saleable product. By the end of this process, they had created nodes capable of efficiently producing dozens of products and have been highly successful, both socially and financially, for over fifty years.

Nodes focus on continuous improvement in products, processes, and relationships; rapid response time; and developing employee capacity. Once a goal or target has been met, the node evolves into a new form or dissipates, allowing employees to link up with other nodes. Because they are fast forming and impermanent, they resist creating rigid, bureaucratic power bases or battling over turf. Nodes combine a focus on enhancing individual and team capacity with a willingness to be flexible and creative. They continuously evolve, reshape work relationships, and adapt to rapidly changing demands and possibilities.

2. Transform Autocratic Managers into Ubiquitous Leaders

Leaders in webs of association are ubiquitous stimulators of vision and collective energy, facilitators of teamwork, nurturers and mentors of individual talent, coaches of potential new leaders, guides and models for constructive feedback, and resolvers of conflict.

Leaders in webs are located throughout the organization and play a variety of roles, such as

- Forging links between people at the cores, as well as at the peripheries, edges, and corners, increasing collaboration among all employees and leaving no one out or behind
- Identifying talent, nourishing its development, clearing paths for achievement and recognition, acknowledging successes, and learning from failures
- Facilitating exciting, innovative visions that energize work and are owned by everyone and implemented everywhere
- Stimulating the flow of energy and information that link nodes to one another, continually removing roadblocks, resolving conflicts, and redirecting miscommunications
- Prompting deeper associations, strategic alliances, and links with other parts of the web, with customers, suppliers, competitors, and society

- Locating resources, linking them to action, and stewarding them to protect the environment and meet demands for a sustainable future
- Challenging the status quo and asking questions that suggest fresh solutions

These roles grow organically out of the self-identified needs and requests of each team, the diverse skills of individuals, the division of labor, and the flow of energy within the team and throughout the web. As in political democracies, citizen-leaders at every level are chosen by those who follow them and are regularly evaluated by peers, subordinates, clients, and customers based on mutually negotiated criteria. These ideas are developed further in the next chapter.

3. Eliminate Need-to-Know and Organizational Secrecy

Eliminating organizational secrecy while protecting personal privacy is an essential element in democracy. In democratic organizations, all information, from financial and strategic plans to thoughts and feelings of employees, can contribute to strategic thinking, efficiency, and problem solving. When organizations shift from traditional hierarchical structures to democratic ones, it becomes essential that information be decentralized, accessible, reliable, practical, modifiable, and strategic, while at the same time not violating personal privacy.

Shared information is critical in shaping the actions, processes, and relationships that define organizations. It is essential for evolution, learning, and improvement, for promoting skill development, learning organizations, self-management, teamwork, and synergy. Employees in heterarchical organizations participate at all levels in collectively identifying the information they need. They have instantaneous access to everyone in the organization at all levels through a wide variety of electronic and nonelectronic media.

Technological innovations and computerized processes support open information in webs by automating traditional administrative and managerial functions and creating access to data through portals that allow employees to modify, correct, and transmit data. Decentralized structures, home offices, telecommuting, distance learning, and extensions of the workplace create new communication and relationship patterns that redefine the role of leadership and require open information, self-management, and teamwork in order to bridge isolated work environments.

Through intranets, teams can gain immediate, direct access to important financial information, including customer profiles, resumes of applicants for available positions, daily schedules for team members, salaries and bonuses, accounts receivable, and to-do lists of executives. They can participate in on-line dialogues and instantaneous decision making. They can form direct links with customers and suppliers, conduct action research, develop alternative models, project and test them for years, and try them out in a series of hostile evolutionary computerized environments before making a final decision.

Peter Drucker has described the strategic role of information and its implications for future organizations:

> So far, for 50 years, the information revolution has centered on data—their collection, storage, transmission, analysis and presentation. . . . The next information revolution asks, What is the MEANING of information, and what is its PURPOSE? And this is leading rapidly to redefining the tasks to be done with the help of information, and with it to redefining the institutions that do these tasks. . . . It is forcing us to redefine what business enterprise actually is and should be.

As Drucker suggests, it is the *interpretation* of data that is key to successful organizations. Interpretation requires that open access, responsibility, strategic thinking, and self-management be exercised by employees who traditionally only collect, file, and report data. Data clerks are being replaced by business analysts who interpret, shape, analyze, and act on the strategic implications that flow from information. With the rise of these new analytic functions, the need for command-and-control managerial practices increasingly dissipates. Analysts cannot be successfully managed as though they were data entry clerks performing routine mechanical tasks. They require weblike structures that facilitate access to information and expand rather than control and constrict their responsibilities and power.

As the sheer complexity and mass of information grows, interpretation becomes increasingly strategic and critical to successful, coordinated organizational evolution. In democratic organizations and webs of association, data functions are no longer separated into silos or departments. The rigidity and information-hoarding role of hierarchical bureaucracies become increasingly counterproductive as universal access and direct transmission of information proliferate.

Self-managing teams and advanced technological resources reinforce one another. New technologies geometrically expand information sharing, allowing cross-fertilization, democracy, and strategic integration. Applications connect finance and human resource functions, integrate order processing and product manufacture, and encourage cross-organizational communications. With these applications, there is no longer a need for managers to coordinate schedules, make sure bills are paid on time, administer recruitment, arrange business travel and vacation allotments, track orders, and control delivery times.

As software applications automatically regulate the flow of traditionally managed transactions, teams are able to track business performance, streamline supply chains, oversee call center support, and interact directly with customers. Software automatically checks contracts and warranties when customers ask for data, lets employees alter their benefit allocations on-line without sending forms to human resources, and manages depreciation of tangible assets without the intervention of managers. With every technological development, management becomes less necessary and self-management more crucial.

4. Develop Transorganizational Meridians

Every organism consists not only of nodes that consolidate groups of cells into systems, but methods for linking these systems into symmetric, balanced wholes. In webs, we call these links between diverse systems *meridians,* which informally bridge conflicting information, reconcile differing agendas, balance the tension of paradoxically opposed values, rationalize alternative priorities, and translate a variety of technical languages and jargons.

Meridians in the body are pathways along which energy travels, connecting diverse organ systems. They mirror the body's symmetry, as depicted in acupuncture charts. In webs of association, meridians permit the energy of communication and collaboration to flow freely across teams and nodes and provide strong, accessible bridges linking them throughout the organization. Webs possess multiple potential pathways along which information can flow. These meridians can be used to encourage learning, feedback, conflict resolution, and other forms of self-correction that allow organisms to evolve naturally in ways that could not be achieved bureaucratically.

Openness, accessibility, and flow of communication, information, and energy along meridians are key to unifying webs of association. Here are some examples of meridians:

- Team forums where team representatives meet regularly to discuss common problems, make decisions that affect all teams, carry information back to team members, and link diverse people in a single democratically run decision-making body
- Inter- and intradisciplinary chat rooms, where team members and employees across disciplines share information, link up with each other as individuals, and engage in dialogue
- Team ambassadors, who travel personally and electronically among teams and nodes carrying messages, transmitting data to be analyzed, posing clarifying questions, relaying information to and from home teams, facilitating dialogue, and developing common goals and strategies
- Strategic planners, who envision, lead, stimulate, and track the process of strategic planning and then implement, monitor, evaluate, and revise strategic plans
- Fast-forming teams, often cross-functional and voluntary, which form across meridians to solve problems that cannot be adequately addressed by a single team or department and achieve rapid results through high-energy involvement and then dissolve quickly
- Mediators, coaches, and facilitators, skilled in group process, conflict resolution, problem solving, and organizational communication, who bring team members, teams, or nodes together to resolve conflicts and improve collaboration, facilitate

consensus, translate decisions into action, and help align behaviors with values

- Affinity groups, which emerge on an as-needed basis, formed
  at will by anyone on any topic at any time, to address common
  concerns or issues that lie outside the scope of other processes
  and come up with creative solutions
- Labor-management relations committees that work year-round
  to improve communication and relationships between labor
  and management and solve problems informally
- Solution centers and SWAT teams, which are focused on customer service and fixing problems quickly

Meridians can be shaped to respond to changing organizational needs and used to promote faster, high-energy collaborations among, within, and between nodes.

Size Matters

In webs, size matters. A key variable in every organization is the
number of people who work together, combined with the degree
of specialization, decentralization, differentiation, and isolation
dictated by the organizational structures in which they work. Communications, interpersonal dynamics, group processes, and relationships differ dramatically when the numbers change. With
increased size, there is a greater need for formality, regularity, and
control in order to make the system function as a coherent whole.
There are substantial differences, even between groups of two and
three or five and six. Quantity significantly affects a range of qual-
itative issues, including group energy, teamwork, communication,
leadership, motivation, trust, and conflict.

Many large organizations have dramatically improved productivity by restructuring into smaller units. Behemoth corporations like
General Electric and AT&T have reinvented themselves as multiple
companies linked by ownership but separated by function, customer
base, and product line. Just as there are well-known economies of
scale that improve as groups increase in size, there are also reverse
economies of scale, including inefficiency, likelihood of error, loss
of creativity, alienation, miscommunication, irresponsibility, distrust,
and conflict. The real difficulty is determining the optimal economy

of scale for a particular purpose. The smaller the scale, the more agile, adaptable, democratic, creative, and flexible an organization can be. Small-scale structures, systems, and functions make it possible for teams and webs of association to operate organically.

Difficulties with size occur not only in stable organizations but those that merge, combine, or experience rapid growth. When contrasting organizational cultures, individuals with different backgrounds, or teams with unique specializations merge into larger units, five outcomes are possible:

1. Subjugation (suppression of differences)
2. Plunder (appropriation of differences)
3. Amalgamation (disappearance of differences)
4. Coexistence (continuity of differences)
5. Collaboration (synergy of differences)

The challenge democratic organizations face is to combine small, diverse, team-based cultures in ways that do not result in the first four outcomes but produce collaboration and synergistic connection. Webs encourage collaboration by creating a context of values that support diversity and unity, equality and uniqueness, and transform conflicts between cultures into opportunities for improvement.

Hierarchical organizations typically seek to mitigate the negative effects of merger by creating bureaucratic rules and procedures and narrowly defining horizontal boundaries. These are eliminated in living, evolving webs, which require organizations to negotiate their differences and to do so on a human scale. These methods allow teams to link with each other synergistically without succumbing to reverse economies of scale that result from larger sizes. Multiple webs of association can then be linked in a single organization, yet still function as small, flexible, responsive units.

The Soft Stuff *Is* the Hard Stuff

In hierarchical organizations, democracy, teamwork, relationship building, consensus, communication, collaborative negotiation, and conflict resolution are often portrayed as soft, touchy-feely, and simple-minded. In contrast, giving orders, jockeying for power, making unilateral decisions, brow-beating employees, and crushing the competition, even within the same organization, are seen as hard, courageous, and difficult. In reality, as Mary Parker Follett wrote during the 1920s, this is completely backwards:

> We have thought of peace as passive and war as the active way of living. The opposite is true. War is not the most strenuous life. It is a kind of rest cure compared to the task of reconciling our differences. From War to Peace is not from the strenuous to the easy existence. It is from the futile to the effective, from the stagnant to the active, from the destructive to the creative way of life. . . . The world will be regenerated by the people, who rise above these passive ways and heroically seek, by whatever hardship, by whatever toil the methods by which people can agree.

Taking responsibility for work and refusing to be infantilized by managers is far more difficult than being told in detail what to do and how to do it. Hierarchy allows employees to take the easy way out and let management solve their problems. Self-management, teamwork, and webs of association require *all* employees to learn how to participate in collaborative, consensus-based relationships and exercise democratic responsibility, whether in public or private life.

Employees create not only products, processes, and relationships but themselves. This requires not tough, top-down management but responsible, living, evolving, self-managing webs of association. Webs ask all employees without exception to elect their leaders, work in self-managing teams, use collaborative processes, self-correct, and resolve their conflicts. In other words, they ask everyone to become responsible for managing the whole organization—not as individuals arranged in competitive hierarchies but as democratic communities of self-managing teams.

In other words, webs ask everyone to see organizations as belonging to none other than themselves. Warren Bennis and Patricia Biederman, in their book about creative collaboration, *Organizing Genius: The Secrets of Creative Collaboration*, cite a powerful argument for doing so:

There are simply too many problems to be identified and solved, too many connections to be made. . . . In a global society, in which timely information is the most important commodity, collaboration is not simply desirable, it is inevitable. In all but the rarest cases, one is too small a number to produce greatness.

Creating webs of association is a complex process. Like other relationships, it calls for constant renewal, clarity of commitment, and the development of high-level skills in collaboration, communication, negotiation, and conflict resolution. This commitment takes place naturally within webs of association, where ubiquitous linking leaders give these structures coordination, direction, and self-awareness.

Chapter Eleven

Develop Ubiquitous, Linking Leadership

Who built the seven gates of Thebes?
The books are filled with the names of kings.
Was it kings who hauled the craggy blocks of stone?
And Babylon, so many times destroyed,
Who built the city up each time? In which of Lima's houses,
That city glittering with gold, lived those who built it?
. . . Young Alexander conquered India.
He alone?
Caesar beat the Gauls.
Was there not even a cook in his army?
Phillip of Spain wept as his fleet
Was sunk and destroyed. Were there no other tears?
Frederick the Great triumphed in seven years war.
Who triumphed with him?
Each page a victory,
At whose expense the victory ball?
Every ten years a great man,
Who paid the piper?
BERTOLT BRECHT, *Poems: 1913–1956*

If we want to create alternatives to hierarchy, bureaucracy, and autocracy, who, other than managers, will design, build, and sustain these organizations? Who will create a context of values, ethics, and integrity? Who will form living, evolving webs of association? Who will build innovative self-managing teams? Who will implement streamlined, open, collaborative processes? Who will create complex self-correcting systems? Who will integrate strategically and change the way we live? The answer, in collaborative, democratic, self-managing organizations, is ubiquitous, linking leadership: in other words, *we will*, together.

Democracy and Ubiquitous, Linking Leadership

Democracy as a collaborative form of self-government uniquely requires everyone to participate in leadership and "followership" as well. Because democracies thrive on diversity, they need leaders who can bring diverse talents, perspectives, and constituencies together to form an integrated, dynamic whole. They need leaders who stand with, not above, those who follow. For this reason, democratic organizations require leaders who listen, empower others, generate trust, build relationships, negotiate collaboratively, and resolve conflicts—leaders who are also able to follow and let others lead. As Chinese philosopher Lao Tzu wrote centuries ago, "To lead the people, walk behind them."

Unlike hierarchical management, democratic leadership is exercised not only at the top but throughout the organization. Indeed, it challenges the very existence of top and bottom. Every employee in a democratic organization needs to become not only a responsible, self-managing team member but a leader who helps run the show.

Democratic leaders embody a clear commitment to values, ethics, and integrity. They inspire collaboration, stimulate synergistic connections, support honest interactions, build trusting relationships, and encourage self-management and strategic integration across organizational lines. Democratic leaders link people through dialogue and collaboration so they can intelligently choose the right direction and become responsible for the results they produce.

Democratic leaders develop the leadership capacity of every employee. They make connections between planners and implementers, responsibility and possibility, reality and dreams, order and anarchy. They build bridges across disparate, potentially conflicting, unrelated ideas, processes, and individuals. They synthesize diverse approaches, theories, orientations, and discoveries;

spark innovative programs; and create synergies that inspire extraordinary efforts.

Linking leaders cross organizational boundaries to invigorate collaboration, develop fresh ideas, and excite participation. They encourage authenticity and integrity and model the values and principles to which they are committed. They consider themselves responsible for the whole and accountable to those who selected them for the results they produce. They blaze trails to unknown, unimagined futures. These leaders are present without title or designation, and often without anyone knowing it, in every organization at every level.

Linking leadership is a skill that is already present and can be improved in every employee through experience, empowerment, and education. It is not inborn, dependent on titles, or wrapped in mystery. It is something everyone does at multiple points throughout their lives, whether they consider themselves leaders or not. We all have led someone somewhere sometime, and we can all do it again—consciously, collectively, intelligently, and effectively.

The Transformation of Management into Leadership

In practical experience, management assumes different forms as it evolves in response to external and internal conditions. As management becomes more capable and self-conscious, it gradually and automatically begins to evolve into leadership.

As management grows in strength and capability, it is able to move from crisis management to administration, which merely reinforces the status quo. It then moves to management by objectives or goals, and then to management by strategic planning. At this stage, it begins to evolve into something new, something that can no longer be called management, and transforms itself into strategically integrated, values-based leadership.

This transformation takes place by degrees, moving forward and backward in the space of a day. But over time, there is a clear evolutionary pattern of movement from management based on authoritarian principles to leadership based on democratic values. Figure 11.1 distinguishes the primary forms, styles, and varieties of leadership, as contrasted with management, based on the degree

Figure 11.1. Varieties of Leadership and Management.

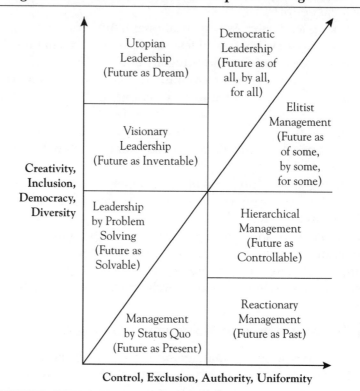

of managerial control, exclusion, authority and uniformity, versus team creativity, inclusion, democracy, and diversity present in the organization. It also identifies alternative attitudes toward the future that flow from these distinctions.

Democratic leadership seeks to maximize creativity, inclusion, and diversity and to minimize control, exclusion, and uniformity, while working to maintain a dynamic tension between these opposite orientations or concerns. It is utopian to think that control can be completely surrendered, just as it is reactionary to suppress all creativity. What is required is a synthesis that is no longer management but leadership.

For organizations to develop leaders who can create a collaborative, democratic future, organizational self-management is essential. Yet hierarchy limits the ability of low-level employees to develop leadership skills. By assuming sole responsibility for solving problems, directing group attention to preselected issues, assigning tasks, and correcting employee behaviors, hierarchical managers send a message that *they* will make the decisions, stripping others of that responsibility and the learning experiences that result in increased skills.

What Cannot Be Managed and Must Be Led

Some skills, behaviors, and outcomes can easily be mandated by others, such as attendance ("Be here at 8:00 A.M."), sequential actions ("Do this first and that second"), politeness ("Don't yell"), and repetitive movements ("Tighten this nut"). Yet there are certain fundamental skills, behaviors, and traits that simply cannot be managed and an equally fundamental set of outcomes that lie entirely beyond management's reach and must be led, facilitated, encouraged, supported, mentored, or coached. Here are some examples of things that cannot be managed and must be led:

• Trustworthiness	• Attitude
• Caring	• Dedication
• Creativity	• Leadership
• Curiosity	• Honesty
• Insight	• Courage
• Synergy	• Empathy
• Integrity	• Compassion
• Consensus	• Understanding
• Craftsmanship	• Wisdom
• Values	• Passion
• Perseverance	• Forgiveness
• Initiative	• Unity
• Flow	• Fortitude
• Collaboration	• Follow-through

Hierarchical management interferes with every one of these fundamental work characteristics. People cannot be ordered to be creative, nor do policies and procedures uniformly generate trust. This does not mean creativity and trust cannot be enhanced through leadership. It means they cannot be commanded, controlled, ordered, predicted, mandated, regulated, administered, or required, because they depend on spontaneous, voluntary, unregulated activity, on choice, and on play.

These skills, behaviors, and traits represent the most important elements in every organization. If the essence of democratic organizations consists of webs of association and collaborative self-managing teams, leadership cannot be effective without the participation and acceptance of those who create, define, and follow it. By creating a distinction between what can and cannot be managed, we identify a human bottom line of leadership and organizational development. To improve, it is essential that organizations decide to develop ubiquitous, linking leaders.

Leaders Are Chosen by Followers

One of the central tenets of democracy is that leaders are chosen by the people they lead rather than being selected by self-designated superiors. Governing fundamentally belongs to those who are governed, and leadership to those who are led, whether the organization is political in the public sector or economic in the private sector.

Organizations can use a combination of consensus, open dialogue, teamwork, and elections to encourage full participation by all employees in making decisions regarding leadership selection. This includes picking their CEOs—not alone but with others who also have an interest in the quality of their leadership, including members of the community in which the organization is located. A small group of majority shareholders or directors who traditionally make these leadership selections actually know far less about the qualities of leadership required by their organizations than those who work on their front lines.

Employees also have a stronger, more socially and environmentally responsible long-term interest in financial success than do shareholders, who have a built-in short-term interest in maximizing their profits and can leave the organization more easily. There is no logical reason, other than the preservation of unequal power, property, and privilege, why all the people immediately affected by leadership decisions should not participate in selecting their leaders and making leadership decisions themselves.

Although corporations are privately owned, they are nonetheless chartered by state laws and subject to legal restrictions. The rights of ownership do not permit discrimination based on race or gender, for reasons of public policy. In a similar way, public policy can be extended to include the right to vote by secret ballot for key organizational leaders who in many cases control assets larger than the gross national products of entire countries.

Nor is there any reason why everyone, from top executives to janitorial staff, should not be eligible to run for these positions and participate equally in dialogue and decision making, or why other democratic devices such as one-person/one-vote, leadership rotation, proportional representation, regulation of campaign activities, initiative and referendum, instant recall, and term limits could not be tried as well.

In the United States, we have extended suffrage to propertyless citizens under the theory that better decisions regarding the selection of leaders will be made through popular democracy than through ownership and privilege. With each great extension of the right to vote has come a broadening of democracy, social equality, and general prosperity. The same principles can be applied with equal effect to corporations.

Elected leadership would stimulate an enormous expansion of democracy in organizations and motivate employees to speak without fear, threat, or coercion. The process of electing leaders would make them responsible to the employees who select them and incline them to encourage democratic practices. Elected leaders are more likely to develop organizational democracy than those selected by a handful of investors interested in turning a quick profit, even if it means gutting the organization, sending jobs overseas, creating social havoc, or destroying the environment.

While it may be objected that this would turn management into a popularity contest, we have several responses. First, managers are already selected based on popularity—only with upper management, not low-level employees. Second, this assumes employees cannot act responsibly or do not deserve democracy, assumptions we have rejected as a nation. Third, popularity is not a bad thing when it comes to leadership, since it reflects a willingness to follow. Fourth, certain outcomes require consent and are far better led than managed. Fifth, other methods simply do not work as well, but produce apathy, cynicism, conflict, and resistance. Sixth, by appointing managers and asking them also to be leaders, hierarchies ensure that they cannot be both and will always remain managers to those they try to lead. Occasionally, managers can overcome these handicaps and become genuine leaders, but it is in spite of, rather than because of, the way they are selected.

In addition to voting for individual leaders, it is possible to use a variety of other more or less democratic methods to select leaders. A team of potential leaders can be identified, each of whom takes a turn at the helm. Leadership positions can be rotated frequently. Candidates' skills can be tested, and those who have the highest qualifications can divide their tasks based on who is best at each. A tag team approach to leadership can be used; everyone occupying a leadership position can be required to step down in favor of anyone who thinks he or she can do it better and give that person a grace period to prove his or her ability. And regardless of who the leader is, important organizational decisions can be submitted to dialogue and consensus or voting.

Three clear facts about leadership are useful for organizations to remember. First, the more practice anyone has exercising leadership, the better he or she becomes at it. Second, the more employees learn to think like leaders, the more creative, strategic, and responsible they become. Third, leadership is not a single skill but a collection of diverse, sometimes contradictory skills that no one person can exercise better than others and that fluctuates based on circumstances.

A more intelligent approach to leadership would therefore be to see every employee as possessing nascent leadership skills that can be developed through practice, to situate leadership not only at the top but throughout the organization, to adopt a team approach to setting organizational direction that allows different individuals to perform different leadership tasks, to give those who follow a voice in deciding whom they think should lead, and to allow leadership to rotate based on circumstances. None of these approaches is supported by confusing leadership with management.

What Are Ubiquitous, Linking Leaders?

We find it useful to distinguish three styles of leadership: *autocratic,* controlling leaders who take responsibility and make decisions for others; *anarchic,* detached leaders who administer but abdicate responsibility and let others take the blame; and *democratic,* linking leaders who inspire, encourage, empower, critique and support, and take final responsibility for decision making along with others. The ancient Chinese philosopher Lao Tzu described three similar forms of leadership:

> The best of all rulers is but a shadowy presence to his subjects.
> Next comes the ruler they love and praise;
> Next comes one they fear . . .
> Hesitant, the best does not utter words lightly.
> When his task is accomplished and his work is done
> The people all say, "It happened to us naturally."

Ubiquitous leadership is precisely a "shadowy presence" that is everywhere in all organizations at all times, and feels as though it happens naturally. It is always available, especially in emergencies. It is democratic, and not separated by status, money, power, or privilege from those who follow.

The more agile, responsive, and creative organizations become, the less possible it is for leaders to be imposed on passive subordinates from above. In order to function, they need to secure the consent of those with and for whom they work. Certainly, upper management ought to have a role in identifying the leaders it needs. But theirs should not be the only voice. Those who are led also ought to participate in selecting the leaders they need.

Employee needs for leadership can change rapidly. At any moment, they may need innovative leaders who can search for unseen answers to questions that may not have been formulated; leaders who are comfortable with diverse constituents, cultures, skill sets, and thinking styles; leaders who are excellent communicators and can create connections, promote collaboration, and build alliances; leaders who can link them together; or leaders who can act decisively.

Democratic leadership needs to be diverse not only in terms of race, gender, age, culture, and sexual orientation but in experience, perceptions, thinking preferences, communication styles, character, emotional makeup, and personality. The best strategy is clearly to have a rich, broad array of leadership styles on call throughout the organization.

The emphasis on developing ubiquitous, democratic, linking forms of leadership does not mean that other forms of leadership are not also useful. There is always a need, for example, for courageous, visionary leadership, which is not always ubiquitous. Courageous, visionary leaders can appear anywhere in an organizational hierarchy. They may have little charisma but great clarity when it comes to articulating or championing a powerful idea. An example of a visionary linking leader is Jerry Cooper, former executive vice president at Showtime Television Networks, who spearheaded a major corporate reorganization to create customer-oriented self-managing teams. Here is how he describes what he did:

> I had a two-fold vision. I figured, let's have the finance department add value to the organization. I saw that where we might add value was by being very customer service oriented. What I did was to take a traditional accounting department and traditional planning department and merge them into a "one-stop-shop." In a traditional accounting department you have senior accountants who do the work and financial analysts who do the budgets, plans and estimates. You take those two disciplines and merge them into a "business analyst unit" which is responsible for all accounting, budgeting and planning for the business unit.

> Then we aligned this new business analyst unit section by section with our customers. That really added value to the organization, so when our financial department was integrated with the rest of the organization we had people in these various financial groups working on the same floor as the business units. The business units found space for them to work so that you could not tell who originally belonged to which organization.

> Then we wanted to raise overall performance. The next level was to change the way we worked, culturally speaking, to give the employees an environment that would enrich and enhance not only their careers, but service to the organization. So we went to the team concept, [and] a self directed, empowered environment. It was not an easy process but we had a vision as to how we would get there and a team environment offered us a couple of things: it enabled us to take people to that next level, and at the same time, people on the teams were being supported by their teammates. The teams were lined up with the business units they supported, and we expanded their strategic responsibilities.

As a result of these changes, employees were able to link with each other across traditional job descriptions, departmental silos, and professional boundaries. They linked with customers across business units to provide direct, high-quality customer service, and with each other in self-directed, empowered teams. Everyone was encouraged to become a leader, support collaboration, think strategically, broaden career opportunities, and develop leadership qualities in themselves and others throughout the organization.

The Roles of Linking Leaders

The practical work of ubiquitous, linking leaders includes playing the following roles:

1. *Shape a context of values, ethics, and integrity.*
   - Keep alive the spirit, heart, and soul of the organization.
   - Develop values, ethics, and integrity throughout the organization, and live by them.
   - Represent human qualities, not just market demands.
   - Stimulate visions, innovation, and creative problem solving.
2. *Form living, evolving webs of association.*
   - Build high-energy connections between teams, individuals, and nodes.
   - Focus on producing high-quality products, processes, and relationships.
   - Encourage all employees to be and express their authentic selves.
   - Provide diverse avenues and forums for the communication of personal and organizational information.
3. *Develop ubiquitous, linking leadership.*
   - Be consistently, authentically, and actively available to all staff.
   - Identify candidates for leadership development and skill expansion.
   - Improve awareness, intelligence, and wisdom across the organization, and champion personal and organizational renewal.
   - Create open opportunities for cross-training, personal development, and skill sharing.

4. *Build innovative self-managing teams.*
   - Stimulate high-performance teams that are innovative, empowered, and responsible.
   - Link motivation and morale with leadership, growth, and learning.
   - Model honest, open, empathetic communication and supportive feedback.
   - Create a variety of democratic forums and team support systems that foster participation and self-management.
5. *Implement streamlined, open, collaborative processes.*
   - Streamline processes to eliminate waste and inefficiency and create opportunities for human interaction and collaboration.
   - Clarify which decision-making processes will be used for different kinds of decisions, and make important decisions by consensus.
   - Engage everyone in strategic planning and designing the future.
   - Conduct open, relevant, democratic meetings in which all participants are able to make constructive contributions.
6. *Create complex self-correcting systems.*
   - Provide honest, open, timely supportive feedback as issues arise.
   - Assess everyone's performance through a 360-degree evaluation process.
   - Develop conflict resolution skills across the organization.
   - Inspire organizational learning through honest reflection and feedback.
7. *Integrate strategically, and change the way we change.*
   - Integrate organizational operations across functions, departments, and roles.
   - Transform the change process by making it collaborative, democratic, and self-managing.
   - Nurture change agents and organizational revolutionaries.

These roles are holistic, integrated expressions of the complex processes employees need to master in order to lead collaborative, democratic, self-managing organizations.

The Skills of Ubiquitous, Linking Leaders

Our friend and mentor Sidney Rittenberg, who spent many years as a leader in China and later as an international trade consultant, believes that linking leaders require unique skills:

> A key role of leaders is listening intently to customers, employees and the public, and getting them to speak freely. This is the basis of any sound leadership orientation and policy. It is also crucially important that leaders maintain an attitude of scientific humility, so that they keep their ears open, their noses in the wind, and their minds continually absorbing new wisdom and experience. Bureaucratic arrogance, inherent in old management systems, is the enemy of learning and of consistently effective leadership.

At a deep level, the values, behaviors, and skills of leaders cannot be fragmented or separated from one another, any more than leaders can be separated from followers. Linking leaders in democratic organizations deploy their skills strategically, integratively, and holistically to build and sustain collaborative, democratic, self-managing possibilities. In doing so, they require the following skills:

- *Character skills,* which build integrity through self-knowledge, ethical sensitivity, values-based action, personal balance, kindness, spiritual openness, trustworthiness, and responsibility
- *Relational skills,* which sustain interconnections among people through dialogue, social inclusion, consensus, acknowledgment, constructive feedback, and collaborative problem solving
- *Mediation skills,* which turn conflicts into opportunities through penetrating honesty and empathy, supportive confrontation, courageous dissent, valued diversity, emotional intelligence, empathetic listening, interest-based negotiation, and conflict resolution
- *Wisdom skills,* which increase understanding, such as imagination, intuition, judgment, innovation, critical reasoning, paradoxical problem solving, and revolutionary strategic planning

- *Elicitive skills,* which motivate people to act, such as involving others, building coalitions, facilitating, coaching, mentoring, nurturing talent, inspiring passion, and empowering leadership
- *Action skills,* which commit to achieving dramatic results, such as dedication, responsibility, self-correction, concern for quality, commitments, perseverance, and evaluating results

All employees can improve their leadership skills simply by bringing the life experiences they already have to work. In families, communities, hobbies, sports, and social gatherings, employees exhibit virtually all the skills required by self-managing organizations. When it comes to something they want to do, employees regularly and without prompting take responsibility, act creatively, solve problems, collaborate to achieve common goals, build consensus, and resolve conflicts.

Everyone wants to create a context of values, ethics, and integrity in their families, schools, and communities that inform their actions at a deep, subconscious level. Everyone has taken responsibility, been on a team, experienced webs of association, exercised linking leadership, used collaborative processes, received feedback, taken risks, solved problems, negotiated differences, changed, and resolved conflicts. What they have not necessarily done, as a result of the way their organizations are structured, is exercise these skills at work.

The skills of linking leaders coalesce into five fundamental configurations.

1. Linking Integrity with Behavior: Skills in Leading by Values

Every revolution starts with a personal transformation, in which courageous leaders see that something is not working and develop the determination to change it. As soon as they begin to take action, they are brought face-to-face with themselves and discover that courage, integrity, and a host of skills and character traits that remain untapped in less demanding times now become essential to success. What they seek to change starts changing them.

Many changes start as a vision of what might be. Visions cause people to grow, learn, and expand their abilities in order to achieve what they desire. As they do so, they are transformed into leaders. They find it necessary to create confidence in others and convince them that the change is going to mean something, that the process will be open and hospitable, that the environment within which the change takes place will also be transformed, and that means will be consistent with ends.

The skill of leading by values starts with personal integrity and the ethical behaviors that flow from it. By *integrity*, we mean being congruent and true to one's values. Ethical behavior stems from a personal commitment to integrity, which is at the heart of all values-based leadership. Leaders who demonstrate these skills are clear that human values are the highest priority, and not dependent on other people's attitudes, circumstances and events. As Warren Bennis has observed, leaders "do the right thing," as contrasted with managers who "do things right."

Those who lead by values are guided by ethical commitments that are integrated into every action they take. Values help leaders create strategies, identify goals and objectives, set standards, shape human resources, design systems and structures, and integrate finance and technology with operations. Values-based leaders model integrity and articulate their values so others can identify and align with them. They ask questions and probe inconsistencies in policies, structures, systems, and behaviors. They drive others to clarify their values and connect with colleagues who have similar commitments. They spark dialogue and are honest in their communications. In a sense, all effective leadership is leading by values, because respect for the values of leaders draws people to follow rather than obey them.

Leading by values means empowering others, promoting self-management, and encouraging employees to define and express themselves in diverse ways. It means building trust, communicating honestly and empathetically, and inspiring personal commitment. It means respecting diversity, assessing social and environmental impact, and balancing economic and human factors. Most important, it means being true to one's self.

2. Linking Change with Ideas: Skills in Revolutionary Thinking

Just as advances in technical skill drive innovations in technology, advances in thinking skills drive innovations in linking leadership and self-management. New organizational contexts, structures, systems, and processes demand that the human side of enterprise be consciously developed. This requires skill in understanding both what needs to be changed and how to make it happen, which we call revolutionary thinking.

Every social, political, and organizational revolution traces its origins to a conceptual revolution in which someone had a new idea. Revolutionary thinking begins in the mind, then seeks ways of translating this vision into reality. It means being open to ideas that fundamentally critique the existing paradigm and seek to transform it. It means questioning stock answers and being committed to altering fundamentals. Because fresh ideas always come from outside the existing paradigm, imagination is the most precious resource for leaders.

Every discovery transforms its discoverer, calling forth the skills needed to make it real. Additional skills are then demanded, including a willingness to take risks; an acceptance of paradox, complexity, and nondualistic thinking; a capacity to dissent with integrity and argue passionately without creating unnecessary enemies; a talent for communicating differences and similarities; and an ability to keep people focused on the big picture.

Revolutionary thinking often originates in young people, newcomers, outsiders, and those at the bottom with little to lose, who bring a celebration of dissent and a wellspring of new ideas. All revolutions, even scientific ones, start with an expanded awareness of anomalies, mistakes, disharmonies, and problems. Leaders who challenge old paradigms seek out the connections between these conflicts and dysfunctions, and treat them simply as the sounds made by the cracks in a system.

Most people think of revolutions as single isolated events. But the history of revolutions reveals that the process of bringing about far-reaching change is much more complex and requires a number of semi-independent, multistaged, interdependent revolutions:

- A revolution of *vision,* which gives rise to the understanding that it is possible to change and a set of ideas and strategies for making it real
- A revolution of *power,* which gives access, permission, resources, and encouragement to put these ideas into practice

- A revolution of *implementation,* which transforms reality by conforming it to the ideas that inspired the change and translating them into organization and action
- A revolution of *completion,* which brings change to everyone, makes them part of a team responsible for results, and leaves no one behind
- A revolution of *being,* which changes not just ideas but the ways people think and transforms not only institutions but relationships, spirits, hearts, and minds
- A revolution of *renewal,* which finds, with implementation and acceptance, that not all problems have been solved and that deeper revolutions must follow

3. Linking Feelings with Balance: Skills in Emotional Intelligence

In hierarchical organizations, employees are expected to check their emotions at the door. Yet they cannot do so without damaging themselves and others or reducing their relationships to superficially polite exchanges that do not reveal who they actually are. In democratic organizations, emotions are accepted, acknowledged, and expressed responsibly and constructively. Linking feelings with balance means being emotionally authentic and not repressing feelings. Applying skills in emotional intelligence allows leaders to transform organizations dramatically by bringing humanity and authenticity to leadership, making work life more compassionate.

Emotional intelligence skills were developed by Daniel Goleman, whose book *Emotional Intelligence* created a new paradigm for assessing leadership. Goleman critiqued traditional IQ tests based on their assumption that intelligence is purely a result of abstract thinking, and in the process identified new roles for leadership. Understanding one's own emotions and those of others is a critical skill for leaders in self-managing organizations, as set out in Table 11.1.

Emotional intelligence is a practical skill that everyone can develop. During crises, conflicts, adversarial negotiations, and competition, people with low emotional intelligence easily reach the limits of their capacity for self-control, self-awareness, self-management, empathy, and collaboration, leading to considerable losses for themselves, other employees, and the organization as a whole.

Table 11.1. The Components of Emotional Intelligence.

	Definition	Hallmarks
Self-awareness	The ability to recognize and understand your moods, emotions, and drives, as well as their effect on others	Self-confidence Realistic self-assessment Self-deprecating sense of humor
Self-regulation	The ability to control or redirect disruptive impulses and moods The propensity to suspend judgment—to think before acting	Trustworthiness and integrity Comfort with ambiguity Openness to change
Motivation	A passion to work for reasons that go beyond money or status A propensity to pursue goals with energy and persistence	Strong drive to achieve Optimism, even in the face of failure Organizational commitment
Empathy	The ability to understand the emotional makeup of other people Skill in treating people according to their emotional reactions	Expertise in building and retaining talent Cross-cultural sensitivity Service to clients and customers
Social skill	Proficiency in managing relationships and building networks An ability to find common ground and build rapport	Effectiveness in leading change Persuasiveness Expertise in building and leading teams

Source: Harvard Business Review, Nov.–Dec. 1998.

Democratic organizations allow emotions to be expressed openly and are far less emotionally charged than autocracies because emotions are not suppressed and made a source of isolation, depression, poor morale, distrust, and deteriorated capacity for self-governance. In democratic organizations, these simple truths are recognized: that people *are* emotional, that self-managing organizations need to be designed with human beings in mind, that emotional intelligence is an essential element in self-management, and that democratic leaders require high skills in sensing, acknowledging, and processing emotions.

4. Linking People with Each Other: Skills in Relationship Building

Author and organizational theorist Peter Senge has observed, "Everyone knows that no work ever gets done by following rules. It gets done through the informal networks." Democratic organizations make rules conform to human relationships, while hierarchies and bureaucracies strive unsuccessfully to make human relationships conform to rules. Relationships are the life of collaborative, democratic, self-managing organizations. Informal information networks and natural communication channels can be enhanced to sustain work processes, build unity among staff, reflect implicit and explicit values, and provide ongoing pathways for collaboration.

Self-managing organizations require linking leaders with strong relationship skills in order to balance unity and diversity, deepen trust and mutual support, keep collaboration alive, support difficult decisions, struggle for consensus, develop emotional intelligence, negotiate differences, and resolve conflicts in ways that repair relationships and end in reconciliation. A key leadership skill in relationship building is supportive confrontation, or giving feedback in risky, straightforward, yet supportive ways. This approach to feedback requires empathy to encourage listening and honesty to say what needs to be heard.

Ubiquitous, linking leaders require skills in building relationships, including fostering and developing natural leadership abilities in all employees, convening and facilitating dialogue, encouraging participation, improving morale, developing latent capacities, supporting personal and organizational learning, and enlisting everyone in strategic integration and renewed and improved forms of practice. At the heart of relationship building is the ability to stimulate dialogue between people with opposing views. Leaders use dialogue in the following ways as a catalyst to build better relationships:

Inquiring	"What do you think should be done? Why do you think so?"
Supporting	"I appreciate your willingness to express your opinions. Here is an example that supports your point . . ."
Acknowledging	"You took a risk in making that concession."
Refereeing	"What ground rules do we need so everyone can perceive we are behaving fairly?"
Concretizing	"Can you give a specific example?"
Exploring	"Can you say more about why you feel so strongly about this issue?"
Summarizing	"Is this what you are trying to say?"
Challenging	"Isn't that inconsistent with what the group has already decided?"
Coaching	"Is there a way you could respond less defensively?"
Connecting	"That point connects directly with what was said earlier, that . . ."
Reorienting	"I think we're lost. Can we get back on track? Are we talking about the real issue?"
Problem solving	"Let's brainstorm for a minute. What are some possible solutions?"
Uniting	"What have we agreed on so far? Why have we come together to discuss this issue? Don't you both agree that . . . ?"

Linking Intention with Results: Skills in Committed Action

The success of organizational democracy will be measured by the results it produces and the quality of work life it fosters. We can articulate countless reasons for collaboration and self-management, but unless they produce positive, concrete, measurable results in both economic and human terms, their future will remain insecure.

In self-managing organizations, everyone forms clear intentions regarding what needs to be done, commits to making it happen, and locates intention as close as possible to action; in hierarchical organizations, intention is separated by vertical layers of management from the point where action occurs. This reduces the level of commitment of those engaged in action and differentiates results from the intentions that create them.

Leaders link commitment with action. By *committed action*, we mean that people are willing to take a stand, put their integrity on the line, and sacrifice time, energy, and resources to achieve a goal. Committed action is sustained over time, strategic regarding obstacles, and focused on achievement. To encourage committed action, linking leaders radically expand participation and the range of options for organizational direction. They winnow these options down and prioritize alternatives through consensus, then mobilize for action, or design experiments and pilot projects if consensus fails.

Strategic planning similarly requires ubiquitous leaders who stimulate creativity and imagination, problem solving and collaborative negotiation, consensus and conflict resolution; who inspire courage and commitment to implement the vision, goals, strategies, and actions that result from planning. These leaders model working across organizational boundaries. They strategically integrate envisioning, evaluating, benchmarking, measuring and tracking milestones, correcting midcourse, receiving feedback, learning from failure, and continuously improving the quality of products, processes, and relationships. Finally, it is committed action that links intention with results. When all other aspects of self-management are working effectively, employees naturally link intention with results and engage in committed action.

Learning Leadership Skills

The difficulty with learning leadership skills, as Oscar Wilde quipped, is that "anything truly worth learning cannot be taught." Perhaps leadership cannot be taught, but it can be learned, and indeed has been learned by all of us. We each learn best in our own way and pace and under conditions we choose, rather than out of fear of not succeeding, or of forfeiting pay, or of being fired.

Management traditionally defines the process by which skills are perfected, often by transforming each skill into an ideal to which employees, regardless of natural abilities, are expected to conform. But creating ideals and perfect standards makes everyone feel like a failure and inhibits learning. We need to surrender the dream of perfection, except in the sense that imperfection forms an essential part of what makes us perfect. Whereas bureaucratic organizations strive for uniformity because it is predictable and easy to control, democratic organizations strive for diversity because it is innovative and leads to unexpected results and organizational learning.

Learning the skills of ubiquitous, linking leaders may seem to be an overwhelming task, especially if we believe that leaders are superior beings rather than natural by-products of collaborative, democratic, self-managing processes. Our friend and colleague Jean Lipman-Blumen has identified a number of pernicious myths regarding leadership, which prevent employees from seeing their own natural leadership potential:

- Leaders are stronger and know more than we do.
- The gods favor leaders, so it is dangerous to cross them.
- If leaders make tough decisions, we can remain blameless.
- Leaders have our best interests at heart.
- We can share in the resources that leaders control only if we remain loyal.
- It's just the way things are and have always been, and we have to accept it.
- Leading is much too difficult for people like us.
- The odds overwhelmingly favor leaders.
- Others seem to think our leaders are doing a good job.
- We are alone in thinking our leaders are doing a bad job.
- If we oppose our leaders, we will be exiled from where the action is.
- We would be afraid to do what leaders are doing, and do it badly.

In fact, each of these statements appears true only in hierarchical organizations. Hierarchy, bureaucracy, and autocracy depend on the maintenance of these myths; democracy requires that they be dismantled. The only way people can learn that the opposites of these myths are true is through the *practice* of democracy and the discovery that leadership is a diverse skill everyone possesses. This is a lifelong learning process that flourishes only in democratic organizations and leads to another truth: that we need new skill-building processes in order to develop ubiquitous, linking leadership. There is, for example, a fundamental difference among the following methods for improving leadership skills:

- *Lectures,* which involve rote memorization and recall of facts and result in knowledge and information
- *Training,* which involves group discussion and results in technical competency and confidence
- *Education,* which involves exposure to ideas and results in learning and understanding
- *Development,* which involves discovery, self-awareness, and dialogue and results in wisdom, integrity, and freedom

As our colleague Ken Anbender points out, these forms of learning shift our focus from knowing, to doing, to understanding, to being. As we make the transition to deeper forms of leadership, we need to develop learning methods that are successful in creating collaborative, democratic, self-managing leaders. Certainly, all learning processes perform a valuable function, but development produces the greatest results in values, integrity, and democratic leadership. Development is the application of democracy to learning. Ubiquitous, linking leadership skills such as integrity, honesty, and emotional intelligence are not greatly improved through lectures, education, or training, but require education and development because they are voluntary, personal, diverse, relational, practical, and within the capacity of every employee.

Questions About Linking Leadership

In order to develop linking leadership skills, we pose a number of questions that highlight the distinctions between linking and other forms of leadership:

1. *If leaders are not born, how are they made?* Linking leaders are made by developing their capacity for vision, caring about people, commitment to results, integrity, and overcoming fear of failure. They learn how family patterns, childhood expectations, and incomplete experiences from the past block development of their leadership potential. They explore the elements in their family histories, attitudes toward failure and success, and stumbling blocks that inhibit or obstruct their continued learning. They develop the leadership styles, modes of operating, expressions of values, and personal strategies that allow them to escape these patterns and create new ones.

2. *What is required to develop linking leadership?* As organizations challenge employees to identify their leadership needs and capacities, envision specific forms of linking leadership, and brainstorm what it would take to make them explicit, employees naturally begin to develop leadership skills. As they collectively identify their diverse leadership styles, find out what their followers want them to do, clarify what they are prepared to do to meet those needs, specify what they plan to deliver, and commit to action, their leadership skills link and expand to fill the gaps.

3. *What is leadership by values?* Leadership by values is acting always on the basis of commitment and integrity. It is shaping a context of values, ethics, and integrity, making principles the basis for organizational decision making, and not considering oneself separate from the physical, cultural, social, and political environments in which one lives. It means being willing to take unpopular stands to support one's beliefs while keeping an open mind and being willing to listen to those who disagree.

4. *What obstructs walking the talk?* Mostly it is pretending to be something or someone we are not, failing to acknowledge our shortcomings, hiding parts of ourselves, and suppressing our core values. It is losing touch with what it means to be a human being and turning people into roles and titles. It is ego, fear, anger, guilt, shame, and trying to be perfect. Walking the talk means not blaming others for our decisions or conditioning our integrity on someone else's choices.

5. *How do leaders respond to conflict?* Linking leaders see conflict as a sign that something is not working for someone, and turn conflict into an opportunity for learning, growth, and improvement.

Linking leaders use conflict to expand their skills in communicating, creating new solutions, negotiating, mediating, and responding to difficult behaviors. They do not avoid conflict or act aggressively toward people; instead, they focus on problems, solutions, and the future.

6. *Is a balanced life possible for leaders?* Most leaders encounter difficulties leading a balanced life. As leaders figure out how to free themselves from the need to control everything, be superstars, and represent all things to all people, they find greater balance in their lives. Leaders need to be committed and responsible but also authentic; to achieve results but also have values; to assist others but also expand their horizons; to clarify their priorities and commitments but also balance financial security and personal achievement with family life, community involvement, and spiritual growth.

7. *How do leaders learn to manage time?* There is never enough time. Therefore, the issue is not how much time there is, which is fixed, but how to develop focus, identify priorities, cultivate patience and determination, and do so strategically. Leaders often learn to manage time by filling their plate so full that they are forced to learn how to work more quickly or by learning to use delegation, education, development, and empowerment to replace themselves.

8. *Is there room at the top?* The top of the organization should not be the sole or even the primary location for strategic thinking and committed action. This is why democratic organizations require ubiquitous leaders and seek to eliminate the destructive competition for top positions that characterizes hierarchical leadership. Indeed, the first responsibility of democratic leaders is to replace themselves and help others step into their shoes. Linking leaders coach, guide, support, mentor, and counsel others on how to make a difference wherever they are and share whatever they have learned.

9. *How should leaders respond to changes and losses in the work environment?* Death, loss, and transition are natural experiences in every organization. Emotionally intelligent linking leaders develop skills in accepting these natural parts of life, pass these skills on to others, and use their experiences to increase their capacity for empathy, compassion, availability, integrity, and presence.

10. *What are the most important responsibilities of linking leaders?* The most important responsibilities are not simply getting the

work done, which is essential, but supporting everyone in the organization in reaching their full potential, improving their skills in leadership and self-management, and maximizing their capacity for finding joy in their work.

How Leaders Generate Flow

Ubiquitous leaders are skillful not only in linking employees and improving relationships but in transforming apathetic, disengaged, cynical workers into caring, goal-oriented, strategic self-managers by creating optimal experiences at work. As employees learn skills in self-management and develop themselves as leaders, their capacity for synergy, joy, fulfillment, and artistry steadily increases.

Sociologist Mihaly Csikszentmihalyi, in *Flow: The Psychology of Optimal Experience,* has described how challenging work, skill building, and self-fulfillment combine to create optimal experiences, or "flow." The elements of flow, which can be thought of as design criteria for the creation of optimal work environments, include identifying challenges that lie a little beyond skill; merging action and awareness; clarifying vision, goals, and objectives; providing immediate, ongoing, supportive feedback; encouraging high concentration on tasks and committed action; believing in the ability to control actions or outcomes; reducing ego and self-consciousness; and creating an experience of the stretching of time.

Developing ubiquitous, linking leadership skills generates a feeling in employees that they are growing and learning, which increases their self-esteem, results in higher morale, improves their task concentration, and creates improved work environments. At any moment, however, employee skills may be greater than the challenges they face, and boredom sets in. Or their skills may be inadequate to the challenges they face, and they experience anxiety. Flow takes place when skills nearly match challenges, as diagrammed in Figure 11.2.

The value of Figure 11.2 is not simply that it reveals the relationship between skills and challenges, but that it identifies solutions to two common leadership problems. If employees are bored, leaders need to increase the level of challenge; and when they are feeling anxious, leaders need to coach, train, mentor, and develop their skills.

Figure 11.2. Flow, or Optimal Experience.

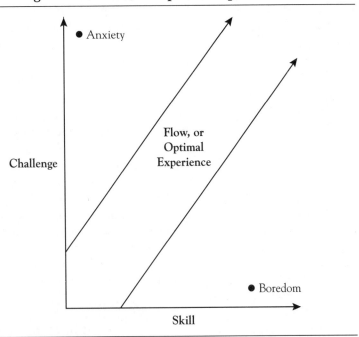

Challenge

• Anxiety

Flow, or
Optimal
Experience

• Boredom

Skill

Owning the Problems Means Owning the Organization

Most private sector hierarchical organizations are owned by their stockholders, CEOs, directors, and executives; public sector organizations are owned by the state, in the name of the public. These organizations routinely send their staff conflicting messages separating them from the ultimate responsibilities that flow from ownership, while at the same time asking them to take risks, be accountable, and own their organizations.

When employees are expected to become leaders and act as though they own their organizations, everything from motivation to rewards and responsibility needs to change rapidly and dramatically. By becoming leaders, employees automatically increase their sense of emotional investment in the organization and naturally seek to expand their financial investment as well. The end of management and the rise of collaborative, democratic, self-managing organizations will therefore inevitably result in a dramatic transformation in the nature and extent of organizational ownership.

Many adventurous organizations have already altered traditional patterns of ownership by giving even low-level employees stock options that allow them to own shares in their companies. This has resulted in a dramatic increase in motivation, morale, commitment, ubiquitous leadership, and responsibility for results. In an article in the *Harvard Business Review,* Bill Gross, the founder and chairman of Idealab, described how, for tax reasons, he reluctantly kept only 19.9 percent of equity in a new spin-off company and turned the rest over to employees. The results, he claimed, were astonishing:

> Within a year, [the company] grew almost as large as [the parent company] itself. Its employees seemed to rise to new heights of creativity and passion—putting in Herculean efforts to close deals, to improve the product, and to recruit new star employees. My earlier reluctance suddenly seemed laughable: instead of owning 80% of a $5 million business, [I] now owned 19.9% of a $77 million business.

Similar results have been documented in many employee-owned companies and cooperatives, especially where ownership has been accompanied by a simultaneous shift to self-managing teams. For these efforts to succeed, staff need to see themselves not only as leaders but as owners of their organizations. When employees move from feeling owned by someone else to feeling like owners themselves, the results in output and work satisfaction increase dramatically.

The implications of broadening and democratizing the forms of organizational ownership are many. Anyone who has moved from a rented apartment to a home they own themselves will immediately understand the differences in motivation and initiative. A sense of ownership consistently produces higher levels of commitment and responsibility, greater creativity and imagination, finer attention to the quality of work life, and a deeper commitment to common values.

For these reasons, it is clear that the highest levels of ubiquitous, linking leadership are achieved when employees become financial as well as operational owners of their organizations. But there is a fundamental difference between the historic definition of ownership as the legal right to exclude others from making decisions and sharing in the profits, and ownership as the right to participate in making decisions and sharing profits with coworkers and contributing back to the community and environments that organizations exhaust and on which they depend. This way of thinking about ownership transforms it from a measure of individual power and wealth to a measure of team empowerment and community responsibility.

This distinction reveals the hidden consequences of expanding organizational self-management. The democratization of organizational power and ownership are prerequisites for the highest levels of motivation and organizational development and cannot remain untouched by their expansion. Ubiquitous, linking leaders can be fully developed only by sharing the power and profits that flow from organizational success. Democracy is, above all, a sharing of power, and for organizational democracy to become consistent and widespread, employees need to become owners and not merely renters of their organizations, and of their work lives as well.

Chapter Twelve

Build Innovative Self-Managing Teams

Every so often a Celtic game would heat up so that it became more than a physical or even mental game, and would be magical. When it happened, I could feel my play rise to a new level. It would surround not only me and the other Celtics, but also the players on the other team, and even the referees. At that special level, all sorts of odd things happened. The game would be in a white heat of competition, and yet somehow I wouldn't feel competitive—which is a miracle in itself. I'd be putting out the maximum effort, straining, coughing up parts of my lungs as we ran, and yet I never felt the pain. During those spells, I could almost sense how the next play would develop and where the next shot would be taken. My premonitions would be consistently correct, and I always felt then that I not only knew all the Celtics by heart, but also all the opposing players, and that they all knew me. There have been many times in my career when I felt moved or joyful, but these were the moments when I had chills pulsing up and down my spine. Sometimes the feeling would last all the way to the end of the game, and when that happened I never cared who won, I don't mean that I was a good sport about it—that I'd played my best and had nothing to be ashamed of. On the five or ten occasions when the game ended at that special level, I literally did not care who had won. If we lost, I'd be as free and high as a sky hawk.
BILL RUSSELL, *Second Wind*

We have all belonged to teams and felt or sensed the synergy Russell eloquently describes—the seamless connections that meld our skills, link us intuitively, and allow us to surpass our expectations. And we have all experienced the frustrations, conflicts, disappointments, failed expectations, and pressures to conform or suppress our individuality that can occur on teams. These contradictory experiences with teamwork pose challenges for team-based, democratic, self-managing organizations.

What Are Teams?

To understand the strength and potential of teams and why they are the fundamental work units of all successful organizations, we need to start with a question: How do teams differ from groups? The answer can be found by posing another set of questions: How is a home different from a house? How is a community different from a city? How is a neighborhood different from a block?

Teams, communities, neighborhoods, and homes all describe relationships—intimate human connections in which the whole emerges as greater than the sum of its parts. Each provides something extra—an energy or synergy that springs from the quality of interactions between the people who create them. By contrast, groups, cities, blocks, and houses represent mere collections, composites, or conglomerates of fragmented, individual parts that have not yet been integrated into a whole but remain sums of parts, however much they may strive to achieve a common purpose.

Teams are affective, emotional relationships and personal connections between people. They mix diversity and unity, openness and acceptance, honesty and empathy, criticism and acknowledgment, trust and risk taking, to create something larger than would be possible by simply adding individual pieces together.

In groups, power is usually distributed hierarchically, and decisions are made by a small circle of individuals to whom others surrender their power and responsibility. A single primary person in charge has the capacity to pressure, coerce, and manipulate others into adopting a single direction. Groups have only a shadowy existence apart from their leaders and a few stalwarts who can be counted on to follow them. For this reason, unquestioning loyalty is in high demand, and disloyalty is punished in overt and covert ways.

Teams have no need to coerce people or require loyalty. A common direction flows automatically from the act of identifying and integrating vision, goals, and strategies. Teams do not seek subordination, fear, or deference. They rely instead on independence, self-confidence, and critical feedback. They do not value uniformity or obedience to the leader's will but rely on diversity, dialogue, and negotiation to achieve consensus and a common direction.

Groups are most successful when there is an external threat requiring quick, coordinated, decisive action. In the absence of a clear threat, they rely on fear and coercion to produce a transient unity. Followers are often poorly motivated, lack creativity, and take only piecemeal initiative and responsibility. They relate to those at the top as children do to surrogate parents, in hopes that, through fealty, their personal needs will be satisfied more thoroughly than would be possible on their own.

Teams do not obey leaders as children do surrogate parents. Each member accepts responsibility and behaves like an adult. Teams are ultimately defined by the clarity of their cohesion; their collective, task-oriented spirit; the vulnerability and affection members manifest in their relationships; and the quality of their enjoyment of the work process. It is this quality of acting together that gives teams power. As Hannah Arendt wrote, "While strength is the natural quality of an individual seen in isolation, power springs up between men when they act together, and vanishes the moment they disperse."

As teams increasingly constitute the fundamental units of organizational energy, values, and strategy, the capacity of individual team members to think and behave as responsible members of a collaborative, strategically integrated network becomes crucial. This requires each team member to abandon excessively competitive, individualistic, egocentric, self-aggrandizing behaviors that regard freedom as the absence of social restraint rather than the presence of social synergy.

Successful democratic organizations require a context of values, ethics, and integrity, living, evolving webs of association, innovative self-managing teams, streamlined, open collaborative processes, and complex self-correcting systems, and each of these requires linking leadership. Showtime Networks CFO, Jerry Scro, reflected in an interview on his experiences in creating self-managing teams:

> In working together as teams, everyone really has to be able to trust each other. They have to be able to break down political barriers, organizational barriers, and barriers of competition. What we did here created competition in a different way. Competition is very good, but it is not self-competition. It is a competition of "we all want to be the best we can and succeed and if we all work together we'll all succeed together." It requires a lot of work, nurturing, continuous involvement, and evolving, and it is not easy. It seems easy to say "I don't have to tell anyone to do anything anymore." On the other hand, everyone has to make sure the work gets done. The role of the senior-level manager in this organization is a lot different than it was in the past—it's obvious, it's a radical change. From a person who directs and tells people what to do and how to do it, to a person who facilitates, leads, guides, sets the tone, helps the environment, and culture—it's an entirely different style, an entirely different demeanor, an entirely different attitude. And the leaders really have to believe that this is the right way to do it, because if a leader doesn't, it gets picked up very quickly by the rest of the organization and they feel, well, this is just not real.

Without a clear recognition that committed leaders are needed throughout the organization regardless of title or position, without a commitment to linking people in creative collaborative ways, democracy will remain imperfect, and possibilities for improvement will be lost.

Team membership does not mean abandoning individuality or surrendering the critical insights that can improve a team's products, processes, and relationships. It means being willing to invest that individuality and critical insight in the team, combine them with similar investments by others, and allow the mixture to turn into something new and qualitatively different.

How Teams Produce Quality Results

Teams form the fundamental units of interconnected action that lie at the core of all democratic, self-managing organizations and provide them with strength, flexibility, creativity, and endurance.

Teams are where values are translated into action. They are the hearts of webs of association. In addition to correcting the mistakes and difficulties created by hierarchical, bureaucratic, autocratic management, teams help organizations provide higher-quality and more responsive, accessible service to internal and external clients. How do they do so?

Teams create a feeling of ownership that increases competitive advantage and a collaborative environment in which members cross-train and back one another up, increasing their efficiency and effectiveness. Teams improve turnaround time and responsiveness in solving customer problems. They develop leadership qualities among all their members, resulting in broader responsibility for achieving goals, greater buy-in, and higher retention rates.

Teams increase flexibility and speed in decision making and responding to changing conditions. They reduce unnecessary conflict, distrust, and miscommunication, and improve working relationships through consensus and collaboration. They encourage employees to continue developing their skills by accepting new challenges and improving morale.

Research cited in earlier chapters supports these assertions, demonstrating that teams are more rapid, creative, accurate, and productive than individuals working alone or in hierarchical work units. Teams eliminate the need for most managerial functions by making everyone responsible for results; reducing disharmony, passivity, and resistance; improving the quality of products, processes, and relationships; encouraging creativity; and correcting errors before they become costly to fix.

Teams take pleasure from overcoming their obstacles, solving problems, and acquiring new skills. The affection team members often develop for one another contributes to the intuitive, unspoken quality of their communications. In team environments, people behave more naturally in nonhierarchical team environments, with less pretension and show. They feel less need to conform to universal standards that ignore their individuality or create rules without consensus. Relationships on teams are more grounded in respect and appreciation for contributions than in hierarchical organizations.

Teams encourage ubiquitous leadership and allow everyone to participate in setting direction. Leadership in teams is floating, situational, and diverse rather than fixed. Leaders are not predetermined or selected from above but promoted by peers based on ability. A leader in one task may be a follower in the next. The natural desire to learn and the team's need for internal backup combine to encourage the development of improved individual and team skills through cross-training, feedback, and mentoring. This makes leadership a shared responsibility that can be exercised without ego aggrandizement or self-promotion.

In quality improvement processes, teams make more accurate decisions using consensus than do hierarchies using directives. They ensure that actions are synchronous, resistance is minimized, and results are sustained. When disputes emerge during the consensus-building process, they are less likely to be accompanied by personalization, polarization, fear, defensiveness, or distrust. Instead, objections and disagreements are turned into dialogue and mined for alternative perspectives, creative solutions, expressions of paradox, challenges, and complex insights.

From Organizational Teams to Team Organizations

Teams naturally arrange themselves into webs of association, which are the crucibles in which strategic integration takes place, where all the elements in the productive process are creatively combined to produce something new. Webs form a matrixed environment in which activity flows between diverse teams yet is centered in a home team. One way of picturing this relationship is given in Figure 12.1.

While not all employees may work on all these teams at the same time, the four teams in the diamond represent primary sources of ongoing organizational learning and development that are critical for collaborative, democratic, self-managing organizations. They allow every team member to feel connected and responsible for the life and direction of the organization as a whole.

For teams to be fully self-managing, they need to communicate with one another, integrate across organizational lines, and think strategically. For these reasons, leadership, facilitation, and coordination skills are essential. As employees increasingly participate in making important organizational decisions, their experience and skill in handling a wide range of organizational issues improve rapidly, helping organizational teams transform themselves into team organizations.

Figure 12.1. Team Matrix.

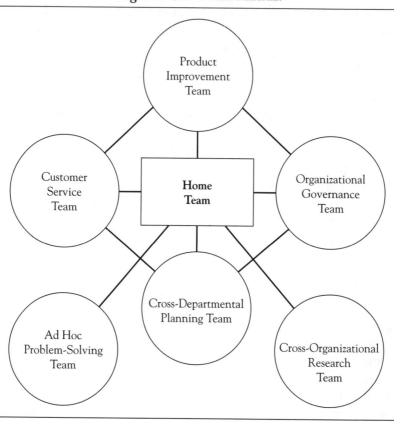

At the beginning of the team-building process, there is often a period in which team members go through the motions, giving only lip-service to participation and responsibility. This can make the entire process seem fraudulent, producing cynicism and a desire to return to managerial control. Yet as old habits of obedience and anonymity are broken down, team members accept responsibility for making increasingly crucial organizational decisions. As they do, their responsibilities expand until they gradually become team-based organizations.

To understand how this process works, it is necessary to answer some fundamental questions about the limits of team decision making. How far can employees go in managing themselves? How can typical managerial functions be improved through teamwork? What would a fully self-managing, team-based organization look like? The following ten questions drawn from our book, *Thank God It's Monday: Fourteen Values to Humanize the Way We Work,* highlight the principal categories of decisions commonly made by managers in hierarchical organizations, together with ideas and suggestions for how they might be handled better in team-based organizations.

1. *Who makes the decision to hire?* Hiring has traditionally been a unilateral activity engaged in by managers based on criteria they alone select. Yet better results can be achieved when hiring becomes a collaborative, peer-based responsibility of self-managing teams, for these reasons:

- Teams are usually much better qualified to choose coworkers than are managers who do not actually perform the daily work of the team.
- Employees who are hired by a team feel an obligation to support their peers and perform at higher levels than when they work to satisfy a manager.
- Errors are corrected more quickly, and poor performers are disciplined or replaced with less opposition from other employees.

2. *Who allocates work and assigns tasks?* Self-management and task selection by self-managing teams can dramatically increase productivity by improving motivation, limiting unproductive behavior, and reducing managerial expenses through reverse economies of scale. Teamwork makes assignment flexible and dynamic rather than bureaucratic and static, and oversight becomes a responsibility of everyone on the team, bringing the following benefits:

- Task-oriented self-assigning teams can counter the negative effects of isolation due to the separation and division of labor. Self-assignment can also improve motivation by increasing task and product identity.
- Self-managing teams can allocate work more cheaply, more quickly, with a finer sense of priorities than managers, and an increased ability to change rapidly to meet new demands.

- Teams are more capable of knowing what is required at any given moment in the workday than managers, who are one step removed from problems. Even centralized tasks can be handled more efficiently by team members representing diverse departments.

3. *How is work evaluated and improved?* Feedback, evaluation, self-correction, learning, and improvement ought to be the responsibility of all team members. Contributions to personal and organizational improvement become far more powerful when feedback is received from everyone affected by the work. The benefits of team-based peer evaluation include:

- 360-degree evaluations based on self, upward, peer, downward, and client feedback, together with analysis of differences between assessments, encourage more open, honest, meaningful evaluations.
- Quicker, more supportive, and useful feedback can be tailored by teams to help each person learn and change. This means regular, honest, open, timely discussions of difficult issues, starting from the top. The most powerful and effective feedback always emanates from clients, team members, and ourselves.
- For feedback to be effective, judgments need to be separated from evaluation. Feedback in a team environment has only one purpose: improvement. Whatever does not actually improve individual and team performance is either useless or counterproductive and should be eliminated.

4. *Who selects leaders?* Management is a title, a set of involuntary roles assigned to people selected from above; leadership is a voluntary relationship informed by vision and maintained by skill with people who freely choose to follow. To establish a mandate, leaders should be selected and elected by those they lead. Leadership requires different skills than management does, for several reasons:

- Leadership is a universal job description for team members, who need to be able to facilitate team meetings, track projects, relate well to customers, solve problems, mediate conflicts, make certain nothing falls through the cracks, and perform countless diverse assignments.

- Leadership on teams is situational and shared, based on whatever task needs to be performed, together with individual skills and desires. Leaders who are chosen by their teams can ask for and receive efforts far beyond what is required.
- Traditional managerial tasks can easily be computerized or rotated among team members, allowing managers to move into roles as facilitators, coordinators, supporters, mentors, mediators, or team members with specialized administrative skills.

5. *Who gets promoted, how, and by what criteria?* In hierarchical organizations, promotions are often based on having done a lower-level job well, that is, on technical ability; some guessed-at capacity to succeed in meeting a set of abstract, objective criteria; or purely subjective, intuitive feelings about the personality of the candidate. In a team environment, there are alternative ways of promoting:

- Eliminating grandiose titles, enormous wage discrepancies, autocratic power, hierarchical privileges, and compensation based on title or status. Instead, a flexible matrix of skills, contributions, knowledge, seniority, difficulty of assignment, willingness to perform low-status work, voluntary efforts that benefit the team as a whole, and similar criteria can be used. Applying genuine market principles to employment means that those who perform the least desirable tasks might receive the highest wages.
- Rather than promote people out of jobs they do well into managerial positions they do poorly, teams can create a broad array of rewards, including acknowledgment, job rotation, free time for creative projects, and opportunities to develop natural abilities, leading to leadership roles and career development.
- Allowing teams to select and promote their own leaders encourages teamwork and leadership development. Internal career counseling, aptitude testing, attitude surveys, and team selection can help teams eliminate burnout, elitism, tyrannical management, and the Peter Principle.

6. *Who gets trained in what?* Training should be organized from the bottom up rather than the top down, and focus on team skills rather than those of individual managers. It should improve practical skills in leading, facilitating, coaching, communicating, negotiating, building ownership, giving honest feedback, building better relationships, resolving interpersonal conflicts, and negotiating collaboratively. Expanding training, education, and development, orienting each to teams, and covering the full range of skills required for self-management can:

- Turn every organization into a university in miniature, providing mandatory and voluntary, free and paid education for all employees.
- Create learning organizations that strongly encourage employees to teach those with less experience, knowledge, or skill and become lifelong learners. Enormous skills and knowledge can be recaptured by transforming master-employees into mentor-teachers as they develop and before they retire.
- Design a comprehensive team-based internal training, education and development program focused on training team trainers and on leadership, self-management, teamwork, and change.

7. *Who determines and enforces rules?* Every employee in a team environment has a vested interest in increasing productivity and client satisfaction and is capable of setting rules that advance common interests and result in shared responsibility for preventing future violations. Employee-generated rules counteract the dynamics created by externally imposed rules, which lead to blind obedience rather than creativity and result in resistance, unequal enforcement, cynicism, coercion, and duress. Democratically generated rules improve results for a number of reasons:

- Value-based decisions in self-managing organizations are reached by consensus, with regard to how resources are allocated, money is spent, people are paid, and individuals interact with each other. When team members genuinely agree, enforcement and coercion become less necessary.

- Team members who are included in decision making regarding rules and values naturally develop the cognitive and communication skills that allow them to assume increased responsibility for results.
- Fairness, justice, and democracy mean that teams decide what rules they need, the consequences for breaking them, and how to enforce them without becoming responsible for other people's choices.

8. *Who resolves conflicts and how?* Conflicts provide teams with rich opportunities to reveal the inconsistencies between expressed values and actual behaviors. They offer openings for growth, personal improvement, and increased team effectiveness. When teams own their conflicts and become responsible for resolving them, the entire paradigm of conflict shifts from one of avoidance or confrontation to one of learning. Conflict resolution is far more effective in team-based environments for the following reasons:

- Teams can pinpoint the sources of chronic conflict, design conflict resolution systems, identify early warning signs, create safety nets, develop techniques for prevention and early resolution, and support low-cost procedures such as peer review and coaching as backups.
- Peer mediation can provide a highly effective, voluntary, consensus-based process for resolving conflicts in which team members learn to negotiate differences and resolve conflicts themselves.
- Team-based conflict resolution increases organizational efficiency by improving morale, providing an outlet for emotional venting, reducing resistance, encouraging listening, and making it acceptable to talk openly and honestly about problems. This allows compassion, empathy, forgiveness, transformation, and ethical behavior to moderate differences and the chaos generated by rapid change.

9. *How is compensation determined?* When employees make compensation decisions, productivity increases enormously. Several studies have shown that when employees are permitted to decide

what to pay themselves, they not only set aside adequate sums for investment but make their products and services more competitive. Experience in employee-owned firms demonstrates that pay cuts and reductions in benefits are more readily agreed to in employee-owned firms than in hierarchies. Team-based organizations can restructure compensation in several ways:

- Leadership can train employees in accounting principles and budgets, and encourage broad participation in budgetary decision making, or create an overall budget and let teams decide how to divide it.
- Team members who receive equity or stock, or become partners and co-owners, benefit directly from reduced waste, noninflationary wages, and increased productivity.
- By correlating investments in organizational expansion with future income and reduced investment with lower income, teams can participate in deciding which path to take and accept the financial consequences for their decisions.

10. *How are profits and losses divided?* As self-managing teams become adept at making strategic financial decisions, dividing profits, covering losses, budgeting, allocating resources, and making investments, they should share in the profits and losses that flow from their energy and commitment. In making decisions regarding profit and loss, teams can be more successful than shareholders and CEOs, for several reasons:

- Changes in employee responsibility and self-management are more successful when compensation is redesigned to reward extra effort, including pay-for-learning, pay-for-skills, bonuses, stock options, gain sharing, and outright employee ownership, which stimulate an ongoing interest in the financial success of the organization.
- The success of employee-owned organizations and cooperatives is based on the long-term interests of employees in sustainable growth and customer service. The greater their responsibility is for profits and losses, the more employees want to make it succeed.

- Employees have a natural long-term interest in sustainable growth, environmental protection, and employee safety, and are likely to be better at making decisions regarding socially responsible investments than shareholders who are focused on quarterly dividends, since their lives depend on their choices.

When organizations address these questions from a context of collaboration, democracy, and self-management, their ability and willingness to give team members responsibility for making intelligent choices regarding organizational direction shifts enormously. Team members increasingly regard organizations as collaborative and interdependent, managerial process as learnable, and themselves as capable of the full range of responsibilities traditionally reserved for management. Success in any of the areas described above makes it easier to succeed in each of the others. As these successes accumulate, it becomes difficult to identify a single managerial function that could not be performed at reduced cost and increased effectiveness by combining self-managing teams with leadership and automated technology.

What Makes Teams Succeed and Fail?

Studies of highly effective teams have identified a number of characteristics that make them successful: a strong and compelling performance challenge; clear goals and objectives; a customer orientation; participative leadership shared by all team members; good communication; a high level of trust, respect, and honesty; a willingness to work through and resolve conflicts; respect for diversity; consensus-based decision making; strong organizational support; adequate resources, especially training; adequate authority and empowerment to achieve goals; and individual and team responsibility for results.

Despite the simplicity and apparent effortlessness required to implement these characteristics, they are often arduous to achieve, and their absence causes teams to fail. A number of research studies have identified the most common reasons for team failure:

- Lack of adequate training, resources, and internal support
- Management interference and micromanagement
- Inadequate empowerment and permission to make decisions
- Inadequate skills in conflict resolution
- Lack of vision, goals, strategies, timelines, and action plans
- Making the team too large or too small
- Repeatedly changing team members or assignments
- Absence of a critical mass of dedicated team members
- Lack of a powerful customer, client, or citizen focus
- Traditional managers being assigned as team leaders
- Managers assigning too much work to the team and bogging it down
- Lack of effective communications from management about the team process
- Lack of support from other departments
- Lack of internal feedback and evaluation
- Lack of team-based compensation, rewards, acknowledgments, and promotions

Each of these sources of team failure can be corrected with increased organizational support, commitment, and understanding of the team process, and with increased empowerment of teams to solve their own problems, starting with the problems of composition, leadership, goals, and decision making.

Questions to Consider in Building Successful Teams

How can organizations maximize their opportunities for successful team building and minimize their risks of failure? In spite of innumerable books written on the subject, there are no models or recipes for successful teamwork. Team building cannot be done by designing ideal models and prototypes or outlining seven or ten steps to apply in cookie-cutter fashion.

Successful team formation is an intricate, complex, always unique process. So instead of providing generic models and uniform answers, we prefer to ask a set of questions team members can answer for themselves and return to throughout the team building process. Employees often coalesce into a team simply by having to grapple with difficult questions and take responsibility for shaping the quality of their own experiences:

- *Who are we? (identification of the team).* What individual and team efforts are required to do the job? How should the teams be structured? Who should be on each team? How should they be selected? How should the teams interact? Has everyone's role been collectively considered and negotiated? Have training needs been self-defined? Are external trainers, consultants, facilitators, or mediators necessary? If so, how and by whom will they be hired?

- *Why are we here? (orientation to team mission).* What is the mission of the team? Does everyone agree with it? Is it clear? Is there adequate support, motivation, and commitment? Has covert resistance been recognized, surfaced, and resolved? What alternatives are available for those who chose not to join the team?

- *Where are we headed? (creation of a vision).* What is the team's vision of its direction for the next three to five years? Is it daring enough? What does the team need to do to imagine its future? What are the needs of internal and external customers, and how can they be incorporated into the vision? What are the needs of team members? Have all the possibilities been considered? Have everyone's ideas been heard? Are there opportunities to fine-tune the vision over time? How can the vision be effectively communicated to others?

- *What do we need to do? (clarification of goals and objectives).* What is needed for the vision to become real? What are the top five or six team goals and objectives? Are they measurable? Are they achievable within a year? Are they realistic? What are some stretch goals that will take the team beyond what it thinks it can achieve but that it will nonetheless strive for?

- *What's in the way? (acceptance of the challenge).* What are the obstacles, barriers, or challenges to achieving the team's goals? Has everyone identified the same obstacles? Does everyone agree to work to overcome them? Has the team analyzed, categorized, prioritized, and understood the challenges? Is the problem part of a larger system that also requires change? Are the challenges internal as well as external?

- *How will we do it? (identification of strategy).* What are the criteria for success in achieving the vision, goals, and objectives? What strategies will help the team overcome the barriers and challenges? Has the team identified a strategy for each barrier and challenge? Have tactics been distinguished from strategies? Has each team member taken responsibility for tracking and reporting on the progress of a particular strategy? What will the team do if the strategy does not work? How will they know?

- *Who will do it and by when? (creation of a plan of action).* What actions need to be taken to implement the strategy? By whom? By when? What else needs to change for the plan to work? What resources will be required for it to work? What communications will be needed? Is everyone on the team committed to doing their part?

- *How will we continue to learn? (feedback for self-correction).* What methods will be used to encourage individual and team feedback and organizational learning? How should team successes and failures be measured? How should oversight, monitoring, reporting, and fine-tuning be accomplished? Does the process encourage risk taking, collaborative responsibility, and honesty? What can be done to communicate the team's discoveries to encourage broader organizational learning?

- *What worked, what did not, and why? (evaluation of process).* What worked? What did not? What parts of the organization's structure, systems, processes, and relationships supported the team's effort? What parts undermined it? How was conflict handled within and between the teams? Why was this method chosen? What changes might prevent conflicts from arising in the future? What should change in the organization as a whole? What needs to shift for this to happen?

- *Good work! What's next? (celebration and renewal).* Have individual and team efforts been generously rewarded? Were people who gave critical feedback affirmed and supported? Has everyone's contribution been acknowledged? Have successes been celebrated? Have failures been understood without blaming? Has the team identified its next challenges? Is it ready to revisit and find new answers to these questions?

As team members discuss and answer these questions, they develop in miniature the attitudes, concerns, skills, processes, and relationships needed to create successful teams. Typically, teams focus their attention on completing a set of practical tasks, on "what" needs to be achieved, without sufficient attention to "how" to achieve it. Through these questions, team members work on "how" issues and discover "why" they are on teams in the first place.

Skills for Teamwork

Special skills are required for successful teamwork. Articulating these skills can help teams clarify what they do and how they do it. All of these skills are interrelated, mutually reinforcing, and dependent on each of the others. Here are ten skills team members can develop.

1. The Skill of Self-Management

Teams are flexible structures that evolve and increase their managerial skills with every obstacle they overcome. Team self-management simply means overcoming obstacles together and in the process building a sense of ownership, responsibility, commitment, and efficiency within every team member. It means sparking passion, merging wills, envisioning the future, and cultivating the flow of individual and collective energy within the organization. It means encouraging full participation and collective self-criticism, and actively improving working conditions. Organizations encourage skills in self-management by asking employees to be responsible for what is important to them and by supporting them with leadership, resources, training, coaching, and feedback while they are doing it.

2. The Skill of Communication

Skilled communications in teams means eliminating the facade of politeness and the concealment and duplicity that trivialize hierarchical, bureaucratic, and authoritarian communications. Teams need to collaboratively develop their skills in becoming better listeners, commiserating with others, reframing communications so they can be heard, and communicating honestly about things that really matter.

When we encourage open, honest, empathetic communications, we change the way people relate and work. At the heart of team communications is effective listening. Team members need to develop a full complement of listening skills to keep collaboration and synergy moving. Listening is fundamentally a matter of intention, and when people intend to listen effectively, they can do so in a variety of ways, such as:

- *Contextual listening,* when we listen for background information or unspoken assumptions and expectations, as for example, when we are feeling uncomfortable and someone senses it and welcomes us warmly
- *Active listening,* when we genuinely care about what the other person is telling us
- *Responsive listening,* when we are engaged in a conversation or dialogue that is moving back and forth between us and our colleagues
- *Creative listening,* when we are searching for as yet unidentified solutions or trying out a new approach to understanding a problem
- *Empathetic listening,* when we are listening to another as though we were the person who is speaking
- *Undivided listening,* when we are no longer aware of our own existence as a listener but are completely in sync with the speaker and the story
- *Committed listening,* when we listen as though our lives depend on understanding what is being said
- *Listening with the heart,* when we listen with, by, and through our love or affection for the person who is speaking

3. The Skill of Leadership

Leadership *adores* a vacuum. For this reason, team leadership means creating opportunities for each member to serve as a leader. To create leadership in teams, employees need to be skilled in linking, organizing, coordinating, collaborating, planning, facilitating, coaching, and mentoring. These acts become the responsibility not of managers or individuals but of self-managing teams acting in concert with empowering leaders.

Team leaders continually raise standards, empower others to accept responsibility for their work, shift old paradigms, set new directions, and improve the quality of products, processes, and relationships. They help teams set and harmonize priorities, negotiate differences, resolve conflicts, improve motivation and morale, coach and mentor individuals, give and receive constructive feedback, acknowledge real effort, take risks, and take responsibility for failures. They make sure details do not fall through the cracks, advertise and celebrate other people's successes, and model the values, ethics, and integrity they seek from others. They help teams coalesce as a synergistic whole by:

- Relating team tasks, problems, and responsibilities to a larger vision or context, including organizational, social, and environmental concerns
- Articulating and modeling shared values that underlie team actions and inform team decisions
- Perceiving the needs and skills of individual team members and integrating them to solve individual and team problems
- Creating opportunities and experiences for all team members to expand their latent leadership abilities

In short, leaders create wholes out of the sum of their parts.

4. The Skill of Responsibility

Teamwork means there is no one left to blame. It means everyone is personally responsible not only for their own work but the work of every other member of the team. Employees in hierarchical organizations often find it frightening to make decisions and manage themselves. Team members have to exercise responsibility in order to become self-managing and cease being spectators in their own work lives. Team members encourage a greater sense of shared responsibility by:

- Including everyone in all projects from the beginning and discussing commitments and how they will be met
- Jointly and collaboratively establishing goals and timetables with benchmarks, deliverables, and dates
- Summarizing areas of agreement about what will be done, by whom, and by when

- Making agreements, expectations, timetables, deliverables, and outcomes public
- Having each person declare his or her commitments and asking early on in the process whether anyone needs assistance in meeting them
- Incentivizing commitments through rewards, acknowledgment, and other forms of support
- Jointly clarifying priorities
- Publicly reviewing whether commitments are being met
- Identifying what will happen if commitments are not met or continue to be unmet
- Asking what support is needed to ensure that future commitments will be met
- Using 360-degree evaluation to identify strategies that result in improved responsibility
- Asking each team member to identify what remains to be done and what has not been done but should have been
- Asking each person to say directly how it feels when commitments are not met and what happened to the team as a result
- Providing training in time and project management skills and a way of reminding people of their commitments
- Examining expectations critically to see if they are realistic and have been communicated effectively
- Trying to discover the real, underlying reasons the team member cannot meet his or her commitments and address those directly
- Linking pay to improved performance and asking the person to leave if he or she cannot meet personal commitments

5. The Skill of Supporting Diversity

Valuing and celebrating diversity substantially increases a team's ability to respond successfully and imagine novel solutions for problems. Collaborative experiences allow team members to overcome prejudices and biases and not create winners and losers, reject outsiders, or mistrust people who are different. New ideas, different opinions, contrasting points of view, and diverse experiences, interests, and goals enrich teams and make them vital, living organisms that are able to flourish.

Support for the richness of diversity can be undermined by pressure to become a "team player" or not "rock the boat" in order to preserve harmony, or "go along to get along" in one's career. The first rule of team behavior is that everyone agrees to say what they think, whether the rest of the team likes it or not. Groupthink and the suppression of criticism do not create a capacity for self-management.

Prejudices and stereotypes that arise in the workplace undermine effective teamwork. Prejudice, simply defined, is prejudgment—the devaluation of people who are different based not on who they are but on prior assumptions about who they are. Prejudice justifies acting selfishly based on assumptions about the other person's inferiority. It produces hostility, closed-mindedness, loss of the ability to learn or become close to the other person, and isolation from parts of oneself. People stereotype others by picking a characteristic; blowing it out of proportion; collapsing the whole person into that characteristic; ignoring differences, subtleties, complexities, and commonalities; making it match their own worst fears; and making it cruel.

Teams in which stereotyping and prejudice are discouraged are able to create environments where differences are valued and harnessed to solve problems and increase learning. Teams can reduce prejudice and stereotyping by:

- Asking individuals or teams to identify the stereotypes they think others have of them, present or act these out in a skit, identify what they actually do, respond to questions, and clarify the support they need to be successful
- Asking each person to take a close look at what he or she has done to encourage stereotyping, responded to stereotyping by others, and modeled respect for diversity
- Meeting privately with individuals holding prejudices, asking permission to speak with them, being low-key and nonaggressive, and telling the truth about how it makes others feel
- Assuming good intentions, not shaming or blaming, asking what the other person intended, and trying to understand where it came from without excusing it
- Sharing perceptions, making "I" statements, giving examples from personal experience, and suggesting alternatives

- Strategizing with others on how to reduce stereotyping, telling humanizing stories, and relaying empathy-inducing information
- Asking whether the stereotyper ever felt stereotyped, discriminated against, or harassed for any reason and requesting details
- Telling stories about times when each person felt stereotyped, discriminated against, or harassed for any reason
- Bringing in a third party to mediate or facilitate a dialogue about prejudice and stereotyping

6. The Skills of Feedback and Evaluation

Feedback and evaluation are essential to improving learning, team communication, and the quality of products, processes, and relationships. They can be positive experiences and actually enjoyed if they are delivered empathetically without judgment and offer supportive criticisms that promote growth and change rather than defensiveness and resistance.

In a true team environment, self-critical perspectives are expected, welcomed, acknowledged, and rewarded. Teams recognize that without challenges, they grow stale, and without honest feedback and generous acknowledgment, they become apathetic and cynical.

Feedback is most successful when it is reciprocal, opened with a self-assessment by the person giving it, after requesting permission from the person receiving it. It is best when it is constructive; framed as an "I" statement; specific, detailed, balanced, and fair; and communicated soon afterwards without anger or judgment.

7. The Skill of Strategic Planning

Effective teams transcend reactive forms of crisis management and administration and develop the ability to act strategically. Rather than respond to problems through isolated responses, teams use strategic planning to identify challenges and opportunities collaboratively and influence the environment in which problems emerge. They create visions, define goals (including stretch goals), analyze barriers, select strategies, and generate action plans that commit team members to implementation.

Strategic planning encourages employees to think long term, be proactive and preventative rather than reactive and responsive, and focus on solutions rather than problems. It promotes continuous improvement and consensus decision making, focuses on quality rather than quantity, reduces apathy and cynicism, and increases engagement and commitment. It promotes collaboration over competition, transforms negative personal judgments into useful feedback, and shifts private conversations into public dialogue.

8. The Skill of Shaping Successful Meetings

The most common complaint we hear from employees in self-managing teams is that they spend too much time in useless meetings. Team meetings can be streamlined and made shorter, more satisfying, and more productive, and result in expanded consensus. Team members can rotate facilitating, recording key ideas, keeping time, and observing processes in order to improve the next meeting. Through participation, observation, and correction, team members develop skills in self-management, collaboration, and democracy.

9. The Skill of Resolving Conflicts

It is impossible to belong to a team without experiencing conflict. This reality encourages team members to improve skills in problem solving, collaborative negotiation, responding to difficult behaviors, and conflict resolution by:

- Stopping pointless arguments and sitting down together to talk about the problem
- Taking turns summarizing and listening without interruption
- Summarizing, clarifying, and acknowledging what the other person says and feels
- Saying what they think the other person is saying, asking if they are correct, and if not, listening again
- Assuming good intentions and focusing on effects, as in saying: "I feel _____ when you _____ because . . ."
- Focusing on the future rather than the past

- Focusing on problems and behaviors rather than personalities
- Focusing on interests rather than positions, as by asking, "Why do you want that?"
- Breaking the problem down into smaller parts and starting with the easiest
- Searching for creative answers and brainstorming solutions
- Agreeing on criteria that will make an agreement successful for all sides
- Identifying what each person wants and what each is willing to do to end the conflict
- Splitting the difference and looking for trade-offs
- Saying what will happen if the dispute is not resolved
- Writing down agreements
- Using team or outside mediators to help resolve the dispute

10. The Skill of Enjoyment

Being able to bring our entire selves to work, stretch to our limits, take pleasure in our work relationships, and know we have made a difference lies at the heart of the team experience. Most team members enjoy working together to accomplish difficult tasks. Their pleasure derives from meeting high-performance challenges and producing results that benefit themselves and their teams, organizations, and communities.

Even when teams work hard, it rarely feels like drudgery, because work is seen as a challenge and problems are not addressed alone or in isolation but by people who are working together. Hard-driving, time-obsessed, control-oriented managerial cultures undervalue pleasure or believe it does not belong in the workplace. Yet play stimulates creative problem solving and improves employee morale and should be integrated into the work process.

There is a clear connection between learning, achievement, and play. Sociologist Johann Huizinga wrote in *Homo Ludens* that when we are at play, there is a sense of tension or uncertainty about what will happen next that magnifies enjoyment, levity, and risk taking. Play involves multiple free, unstructured choices within a tightly structured process and an apparent absence of objective purpose, even though outcomes are subjectively highly important. In play, success and leadership vary widely from task to task. Skill or chance, low levels of internal competition, and high levels of cooperation are characteristic features of play.

Organizations can encourage a sense of play by shifting people's attitudes toward mistakes, problems, and obstacles; encouraging intuition; treating projects as contests; hearing conflict stories as myths; and designing organizational culture with an aesthetic orientation. Play occurs spontaneously when people take time to enjoy being with each other. While it is obvious that a commitment to certainty, accuracy, timeliness, and integrity are central to work, team members can also increase productivity and improve the quality of work life by:

- Encouraging curiosity and creating abundant opportunities for learning
- Embracing paradox, enigma, ambiguity, doubt, contradiction, and uncertainty
- Setting aside time for personal networking and social interaction across organizational lines
- Acknowledging, celebrating, and rewarding personal and team achievements
- Encouraging participation, collaboration, democracy, and self-management
- Sharing failures as well as successes
- Assigning unusual, even impossible tasks to small, independent, self-managing teams
- Violating expectations and creating pleasant surprises
- Introducing totally different perspectives from outside the group's work, field, culture, and experience
- Providing training and classes in enjoyable, non-work-related topics
- Consciously inventing myths, stories, and legends and publicizing them broadly
- Inventing rituals, ceremonies, jokes, songs, plays, poems, and stories
- Poking fun at themselves, especially in public
- Rewarding playful, creative, risk-taking behavior
- Using periodic retreats, off-site meetings, and games to relax and enjoy each other's company
- Creating an enjoyable, amusing atmosphere every day

Mastering team skills is a lifelong process, one that requires and contributes to self-discovery, reflection and reinvention. Teams generate opportunities for self-actualization by creating learning environments in which the development of each is dependent on the development of others. This requires teams and organizations to implement streamlined, open, collaborative processes.

Chapter Thirteen

Implement Streamlined, Open, Collaborative Processes

> *The longer I live, the more I realize the impact of attitude on life. Attitude, to me, is more basic than facts. It is more important than the past, than education, than money, than circumstances, than failures, than successes, than what other people think or say or do. It is more important than appearance, giftedness or skill. It will make or break a company . . . a church . . . a home. The remarkable thing is we have a choice every day regarding the attitude we will embrace for that day. We cannot change our past . . . we cannot change the fact that people will act in a certain way. We cannot change the inevitable. The only thing we can do is play on the one string we have, and that is our attitude. I am convinced that life is 10% what happens to me and 90% how I react to it. And so it is with you . . . we are in charge of our attitudes.*
> CHARLES SWINDOLL, *The Grace of Encouragement*

We are all aware of the enormous impact attitude has on the quality of our lives and our relationships with others. Changing our attitude not only affects how we experience life; it changes who we *are* and how others relate to us. As we build collaborative, democratic, self-managing organizations, our attitudes toward work, colleagues, and ourselves shift, and we increasingly require collaborative, democratic, self-managing organizations to reinforce these new relationships.

The cheapest, easiest, and most effective way of changing both attitudes and organizations is by implementing streamlined, open, collaborative processes.

Transforming bureaucratic, authoritarian hierarchies into self-managing, democratic heterarchies means creating a context of values, ethics, and integrity, forming collaborative webs of association, developing ubiquitous, linking leadership, and building innovative self-managing teams. These changes call into question old habits based on hierarchical principles, focus attention on processes, and increase opportunities for employees to develop attitudes of ownership toward their work lives.

Organizations that seek to improve collaboration, teamwork, motivation, and morale are highly dependent on employee attitudes, which are undermined and debilitated by hierarchical, bureaucratic, autocratic processes. Consider the positive effects on attitude of even simple processes like listening, speaking, offering feedback, and negotiating, each of which can generate feelings of respect, self-esteem, participation, excitement, collaboration, and commitment, or their opposite.

As managers are replaced by self-managing teams, employees require open, collaborative processes that allow them to imagine their own futures, make decisions without winners and losers, and negotiate differences without damaging their relationships. This suggests a new understanding of what processes are, how they are created, and what we can do to make them more streamlined and democratic. It means designing paradoxical processes that simultaneously support diversity and unity, dissent and consensus, change and equilibrium, conflict and resolution.

The stakes involved in process improvement often appear petty but are actually immense because organizational structures and systems are subtly shaped by them. The methods by which decisions are made, involvement in strategic planning is encouraged, commitment to diversity is affirmed, team expectations are negotiated, and openness and honesty get communicated all have an enormous impact on organizations. And when we implement collaborative, democratic, self-managing processes in organizations, we automatically encourage them in families, schools, communities, society, and government.

What Are Processes?

It is customary to distinguish process and content, means and ends. These distinctions separate methodology, or *how* a thing is done, from substance, or *what* is done. Process is usually thought of as secondary and having little or no impact on content, while content is viewed as consisting solely of substance, meaning, import, and essence. For this reason, most organizations create hierarchies of values that focus on content and pay little attention to process.

In practice, process cannot be separated from content. The process used to reach an outcome profoundly influences it, minimizing some aspects and maximizing others. The means always affect the end, just as the end always affects the selection of appropriate means. Yet it often happens that people kill for peace, hate for love, and dictate for democracy.

Gandhi clarified the impact of means on ends:

> To believe that there is no connection between the means and the ends is a great mistake. . . . [This] is the same as saying that we can get a rose through planting a noxious weed. If I want to cross the ocean, I can do so only by means of a vessel. If I were to use a cart for that purpose, both the cart and I would soon find the bottom.

In bureaucracies, red tape, knotted procedures, secrecy, and administrative runaround affect the content of decisions, producing predictable results in discouragement, disempowerment, distrust, and dead-end decisions. What is worse, hierarchies and bureaucracies ensure that the only processes that can produce successful results are those that reinforce hierarchy and bureaucracy. The same is true of autocracies, which routinely discourage or punish the use of processes that produce democratic results. Those who are required to live with hierarchical, bureaucratic, or autocratic processes become inured to them and do not develop the skills they need to bring about collaborative, democratic, or self-managing change.

As an illustration, a corporate procurement department created a frustrating, time-consuming process for requesting office supplies. It took two months for requests to be filled, and everyone grew increasingly infuriated waiting to receive their desks, chairs, and pencil sharpeners and exhausted by pointlessly bureaucratic requisition processes. People began hoarding supplies, and an informal black market arose for desperately needed items. The message communicated by this process was that hierarchical power, bureaucratic procedures, and saving money were a higher priority than employee well-being and productivity.

In another example, students at a large university, in the course of registering each semester, had to write their names, addresses, telephone numbers, e-mail addresses, and other details twenty to thirty times, when available technology made one entry enough. The message sent by this process was that students were there to make the work of the bureaucracy easier rather than vice versa.

These examples reveal an indelible connection between process and content. These organizations used all the right rhetoric regarding empowerment, teamwork, customer service, and opposition to bureaucracy, but none of it touched their processes. They offered complex justifications and rationalizations for each step in the process, but their means eroded and undermined their ends, and none of it was necessary.

In truth, every process encodes, reproduces, and communicates a specific content, and every content generates a set of self-consistent processes. Every bureaucratic process supports organizational hierarchy and undermines or sidetracks self-management, and every collaborative process supports organizational democracy and undermines or sidetracks bureaucracy.

Open Processes and Organizational Democracy

Countless organizational processes support hierarchy, bureaucracy, and autocracy, and countless others support heterarchy, self-management, and democracy. Broadly speaking, hierarchies, bureaucracies, and autocracies rely on *adversarial* processes such as competition over resources and top-down decision making; *control* processes such as restricted access to information and expertise; *dominating* processes such as hierarchical reporting relationships, vertical feedback, and controlled meetings; and *coercive* processes such as the power to hire, fire, and discipline.

By contrast, heterarchies, democracies, and self-managing organizations rely on *collaborative* processes such as teamwork and webs of association; *learning* processes such as feedback and dialogue; *empowering* processes such as participatory strategic planning; *relational* processes such as group brainstorming, 360-degree feedback, dialogue, ritual, and celebration; and *consensus-building* processes such as team decision making, negotiation, and mediation.

Democratic organizations open their processes and encourage employees to become aware of their content, consciously design them from a context of shared values, and continuously improve them. Any process that includes others without regard to power, title, or position automatically encourages collaborative, democratic, self-managing relationships and bolsters attitudes that favor participation, shared values, consensus, diversity, creativity, and satisfaction of interests.

Democratic processes support open and honest communication, risk taking, shared leadership, and ownership of results. They value paradox and complexity, quality and service, success and failure, challenge and satisfaction. Self-management can be encouraged simply by asking employees to become conscious of their processes and collaboratively redesign them. Through expanded awareness, they are able to critique and transform processes that do not achieve democratic ends.

Opening Processes and Expanding Awareness

Hierarchical processes are closed, designed without employee participation, and followed without much awareness or conscious attention. They are focused more on results than on how they are achieved. Yet this lack of awareness of organizational process distorts, twists, and subverts the ability of teams and organizations to achieve better results.

Which is more powerful and enduring: the goal or the process of achieving it? The answer is clearly the process. With process, we can achieve the same goal repeatedly. When we make a shoe, we produce not only the shoe but the process we used to make it, so that if something happens to the shoe, we can make another using the process we created.

Process awareness appears innocent but is highly risky because it demands changes in behavior. When we observe the process of communication, decision making, or values implementation, we are forced to critique our own behaviors, assess the consequences of our actions, stop relying on antiquated methods, and adopt others for which we may lack the skill or self-confidence to succeed. If we are not aware of our processes, they quickly become habits, which turn into ruts, as novelist Edith Wharton warned:

> The [main] producer of old age is habit: the deathly process of doing the same thing in the same way at the same hour day after day, first from carelessness, then from inclination, at last from cowardice or inertia. Luckily the inconsequent life is not the only alternative; for caprice is as ruinous as routine. Habit is necessary; it is the habit of having habits, of turning a trail into a rut, that must be incessantly fought against if one is to remain alive.

When we are in a rut and committed to staying in it, we react by making it safe—either by burying it in processes that are secure and predictable or paying lip-service to the change while diluting and undermining it. In this way, bureaucracies convert innovative ideas into "same old used-to-be's," and cynicism deepens with each "flavor of the month" reform. Even revolutionary ideas are transformed into reactionary reinforcements of the status quo, simply because the process of change was not also simultaneously transformed. When it comes to matters of office routine, revolutionary thinkers can behave like the worst reactionaries. Yet it is precisely through routines that old practices are reintroduced.

Hierarchy, bureaucracy, and autocracy are not only structures but routines and processes. When someone stands at attention, relationships of superior to subordinate are created, just as monarchy is brought into existence when subjects bow before a queen. Bureaucracy is created when forms are filled out in triplicate, and democracy when people vote. Every organizational process can be analyzed in this way to determine whether organizational processes are consistent with values and intentions.

By expanding process awareness, we can transform meetings that have become destructive or a waste of time simply by asking participants to say what they think might be done to make them more successful, or agreeing on a set of ground rules for respectful communication, or working in small groups of four or five and brainstorming recommendations for future meetings, or engaging in dialogue over difficult and important issues.

Process awareness is the first step in designing and implementing streamlined, open, collaborative processes. Once we become aware of processes, they can be simplified, allowing waste and inefficiencies to be removed. A useful method for shifting process awareness into process design is process mapping.

Collaborative Process Mapping

To restructure the way we work, it is useful to map or diagram organizational processes in order to calculate their effects on results and modify those that obstruct goals or are inconsistent with shared values. Process mapping is a method for stripping away bureaucratic, autocratic, hierarchical procedures that entangle and entwine organizations and contribute to poor morale, disenfranchisement, and dysfunctional relationships.

Process mapping requires the full participation of everyone who performs the work. It is a democratic, collaborative team methodology for simplifying actions, reorienting priorities to core values, improving quality, and eliminating unnecessary steps. It allows organizations to improve products and services, reduce costs of production, and simplify practices. It helps self-managing teams plan strategically, set priorities, and focus resources for maximum impact. It is a way of transforming bureaucracies into webs of association.

Process mapping begins by establishing a context of shared values; articulating vision, mission, goals, and strategies; and clarifying expectations regarding results. Actual outcomes can then be measured against plans for the future, existing change processes such as quality improvement and reengineering can be evaluated, and methods for responding to customer needs and delivering results can be improved.

Mapping transforms not only processes but structures, strategies, and systems. Process mapping identifies and eliminates bottlenecks, increases capacity utilization and quality enhancement, and lowers unit costs by reducing backlog, inventory, defects, and waste. It shortens completion time, reduces operations to core competencies, improves handoffs, automates tasks, and focuses on customer and team relationships. It generates experiments and pilot projects, improves customer return rates, and rewards and motivates continued improvement.

To implement these actions, mapping teams collaboratively analyze information regarding inputs, outputs, processes, and relationships. They take apart current procedures and invent new ones. Process mapping teams begin by investigating:

- How existing processes encode and recreate content
- How processes interact to reinforce the negative and positive parts of a system
- How process flaws and duplications can be located
- How quality can be continuously improved
- How processes can be evaluated to add value or improve customer or client relations
- How processes can be streamlined and waste eliminated
- How organizational culture can be enhanced
- How collaboration, teamwork, and partnerships can be increased across organizational boundaries
- How conflicts can be resolved
- How processes redesign can be made ongoing

Once these investigations have been made and processes have been tracked against results, the mapping team focuses on process flows within the organization and ways of leveraging goals, values, and results. An analysis is made of each step in the process, breaking it down into its component parts. Figure 13.1 shows a simple example of this analysis.

The mapping team analyzes the map, identifies the best processes, and recommends improvements. These recommendations include eliminating duplicative or unnecessary actions and combining, simplifying, prioritizing, rearranging, and adding actions to increase quality and decrease costs. Each process is analyzed to determine the point where action is taken; how long it takes; what changes afterward; what it costs in wages, inventory, resources, and materials; and how much value is added as a result.

Figure 13.1. Time-Sequenced Process Map.

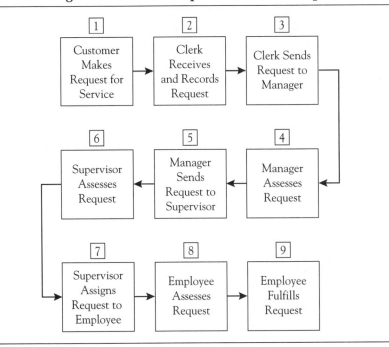

Shortcuts and radical streamlining can improve even minor processes. It is possible to skip steps, combine and reorder them, delegate them to others, or divide them into substeps. Only by mapping and analyzing each step, understanding the entire process, and identifying shortcuts and redundancies can the process be improved. Processes can be mapped against vision, mission, or values to determine whether they benefit customers, employees, and the organization and support behaviors that are consistent with ethics and integrity.

Processes can be improved simply by allowing people to escape rigid bureaucratic requirements. This can be accomplished by giving employees floating assignments, asking them to work outside narrow job descriptions, or empowering them to solve whatever problems they discover. In other cases, teams can be authorized to invent unique processes that eliminate standardization and uniform one-size-fits-all solutions.

It is possible for streamlining to go too far and eliminate important sources of added value. For example, making customers stand in line for five minutes reduces salaries, but it also reduces customer satisfaction and creates process overloads for other employees, who also need to participate in the mapping process. The primary goal of process mapping is to reduce unit costs and increase quality at each step in the creation of goods and services through analysis, planning, strategy, and integration. For this reason, strategic planning, consensus decision making, team meetings, collaborative negotiation, and conflict resolution are priorities for improvement and key categories to map.

Democratic Strategic Planning

Strategic planning processes provide multiple opportunities for employees to experience self-management and participate in creating a shared, democratic future. In hierarchical organizations, strategic planning is largely the prerogative of managers and top executives. In collaborative, democratic, self-managing organizations, everyone participates in strategic planning.

Including employees in the planning process does not mean abdicating leadership. Leaders of all kinds are needed to imagine the future, harmonize diverse perspectives, communicate commitment, and get everyone moving in the same direction at the same time.

Democratic strategic planning is more comprehensive than its hierarchical cousin because decisions are based on more diverse sources of information, making planning more informed and implementation more committed. When strategic planning is restricted to the top, it becomes an empty process. Managers typically go through the motions and agree on a set of empty slogans, then continue doing what they did before. Employees then rationalize their exclusion and assume that strategic planning is unnecessary, that it can be figured out along the way, that it is a prerogative of those with power, or that nothing will change anyway.

Hierarchical organizations spend enormous amounts of time and energy making detailed strategic plans without the participation of the very people whose buy-in is essential if they are going to work. They make executive decisions about content without trying to reach consensus, leaving dissenters feeling excluded and marginalized. They create strategic plans that focus on short-term problems that can be solved relatively easily; or describe futures that are simplistic, pathetic, or uninspiring; or use eloquent phrases to restate the status quo. They condense the creative thinking process, tie it to conformist ends, and cripple it by ignoring new ideas, paradigms, values, and the needs of human beings. They create strategic plans that are unclear about what will change in each person's roles and responsibilities, the effects that changes in one area will have on others, and who will do what by when. They pay little attention to organizational culture or the complex methods that systems use to defend themselves against change. Instead, words are crafted to satisfy upper management, ignoring most of what actually needs changing. They are then turned into bureaucratic policies, filed away, posted on a wall, and quickly forgotten.

By contrast, democratic planning starts by critiquing hierarchical planning processes and improving on them. Unless employees understand the pitfalls of past planning practices, they will return to old patterns that undermine democratic content. At each step there is full inclusion. This makes strategic planning a critical element in self-management, because it asks every employee to become responsible for the results the organization produces. If strategic planning is genuinely to decide the future of the organization, everyone has to participate.

Democratic strategic planning allows managers to reveal whether they are capable of becoming leaders and encouraging employee self-management. It allows employees to reveal whether they are capable of self-management and shift from focusing on partial, routine, isolated changes to holistic, continuous, integrated ones. It allows the organization to spread the process over time and fine-tune the plan based on results, rather than produce idealistic documents that fail due to lack of follow-through.

A simple, democratic model of strategic planning starts with teams using a collaborative, consensus-based, inclusive process to answer questions that identify the organizational elements needed to create a comprehensive plan:

Values	What is important to us?
Mission	Who are we?
Vision	Where do we want to go?
Goals or objectives	What do we need to achieve to get where we want to go?
Stretch goals	What could we produce if we really pushed?
Barriers	What stands in the way of getting there?
Strategies	What approaches can we use to overcome these barriers?
Tactics	What specific actions can we take to implement our strategies?
Action plans	Who is going to do what? By when? What resources do they need to do it?

Even in team-based organizations, there are limits to the application of strategic planning processes. Management theorist Henry Mintzberg has identified a number of fallacies in strategic planning in his classic *Harvard Business Review* article, "The Rise and Fall of Strategic Planning," which we have modified to reflect our experience, including:

- *Prediction* (thinking that you can know what is going to happen)
- *Reductionism* (thinking that complex phenomena can be reduced to simple, bite-sized bits)
- *Separation between planning and doing* (thinking that planning can take place in the absence of action)
- *Formalization* (thinking that formal processes can alter informal realities)
- *Closure* (thinking that it can ever be over)

These fallacies do not eliminate the need for strategy and planning. Rather, they suggest important issues for teams to raise and discuss throughout the process. What matters most in strategic planning is not just finding answers but engaging in dialogue over important questions. Simply by addressing strategic issues, employees are invited to reflect on their work experiences, become responsible for their actions, own the results of their work, collaborate, reach consensus, consciously plan their futures, and engage in coordinated action. In the process, they experience self-fulfillment, fun, passionate discussion, and camaraderie, which can be as important as coming up with strategies. As employees participate in this process, follow through, and track real changes, they learn practical skills in collaboration, democracy, and self-management.

How to Make Meetings
Interesting, Intelligent, and Useful

In hierarchical organizations, meetings are convened and conducted by managers, who set the agendas, do nearly all the speaking, restrict the scope of conversation, and use them to deliver messages, hear reports, or make assignments. It is rare that important issues are discussed, open and honest dialogue takes place, or significant decisions are made by consensus. As a result, these meetings suppress communication, polarize relationships, and undermine morale. Most employees consider them a waste of time and try to get through them without falling asleep or saying something they will regret later.

In self-managing organizations, meetings are an opportunity to build better relationships, recommit to values, create webs of association, inspire team leadership, improve participation and responsibility, resolve low-level conflicts, and increase skills in self-management. Everyone participates in planning and conducting meetings, and correcting them when they become dysfunctional. Participants apply process awareness to meetings and improve them so they become interesting, intelligent, and useful.

It is actually not difficult to make meetings intelligent, interesting, and useful. This can be done by making them democratic and investing those who attend with complete responsibility for making them work. Meetings can be streamlined, made more useful, and expand organizational democracy. Here are some process steps teams can take to conduct better meetings:

- Plan the meeting in advance. Know why you are meeting, who is coming, and why. Meet away from telephones, pagers, beepers, and other interruptions.

- Before the meeting, consult with key participants on roles they might play. Make sure people on the agenda and the facilitator know what they are asking the group to do and how much time they have.
- Set clear expectations beforehand as to time and what people want to take away from the meeting as a whole, as well as for each item. Start and end on time—or have good reasons for not doing so.
- Prepare a tentative agenda, and give it out in advance to everyone expected to come. Structure the agenda according to the shape of the meeting: light at the beginning, heavy in the middle, light at the end.
- Ask people to assist in facilitating and recording important contributions, and rotate these roles.
- If facilitating, arrive fifteen to thirty minutes early to set up the meeting room and discuss problems or conflicts in advance with people who intend to raise them, so they feel included and less aggressive.
- Make certain everyone can see and hear everyone else and that the environment is comfortable.
- Greet everyone as they arrive. Make people feel welcome so they can ease into the meeting.
- Have participants introduce themselves, report on anything new, state their expectations or goals for the meeting, or answer a question with multiple correct answers.
- Have everyone agree on clearly defined roles of responsibilities for the meeting, review and prioritize the agenda, and make changes where needed.
- Have brief reports on what was done since the last meeting.
- Shift from personal attacks to disagreements over ideas. When there is disagreement, do not suppress it, but look for creative solutions, consensus, and win-win outcomes.
- Allow everyone an opportunity to participate, and be sure that no one feels left out.
- Agree that people should not interrupt each other, carry on side conversations, or speak without being recognized.
- Ask someone to record key ideas so everyone can see them, and summarize key points prior to decision making.

- Do not let the facilitator overly control the meeting. Let the group decide what to discuss.
- If the group gets stuck, refer the issue to a subcommittee to come up with a compromise solution, and set a date to meet. Or use straw votes to show what the group is thinking, then brainstorm or discuss the issue further before a final vote.
- Determine who will be responsible for what actions, by when, and what resources are needed for them to be successful.
- Set a date, time, and place for the next meeting, with ideas for an agenda.
- Evaluate the meeting. Look for ways of improving the process. Periodically schedule a retreat to consider how to improve process and relationships in the group, and acknowledge those who objected when the process didn't work.
- Leaders stay afterward to talk to key individuals, debrief the meeting, discuss how to carry out responsibilities, reflect on how to improve the next meeting, and follow through to make certain responsibilities are met.

Democracy takes more time than autocracy and hierarchy, partly because of the complicated, sometimes chaotic nature of what needs to take place during meetings. In building self-managing organizations, it is not enough to declare processes democratic. Participants need to learn how to engage their differences actively, discover the reasons for dissent, explore diversity, and go more deeply into conflicts. Collaboration is always a messy process, yet out of the mess come better solutions, renewed trust, deeper relationships, and mutual respect.

Consensus Decision Making

For employees to participate fully in strategic planning, conduct effective meetings, and engage in other collaborative, democratic, self-managing processes, they require skills in decision-making processes that are open, egalitarian, and inclusive; that encourage disagreements and unity; and that sustain creativity, teamwork, and partnership.

Organizational decision making ranges from hierarchical, authoritarian, unilateral, competitive, bureaucratic, centralized processes at one pole, to heterarchical, democratic, collaborative, authentic, decentralized processes at the other. There are six fundamentally distinct decision-making processes from which individuals, teams, and organizations can choose. Rather than pick one, teams need to become fluent in all of them and be able to choose the right one for each type of decision. These are the basic methods of decision making, together with illustrative phrases:

Notification	"The following decision has been made and will be implemented by Friday."
Consultation	"I would like your thoughts on this issue before I make a decision."
Delegation	"You decide."
Voting	"Let the majority decide."
Consensus	"I am willing to abide by the consensus of the group and believe the decision addresses my most important needs and interests."
Unanimity	"We must reach complete agreement in order to implement this solution."

In considering which decision-making process to use, it is important to note that as the group proceeds from notification to unanimity, the time required to decide increases, as does the degree of unity and ownership following the decision. Decision makers need to be clear about which method they have chosen to use and why, so employees do not believe the process is delegation while managers think it is consultation.

The choice of process depends on the kind of problem to be solved. Rapid, unilateral decision making works fine when issues are clear and stakes are minimal. But organizations that rarely reach consensus or unanimity experience higher levels of conflict and distrust than organizations that periodically take time to make sure everyone is on board.

Conflicts also occur when it is not clear which issues are being delegated, and teams work hard on recommendations that are later rejected, leaving group members feeling disrespected and disempowered. Delegation requires either a statement by the delegator or a question by the delegatee that clarifies the parameters and limits of the delegation.

Voting is usually considered the appropriate form of decision making for democracies, but problems arise whenever a significant minority loses an important vote, causing divisions and bad feelings to undermine unity and ongoing relationships. Because voting permits full participation, it is preferable to notification. Yet it is often competitive, contentious, and adversarial, and is not preferable to consensus, which is based on interests, rather than rights or power. Interests are not *what* people want but *why* they want it. Processes such as consensus aim to satisfy the underlying reasons people are for or against something, create opportunities to modify ideas to meet a broader set of needs, and include dissenters and resisters in owning the results.

Nevertheless, it is clearly inappropriate to use consensus to decide, for example, what someone else is going to have for lunch. It is equally inappropriate to use notification to decide what employees will do in self-managing teams or to vote on whether to act respectfully toward minorities. Each problem needs to be considered separately to select an appropriate decision-making process, so that everyone involved in implementing the decision accepts the way it was made.

Collaborative, democratic, self-managing organizations can ask employees to identify the categories of problems they are likely to face in the future and reach consensus on a comprehensive plan regarding each decision-making process, so that everyone agrees on the decision-making method they will use to make decisions on each problem.

How Consensus Works

Consensus is naturally collaborative because it includes everyone, promotes understanding and ownership, involves them in brainstorming and selecting options, and prevents sabotage after decisions are made. It is democratic because it ensures that everyone has an equal voice regardless of rank or position, allows differences of opinion to surface, and builds unity and a sense of common direction. Here are some typical statements indicating that consensus has been reached:

"I can say an unqualified yes to the decision."

"I find the decision acceptable."

"I am willing to support the decision because I trust the wisdom of the group."

"I can live with the decision, though I'm not enthusiastic about it."

"I do not fully agree with the decision and need to register my disagreement. However, I do not choose to block consensus."

Organizations know that consensus is working when everyone feels that the process was fair, that they had sufficient opportunity to influence the decision, and that they are willing to live with it and support it as though it were their first choice. A lack of consensus can be found in statements like these:

"I feel there is no clear unity in the group."

"We need to do more work before I can reach consensus."

"I feel I haven't been heard."

"I do not agree with the decision and feel the need to stand in the way of it being accepted."

"I strongly [or repeatedly] disagree."

There is a common misunderstanding that consensus requires people to surrender on issues that are important to them. In fact, consensus *requires* the expression of honest differences, preferably in ways that are not unnecessarily adversarial, together with a search for common ground. It is most important in using consensus not to compromise over principles. It is equally important not to rush decisions, vote before it is necessary, withhold participation, dominate the process, or act unilaterally.

Although consensus is the preferred method of decision making for self-managing organizations, sometimes it fails. It does not succeed when people give up too quickly and move on to voting without working in a committed way to resolve the issues that block agreement. If, after ample time for dialogue and committed effort, it is clear that consensus cannot be reached, the following options remain:

- Return to the organization's vision or goals. Then develop procedures or guidelines that flow from the vision and goals, or identify shared values, commonalities, interests, and criteria for decision making.
- Separate out issues over which there is no consensus to return to later, or use brainstorming to expand options.
- Break issues down into separate parts, and try to reach consensus on each one separately, or look at each objection to see if solutions can be created to these while moving ahead with the proposal.
- Take a break or table the decision; then return for additional problem solving.
- Refer the issue to a completely uninvolved group to develop compromise solutions, bring in an outside expert to advise the group, or bring in a facilitator or mediator to bring about consensus.
- Look for hidden issues, and surface hidden agendas.
- Separate into interest groups and engage in dialogue, or ask each group to meet separately and list five suggestions for compromise.
- Create a team of representatives from each side to brainstorm, prioritize, and recommend solutions.
- Vote based on majority rule.
- Prepare majority and minority reports, and allow the minority to continue convincing the majority to change.
- Allow the primary decision maker to decide.

The most important outcome of consensus is not the decision reached or even the process used. It is the development of an ongoing working relationship between majority and minority factions, who come to see each other as partners in a search for better solutions. As a result of this experience, people realize that dissent is not an obstacle but a gift, since it is through dissent that better solutions are discovered.

Collaborative Negotiation Processes

Not only do self-managing organizations need to map their processes, plan their strategies, conduct effective meetings, and decide by consensus; they need to improve their processes for collaboratively negotiating differences and resolving conflicts. If negotiation and conflict resolution are not collaborative, democratic, and self-managing, these processes will begin to degenerate and unravel. The way we negotiate and resolve our differences has a profound impact on our relationships and tests our capacity for collaboration, democracy, and self-management.

In hierarchical, bureaucratic, autocratic organizations, significant differences between managers and employees are rarely negotiated, and conflicts are either avoided or settled by managers who mandate solutions. Conflicts are rarely surfaced, opened up, collaboratively negotiated, or completely resolved, partly because many conflicts that appear to be between individuals or based on personalities actually reflect systemic dysfunctions within the organization.

It is common for people to see conflict as negative and collaboration as positive, yet they are inextricably linked in self-managing organizations. Collaboration without conflict can easily turn into formality and politeness that are inauthentic and lack substance. It is less important in democratic organizations for people to behave politely than it is for them to express their differences respectfully and honestly and work diligently to find solutions based on their interdependence and commonality.

Collaborative, interest-based negotiation and conflict resolution techniques encourage people not to suppress their differences, because doing so results practically in their disenfranchisement. Democracy creates a need to discuss, probe, challenge, engage, debate, and make decisions regarding issues. This cannot be done without going deeper into what divides us and at the same time remaining together in a context of shared values and a common search for solutions.

Creating collaborative, democratic self-managing processes for negotiation and conflict resolution is not simply a matter of having the right intent or attitude, though these are extremely important. It is a matter of using the right processes and separating those that work from those that do not. As we wrote in *Resolving Conflicts at Work*, this means learning to separate

- Positions from interests.
- People from problems.
- Problems from solutions.

- Commonalities from differences.
- The future from the past.
- Emotion from negotiation.
- Process from content.
- Options from choices.
- Criteria from selection.
- Yourself from others.

Separating these elements in a negotiation may appear simple, but it is extremely difficult in practice because each separation requires people to give up being the one who is right. It asks them to acknowledge what they contributed to the impasse and to do so in ways that facilitate a joint search for solutions. In this way, complex problems can be broken down into a series of steps that are focused on one at a time.

Each of the democratic processes we have described requires everyone in the organization to take primary responsibility for improving their work life and the processes, methods, and techniques needed to keep democracy, collaboration, and self-management alive. Self-management would be easy if it were merely a matter of implementing a few democratic or collaborative processes created by others. Instead, self-managing organizations challenge everyone to create complex self-correcting systems that encourage them to continue improving their processes and developing their skills.

Chapter Fourteen

Create Complex
Self-Correcting Systems

*The logic, or perhaps I should say metalogic, of the creative
process is founded on the simple fact that disorder feeds
order. In any system, once a relative orderliness has been
achieved, the only means by which a broader and more
complex interrelationship among the various elements
can be achieved is by introducing or generating disorder.
The system can come apart to be put together in a much
more integrated way. Any system that resists this creative
disintegration and re-integration can only suffer the
gradual erosion of its established order due to the energy
required to protect the system from change.*
GEORGE AINSWORTH LAND, *Grow or Die*

Every successful organism uses a combination of three natural
forces to survive and adapt to environmental change: order, or self-
organization; disorder, or conflict; and balance, or self-correction.
Order and self-organization are required for systems to coordinate
complex functions and perform smoothly and continuously. Disorder and conflict are required to reveal what does not work and
encourage evolution to higher states of order. Balance and self-
correction are required to regulate the stagnation and chaos that
ensue from too much order or disorder.

It is therefore essential for organizations to seek a balance between order and disorder, so that learning and growth can take
place and synergy can occur. They do so by creating mechanisms

that increase awareness and adaptation and integrate complex, contradictory information. This is primarily accomplished through feedback, conflict resolution, and organizational learning.

For organizations to evolve successfully, multiple contradictory tendencies need to be energized and balanced, including order and disorder, control and chaos, harmony and conflict, centralization and decentralization, habit and spontaneity, caution and risk, work and play, responsibility and freedom. Learning, synergy, and evolutionary adaptation allow a degree of chaos to enter an ordered system in order to reveal its inadequacies and transform them into opportunities for growth and learning.

To maintain optimum levels of order, disorder, and balance so as to support sustainability, renewal, and regeneration, organizations require systems for feedback, conflict resolution, and organizational learning that are *at least* as rapid, complex, integrated, and creative as the system, the challenges it faces, and the environment in which it operates. These systems have to be able to continue evolving and produce ever more sophisticated methods of adaptation, self-correction, improvement, and learning.

Organizations automatically become more complex, integrated, and adaptive when they create a context of values, ethics, and integrity; form webs of association; develop ubiquitous, linking leaders; build innovative self-managing teams; and implement streamlined, open, collaborative processes. They then must design complex self-correcting systems to support these new characteristics. Democratic, collaborative, self-managing organizations require systems that promote regular, open, honest, formal and informal, 360-degree feedback; resolve a broad range of conflicts; and promote organizational learning. Ultimately, each of these requires the end of management.

The Self-Referential Feedback Loop

All systems maintain thermostats that help them sense the need for change and aid them in adjusting without upsetting their internal balance. These thermostats need to deliver information that is as complex and diverse as the larger systems they are adjusting, or the information will be insufficient to produce the changes needed to survive. Feedback is a critical element in the ability to make rapid, strategic, integrated choices concerning the pace and direction of change.

Most feedback that takes place inside hierarchical organizations is shallow, distorted, irresponsible, one-dimensional, sporadic, irrelevant, destructive, and self-referential. It is primarily delivered from the top down, causing those below to discount it. It is judgmental, causing those who receive it to become defensive. It is superficial, causing those who hear it to pay no attention. It is connected to promotion and termination, causing those who are ambitious or insecure to fear it. It reinforces the status quo, causing those who are asked to participate in it to distrust its effectiveness. In countless ways, it misses the point.

Perhaps the greatest difficulty with hierarchies, bureaucracies, and autocracies is that they are incapable of recognizing or processing certain sources of feedback. Whenever feedback is offered or received by someone who has a lesser degree of power, status, or position within the organization, it is easy to reject, misconstrue, reinterpret, or rationalize it away. And whenever it comes from someone with a greater degree of power, it is easy to become frightened, hurt, hostile, distrusting, and defensive. Complaints from employees are heard as griping or negativity; corrections from above are perceived as micromanaging or harassment.

Feedback in democratic organizations consists of multiple interdependent, interacting, interrelated, responsive elements, including ideas, emotions, attitudes, myths, stories, unspoken expectations, informal communications, inchoate perceptions, subtle processes, states of energy, and delicate relationships. These require heightened sensitivity on the part of both giver and receiver.

There is only one real reason for feedback, which is improvement. For feedback to supply useful, unbiased information that can lead to self-correction, it has to be free of the taint that comes from unequal power, authority, status, knowledge, and responsibility. This is especially true of feedback between managers and the employees they manage. These difficulties combine to make critical changes, conflict resolution, organizational learning, and self-correction arduous, and frequently impossible.

When feedback is blocked, capacity deteriorates, change dwindles, resistance mounts, and distrust accumulates. Employees begin to see problems as systemic and requiring even deeper transformation, escalating conflicts within the group. Certain subjects become taboo, secrets and gossip proliferate, morale becomes dependent on unfulfillable expectations, and silences spread about things that matter. Roles and responsibilities become less clear, relationships grow more dysfunctional, and evolution freezes.

Democracy, collaboration, and self-management, in contrast, encourage feedback givers to deliver honest information openly and immediately and take responsibility for communicating what is not working. They encourage feedback receivers to listen constructively and nondefensively, accept responsibility for their behaviors and results, receive critical information as a gift, and use it for organizational and self-improvement.

Democratic, collaborative, self-managing organizations deliver higher-quality feedback by eliminating or reducing distinctions based on power and privilege. Democratic principles require that anyone who gives feedback also receive it. Givers and receivers critique their own perceptions, communications, relationships, processes, and behaviors and engage in dialogue and negotiation regarding their expectations and conflicting experiences. In other words, improving feedback encourages organizations to become collaborative, democratic, and self-managing.

Lenses That Distort Feedback

For feedback to be effective, it needs to be open, honest, and unbiased. This requires givers and receivers to see themselves and others accurately. But because our eyes look outward rather than inward, our view of ourselves is nearly always skewed and inaccurate. For this reason, organizations need to elicit feedback from outside each self-perceiving unit. They also need to elicit feedback from inside each person and team—feedback that is integrally connected to the people, problems, and relationships being evaluated.

In order to use these perspectives, it is important for self-managing organizations to create complex feedback systems. Initially, this means identifying the lenses that distort the content of feedback, especially where people are likely to be unaware of them. Some of these lenses are diagrammed in Figure 14.1.

Figure 14.1. Lenses That Distort Feedback.

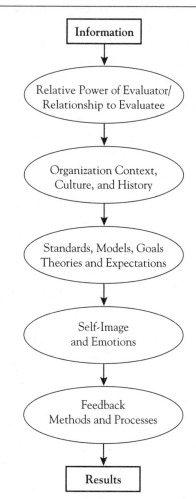

Hierarchy, bureaucracy, and autocracy alter each of these lenses, twisting and distorting feedback content, blocking the flow of information within the organization, and warping the meaning of the message. Organizational problems are then compounded—not only because people cannot see who they are and what they are doing, but because they *do not see* that they do not see.

For this reason, every truly effective method of feedback undermines, and to some extent destroys, hierarchy, bureaucracy, and autocracy. It signifies the end of management, for two principal reasons. First, for anyone to receive accurate feedback, there must be an absence of fear of retaliation, yet hierarchies allow managers to use feedback as a means of punishment and control. Second, effective feedback requires that evaluators also correct themselves, yet hierarchies allow managers to avoid correcting themselves based on feedback from below.

Heinz von Foerster suggests that heterarchical feedback by itself leads to a powerful mutation in the managerial injunction, "Thou shalt," transforming it into the self-managing declaration, "I shall." When givers and receivers engage in open and honest feedback, they automatically become coequal members of a team. And when team members give each other honest feedback, they cease being irresponsible employees and become self-managers, creating the collaborative declaration, "We shall."

Designing Democratic Feedback Loops

Democratic feedback is an essential element in organizational learning for many reasons. First, everyone sees themselves from the inside out and perceives others inaccurately. Second, each person contributes something different to identifying problems and solutions, making combined feedback more accurate. Third, inequalities in power, status, and privilege allow feedback to be dismissed as inaccurate or biased. Fourth, groups feel safer opening up and discussing problems when everyone participates. Fifth, feedback is more effective when self-doubt, poor self-esteem, and failure are tempered with kindness, empathy, and compassion, which occur spontaneously in democratic environments. Sixth, supportive feedback encourages employees to trust the process and the intentions of others.

For these reasons, organizations need to develop democratic methods for giving and receiving feedback and collaborative ways of supporting people in actually changing their behaviors. This means designing democratic feedback loops for maximum personal impact, strategic organizational advantage, and self-managerial potential, based on the following strategies:

1. Search for diverse ideas through multifaceted feedback mechanisms, such as interviews, surveys, and focus groups among

employees, customers, and the community. Discover not only what is counterproductive but what is *missing* that might increase productivity.

2. Collaboratively design the system, including everyone to whom it will apply, and reach consensus on both principles and measures for evaluation.

3. Create multiple systems that encourage customization of systems and methods to meet diverse needs and circumstances. Use a variety of acknowledgment and evaluation methods—for example:

   - *Personal acknowledgment.* Routinely and frequently acknowledge, thank, and compliment everyone for their efforts, without saying "but . . ."
   - *Self-assessment.* Ask everyone to evaluate themselves openly and honestly.
   - *Team assessment.* Help teams assess ways of improving their relationships, communications, and processes.
   - *Horizontal feedback.* Give honest, open, peer-based feedback in real time, not once a year.
   - *Vertical assessment.* Ask managers to evaluate employees, and vice versa.
   - *Customer, client, and citizen assessment.* Elicit feedback from clients and customers regarding products and services.
   - *Task evaluation.* Evaluate performance based on results.
   - *Process evaluation.* Evaluate processes for ways of improving how work is done.
   - *Relationship evaluation.* Evaluate relationships based on what is working and what is not.
   - *Organizational assessment.* Have everyone in the organization come together to examine where they are heading, what is working, what is not, and what can be done to improve it.

4. Keep it short, easy, and relevant by focusing on improvement in a few key areas and limiting rubrics to assessing what is within the person's capacity to change.

5. Evaluate the evaluation process by exploring areas of contradiction and open dialogue to determine the accuracy and success of the process.

6. Evaluate the evaluators to discover whether they communicated clearly, empathetically, and honestly and actually improved the performance of those they evaluated.

7. Openly discuss the evaluations by sharing what was learned individually and as an organization in diverse forums focused on learning.
8. Create linkages to motivation, and reward self-criticism and improvement through a variety of compensation measures.
9. Link the entire process to values by making sure values inform both the content and the process of delivering it.
10. Use information as a springboard for organizational learning by synthesizing, publicizing, and discussing relevant lessons so everyone can learn from others' mistakes.

The methodology that most closely meets these goals is the 360-degree evaluation process, shown in Figure 14.2, which provides a four-dimensional snapshot of individual and team performance. Discrepancies between messages coming from diverse sources can be analyzed and discussed with individuals and team members in an open process led by team facilitators or human resources.

The performance factors assessed under this process usually include task and technical competence; values, ethics, and integrity; responsibility and dependability; relationship and process

Figure 14.2. 360-Degree Evaluation.

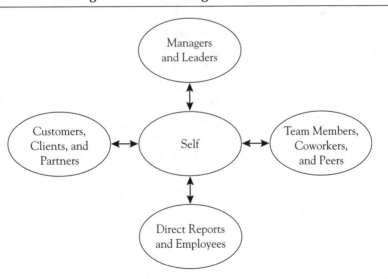

skills; adaptability, resourcefulness, and initiative; respect for others; communication and conflict resolution; and leadership skills. In designing the assessment process, each employee needs to agree on the skill areas to be evaluated, the questions to be asked, the method of asking, and how the answers will be communicated. Individuals can be given simple and immediate feedback using the following statements:

"I would like to compliment you for . . ."

"I feel you could improve by . . ."

"Here is an example: . . ."

"Here is how you might have handled it better: . . ."

"I am willing to support you in improving by . . ."

The purpose of democratic feedback is to shift responsibility for improving performance from managers to employees and involve everyone in contributing to personal and organizational learning. The heart of the process is delivering feedback that cannot be discounted and does not trigger defensiveness drawn from one's self, peers, reports, and customers. In these ways, feedback becomes collaborative, democratic, and everyone's job.

Democratic feedback is essential because secrets are far more powerful than any feedback one can give; because feelings, relationships, and self-esteem are less sensitive when they are normalized and shared; and because negative behaviors disintegrate when they are publicly identified and passed back rather than on to others. It is essential because self-improvement is dependent on the opinions of others; because honesty, humility, and compassion require continuous reinforcement; and because conscious efforts are needed to establish connection and common direction across organizational lines. As Oscar Wilde wrote, "To speak the truth is a painful thing. To be forced to tell lies is much worse."

Attitudes Toward Democratic Feedback

Democratic feedback requires a transformation in personal and organizational attitudes in at least four ways. First, feedback is enhanced when people participate equally in the process and recognize that everyone's perspective is useful. In truth, there is no such thing as neutral or disinterested feedback. Every observer's perspective is based on profoundly subjective experiences, no matter how objective they try to be. This does not make feedback useless but asks those giving it to recognize their truth as one of many and explicitly acknowledge their point of view when evaluating someone else's.

Second, no one completely knows or understands anyone else, especially when observation is limited to the workplace. People behave differently in private than in public, and at most we see only parts of a whole person, which are experienced differently by coworkers, superiors, subordinates, and customers. In democratic feedback, these perspectives form a mosaic that is pieced together to create a larger, more complex picture.

Third, not everything we recommend others do differently works for them. Divergent perspectives, needs, and expectations should be negotiated rather than reduced to commands. Every work of genius and every scientific, artistic, and social advancement was bitterly opposed by someone. Had their creators listened to feedback, they might never have produced anything new. We need to make ample room for genius, dissent, complexity, and uniqueness.

Fourth, individuals are often blamed unfairly for organizational failures, including structural, systemic, procedural, and relational dysfunctions they did not create. Discontent is often channeled into negative feedback because organizations provide limited ways of registering disapproval, as with employees who are yelled at by customers because their products do not work. Feedback becomes a way of venting anger rather than a factual description of what happened or a constructive suggestion about how someone might be more effective. On the flip side, personal loyalty also interferes with feedback, and from the best of motives, employees suppress feedback and cheat each other out of opportunities for learning and improvement.

These difficulties are overcome, and feedback is transformed into a powerful source of improvement when it is:

- Recognized as having a single purpose, which is improvement
- Everyone's responsibility
- Delivered without delay, and there are no surprises

- Welcomed and invited without waiting for others to offer it, and is given directly, without fear, anger, quid pro quo, or dissembling
- Constructive and nonjudgmental, so egos are disarmed, and behaviors are separated from personalities, allowing real listening to take place
- Honest and open and not held back out of fear or friendship
- Accepted without resistance, defensiveness, or withdrawal, thereby losing its sting
- Translated into action, encouraging people to be authentically who they are, and more aware of the effects their behaviors have on others

In self-managing organizations, people are encouraged by democratic feedback to improve their ability to make and meet commitments without managerial oversight. For employees who seem unable to correct their behaviors without managerial intervention, a number of self-managerial approaches can still be used by teams to improve their behavior—for example:

- Honestly and openly discussing failures to correct within the team
- Listening to objections, satisfying underlying interests, and clarifying individual and team responsibilities
- Allowing team members to negotiate and rearrange their work assignments and help each other
- Providing training in time and project management skills
- Periodically reviewing progress and rewarding those who improve most
- Discussing the importance of improvement within the team
- Modeling how to receive feedback and improve based on it

Ultimately, the purpose of democratic feedback is to help people who have been hierarchically managed by others learn to manage themselves responsibly. It is, in other words, to encourage them to grow up and make sure the organization and its culture grow up as well. In the process, conflicts inevitably arise, making mediation skills a critical component in designing complex self-correcting systems.

The Cost of Unresolved Conflict

Conflict often signals the presence of personal and organizational issues that have not been successfully addressed through feedback and are blocking learning and change. In this way, conflict can be understood simply as the sound made by the cracks in the system. It is also the first sign of a new paradigm—a warning light that signals imminent breakdown and a path to transformation.

Managerial organizations are riddled with chronic, unresolved conflicts between employees and managers, providers and customers, unions and management, manufacturing and shipping, sales and finance. Many of these conflicts are triggered by unfair decision-making processes, dysfunctional policies, competitive and bureaucratic relationships, differences in applying rules and standards, unclear roles and responsibilities, adversarial attitudes, false expectations, distorted communications, value and goal differences, responsibility issues, resistance to change, and competition over limited resources.

Countless resolvable conflicts are allowed to fester because managers are seen as responsible for solving them yet lack the skills or desire to do so. There are conflicts between those who are creative and those who are practical, those who are "hang-loose" and those who are "uptight," those who talk but do not listen and those who listen but do not talk, all of which waste precious human and organizational resources.

A survey conducted by the American Management Association, responded to by 116 chief executive officers, 76 vice presidents, and 66 middle managers, revealed that these managers spent at least 24 percent of their time resolving conflicts. They felt conflict resolution had become more important over the past ten years and was equal to or more important than strategic planning, communication, motivation, and decision making. In many organizations, 24 percent is a low-end figure, particularly when minor disputes are included. If we add all the time managers spend listening to complaints, countering rumors, delivering corrective feedback, disciplining employees for conflict-related behaviors, monitoring compliance, and searching for solutions, managerial time spent resolving conflicts easily increases to 50 percent or higher. If we multiply this figure times the average manager's salary, we begin to understand the true cost of unresolved conflict.

It is undeniable that conflict has a significant impact on the organizations in which it occurs, dramatically reduces productivity and morale, occupies a great deal of the conscious and unconscious attention of employees, and creates stress for everyone involved. It often leads to litigation, lost synergy, poor morale, high financial expenditures, wasted time and resources, loss of valuable employees and customers, and reduced opportunities for change and improvement.

As these conflicts are resolved, organizations experience revitalization, reduced waste, improved productivity, innovative solutions, better communications, expanded synergy and teamwork, streamlined processes, and increased trust. Although it takes time and money to resolve conflicts, it also takes time and money *not* to resolve them. Indeed, the time and money spent on not resolving conflicts is far in excess of the cost of implementing the most elaborate resolution system imaginable.

Many organizations have discovered that conflict resolution programs can substantially reduce litigation expenses and create cost savings. Among the examples cited by Karl Slaikeu and Ralph Hasson in *Controlling the Costs of Conflict* are these:

- In the first year of comparison, Brown and Root reported an 80 percent reduction in outside litigation expenses by introducing a systemic approach to collaboration and conflict resolution regarding employment issues.
- Motorola Corporation reported a reduction in outside litigation expenses of up to 75 percent per year over six years by using a systemic approach to conflict management in its legal department and including a mediation clause in contracts with suppliers.
- National Cash Register Corporation reported a reduction in outside litigation expenses of 50 percent and a drop in its number of pending lawsuits from 263 to 28 between 1984 and 1993, following the systemic use of alternative dispute resolution.
- The U.S. Air Force reported that by taking a collaborative approach to conflict management in a construction project, it completed the project 144 days ahead of schedule and $12 million under budget, and an estimated savings of 50 percent

per claim in one hundred equal employment opportunity complaints using mediation.

If we add the costs associated with gossip and rumors, stress-related sick leave, conflict-induced absences and tardiness, reassignments, retraining costs triggered by unresolved conflict, human resources and executive salaries devoted to employee discipline and discharge, and similar conflict-related expenses, the figures become astronomical. In one study of sixteen hundred employees, 22 percent said they actually decreased their work effort because of conflict, over 50 percent reported that they lost work time because they worried about whether the instigator of the conflict would do it again, and 12 percent reported they changed jobs to get away from the instigator.

The Systemic Source of Organizational Conflict

As organizations face increasing demands for change, conflicts accumulate along the fault lines that lie hidden in their systems. These conflicts point directly to what is not working, and their resolution often reveals some new process, principle, or relationship waiting to be born. For this reason, hierarchy, bureaucracy, and autocracy defend themselves or actively suppress conflicts, even at the cost of organizational learning.

Most conflicts in organizations appear purely personal in nature, such as personality clashes. Yet as these conflicts accumulate, what seems unique and personal suddenly emerges as common, widespread, and omnipresent, as by-products of a dysfunctional organizational system. These larger issues often remain hidden, even when countless others are treated the same way.

To understand organizational conflicts, we need to look beyond individual words and behaviors to the *contexts* in which they occur. Chronic conflict is a sign that a system is unable to reform or repair itself and is protecting itself against any resolution that requires fundamental change. As these defenses aggregate, they produce a growing insecurity, a fear that the whole structure will collapse, and a heightened resistance even to minor modifications that might trigger an avalanche. As fear of a systemic meltdown increases, even those in favor of change may retreat and seek to preserve or roll back the status quo or deflect the change by promoting a less serious conflict.

Dysfunctional systems defend themselves against conflict not only by avoidance, denial, diversion, and suppression but by rationalization and the invention of stories that personalize systemic discord. These adversarial stories disguise and distract attention from fixing the holes exposed by the conflict and focus attention on individual victims and perpetrators. Stories that blame people for systemic conflicts are a defense against change, just as confrontation is a defense against vulnerability and bureaucracy against the experience of responsibility.

Democratic organizations resolve internal conflicts by creating complex self-correcting systems that move people from hierarchical power to heterarchical equity, from bureaucratic stasis to collaborative change, and from autocratic coercion to democratic consensus. Collaborative, democratic, self-managing organizations view conflict resolution in its broadest sense and use it to shift organizational life in a collaborative direction. This means revealing and moving toward the heart of the organizational system that generated the conflict. It is here that leverage can be found not only to end it but to transform the values, structures, systems, processes, and relationships that triggered, aggravated, encouraged, and defended it.

Designing Conflict Resolution Systems

Few organizations possess adequate systems for resolving conflicts, and most do not use these systems until after unacceptable loss has occurred. When this happens, the conflict is pigeonholed as someone else's personal responsibility, or beyond the reach of organizational policy, or not within the expertise of people inside the organization to resolve, or the solution does not reach deep enough into underlying attitudes and relationships that emerge later to generate new problems.

What is needed in these circumstances are complex, collaborative, self-correcting conflict resolution systems that are designed to reach all the elements in the organization and provide a rich array of alternatives leading to resolution. These conflict resolution systems allow organizations to respond to a range of conflicts using a variety of techniques.

Based on ideas originally propounded by William Ury, Stephen Goldberg, and Jeanne Brett in *Getting Disputes Resolved,* the conflict resolution systems design approach encourages organizations to see conflicts not as isolated incidents but as parts of a larger system that can be addressed in more than one way. It permits organizations to emphasize integrated approaches rather than discrete procedures, and respond both to single disputes and the stream of disputes that flows through them. It encourages informal problem solving, monitoring, and deescalation throughout the life of the conflict, lets several people work on the same problem from multiple perspectives, employs alternate methodologies in search of synergistic results, and encourages organizational learning and systemic self-correction.

Conflicts in organizations can be resolved by exercising power, adjudicating rights, or satisfying interests. The principal methods adopted by power-based hierarchies are compulsion backed by force, coercion, unilateral decision making and manipulation. Those used in rights-based bureaucracies are litigation, adversarial negotiation, policy notification, and elections. Those used in interest-based, democratic, self-managing organizations are mediation, collaborative negotiation, coaching, and informal problem solving. The conflict resolution systems design approach attempts to shift initial resolution choices from power- to rights- to interest-based alternatives that encourage consensus.

The great advantage of interest-based solutions is that they permit both sides to win, whereas power- and rights-based systems nearly always involve loss for one side or the other, causing damage to relationships. Interest-based systems are far more complex than power- or rights-based systems. They offer multiple opportunities for personal, team, and organizational learning. Their goal is not victory over others but improving relationships, processes, trust, and communication. Conflict resolution systems are often established using the following steps:

1. Analyze the sources of conflict, including its connections to systems, structures, culture, communications, strategies, change, values, morale, styles, and staffing by conducting a "conflict audit" to assess chronic sources of conflict within the organization.

2. Identify the core cultural ideas, traditional approaches, and informal mechanisms already in place for resolving conflict, and supplement them with enriched alternatives that emphasize prevention, and focus on interest- rather than rights- or power-based solutions.

3. Expand the number and kind of resolution alternatives available internally and externally, and arrange these procedures from low to high cost.

4. Include a full range of options from process changes to binding arbitration, with low-cost rights and power backups, and "loopbacks" to informal problem solving and negotiation.

5. Improve consultation, facilitation, dialogue, coaching, mentoring, feedback, and evaluation, and alter behavior patterns that block use of resolution procedures.

6. Provide training, motivation, skills, support, and resources to make these procedures work, continue to improve understanding of how these principles succeed and fail, and improve their design.

The object of the systems design process is to create complex self-correcting conflict resolution mechanisms that match specific organizational needs, resolve individual conflicts, and allow the larger organization to stimulate growth, insight, change, and learning so they are not repeated.

Examples of Conflict Resolution Systems

The most commonly used procedures in conflict resolution systems design include peer counseling, coaching, mentoring, team intervention and confrontation, dialogue and public forums, peer and professional mediation, ombuds investigations, internal appeals, organizational review boards, arbitration and early neutral evaluation, summary jury trials, and similar processes.

Here are some examples of conflict resolution systems we helped design:

• A Fortune 100 corporation decided after a string of costly jury verdicts to develop a comprehensive approach to conflict resolution. Human resource staff created an employee problem resolution procedure that led conflicting employees through a multistep process. Both sides in the conflict were assigned an "executive adviser" from outside their business unit to advocate and coach them or meet informally to resolve it. If this failed, the dispute proceeded to a consensus review board made up of an equal number of managers and employees with power to bind the company. If these processes failed, the issue went to binding arbitration.

• A technology corporation confronted with angry clients and chronic conflicts between staff members and business partners conducted a conflict audit that revealed disgruntled information systems users, skeptical senior managers, and low morale among staff and vendors who did not believe they could implement the new systems. A staff retreat produced consensus on a conflict resolution plan, resulting in more effective customer service, a better delivery system, and a more powerful technology architecture.

• A conflict audit at a manufacturing company revealed multiple disputes between line workers at one of its manufacturing plants. Angry outbursts, competition among team members, and threats of physical attack were disrupting operations. Human resources identified, analyzed, categorized, and prioritized the sources of conflict and observed how it was reinforced by the organization's culture. It was then possible to identify predictors, preventive measures, safety nets, outlets for constructive expression of differences, procedures for resolution, and methods for making them effective. This allowed them to reduce the risks and costs of conflict dramatically, settle disputes before legal costs accumulated, and create a learning environment regarding conflict.

• A large corporation reorganized its staff into self-managing teams. As managers became team leaders and a largely bookkeeping and accounting staff began managing themselves, they became more service oriented and adept at strategic planning. As these changes unfolded, conflicts arose within, between, and among the teams based on false expectations, inconsistencies in implementing team values, lack of equity in team members' pulling their weight, old managerial behaviors, and role confusions. The teams created new governance structures, communications systems, organizational roles, and training programs for managers and staff. They developed innovative strategies to address the systemic sources of their conflicts and conducted an open dialogue about inconsistencies in the team process, resulting in a dramatic improvement in morale and productivity.

• A regulation negotiation process was initiated between city staff and neighborhood organizations to help diverse constituencies reach consensus and avoid a destructive battle over the design of zoning regulations and public policies that directly affected their lives. This months-long process brought together civil servants, merchants, residents, community organizations, and homeowners who had fought bitterly for years. In the course of a few meetings, they produced a vision for the future of their neighborhood, and a proposed ordinance was recommended by consensus to the city council for adoption.

• Similar results were achieved by a homeless task force that brought hostile, opposing parties to consensus on recommendations for public action, and by conflict-ridden schools, college and university departments, and public interest groups where conflict resolution systems design proved to be a powerful process not just for resolving conflicts but learning from them as they moved toward collaboration.

Although some conflicts are unavoidable, most are preventable, containable, and resolvable at lower cost, and all contain information that is critical to personal and organizational learning. When organizations succeed in resolving chronic conflicts, they evolve to experience higher levels of conflict and open up new opportunities for organizational learning.

Systems for Organizational Learning

Creating complex self-correcting feedback and conflict resolution systems not only contributes to personal, team, and organizational learning, it allows each to expand their capacity for learning consciously and systematically. Peter Senge, in *The Fifth Discipline*, describes the process of organizational learning as one in which experience is transformed into improvement. Learning organizations design, detect, and nourish local learning practices; articulate values and create shared meaning; empower staff to analyze the elements of their culture that prevent learning and change them; generate knowledge-enhancing systems; regularly assess the impact of new experiences in terms of results, processes, and relationships; and diffuse important lessons and innovations throughout the organization.

The deciding factor in both individual and organizational learning is the degree to which people are encouraged to regard their mistakes and conflicts as events from which lessons can be learned. Learning is reinforced when mistakes are experienced as leading to improvement in structures, systems, processes, and relationships. In cultures that support organizational learning, strong signals are sent that learning is valued, and everyone is expected to learn. Some organizations have "chief learning officers" responsible for designing and implementing learning strategies that encourage lifelong learners, capture important lessons from mistakes and conflicts, and feed these reflections back to the organization for self-correction and improvement.

Democratic organizations make lifelong learning an integral part of their day-to-day activities. They encourage employees to engage in reflective practices and see themselves as seekers, experimenters, and students. They support staff in being willing to explore their failures openly and honestly. They use performance reviews as opportunities to identify learning goals and project postmortems as occasions for self-assessment.

Many adults consign their learning experiences to schools and trainings and assume that once they are employed, they no longer need to study, learn, or improve. The basic idea of learning organizations is that work is an opportunity to learn and grow and increase wisdom, self-knowledge, and capacity. The support provided by learning organizations encourages employees to become lifelong learners and contribute back to the organization, as well as to colleagues, society, and themselves.

Collaborative Coaching, Mentoring, and Cross-Training

Other self-correcting systems for organizational learning include peer coaching, cross-training, and mentoring. These are self-correcting not only for those being coached, trained, or mentored but for the coaches, trainers, and mentors as well, who reflect on their experiences, draw lessons from observation, and discover ways to communicate their knowledge and encourage others to learn and change. Like teaching, peer coaching, mentoring, and cross-training create opportunities for employees to apply their learning, model how to receive critical feedback, transform their behaviors, improve their relationships, and develop skills in observation, communication, and committed action.

In the process, coaches, mentors, and cross-trainers learn what they really know, how to transmit it, and how to improve their observation and communication skills. Organizations benefit by expanding employee knowledge, increasing flexibility in assignments, improving reliability, and reducing errors. These methods increase the capacity of employees to manage themselves.

Some organizations have created in-house universities offering courses in technical skills, language arts, mathematics, English-as-a-second language, communications, conflict resolution, leadership development, poetry, team building and technical topics. Some offer university credits through alliances with degree-granting institutions. Although in-house universities do not always promote self-correction, they inspire a thirst for lifelong learning and integrate educational values into organizational culture.

Coaching, mentoring, and cross-training similarly promote collaborative, democratic, self-managing organizations. They support initiative, risk taking, and innovation, which make everyone a learner. They are based on the assumption that no one person knows what a team can know and that a community of learning is a rich environment for stimulating success. They honor diversity in background, perspective, opinion, culture, and style. They treat employees as customers, clients, and citizens and cultivate humility by helping people let go of what they think they know.

To create real learning organizations, multiple changes are required, each of which reduces the need for hierarchy, bureaucracy, and autocracy and contributes to the end of management. Learning implies a shift from giving answers to asking questions and from blaming, avoidance, and passivity to responsibility, proactivity, and prevention. It means expecting maturity rather than infantilizing others, facilitating consensus rather than coercing obedience, and creating values-driven rules rather than rule-driven values.

Every effort to create a learning organization results in a more complex, nuanced capacity for self-correction. As it does so, it opens internal lines of communication and decision making, which expand democracy and self-management. In this sense, organizational democracy is both a prerequisite and a cause of organizational evolution, expanded human capacity, and more humanistic work environments.

Organizational Learning and Facilitated Dialogue

Facilitated dialogue is the systematic orchestration of meaning and learning between people. It is thinking together in a coordinated way. In dialogue, a kind of participatory consciousness allows thought to behave like an organism, so that its disparate parts coordinate to produce a single complex message, analysis, or idea. Facilitated dialogue encourages values formation, participation, relationship building, community, teamwork, group learning, and trust. It builds on feedback, incorporates lessons from conflict resolution, and provides opportunities for individuals, teams, and organizations to observe, correct, and repair their mistakes and dysfunctions.

Dialogue happens when teams hold postmortems on projects and look at what succeeded and what failed; when coaches meet to analyze performance, identify future goals, and discover how their relationship can support achieving their targets; when teams meet to develop strategies in reaching shared objectives and revise plans based on feedback and self-correcting discussion; and when isolated departments identify the stereotypes they think others have of them, indicate what they actually do, and state what they need from others to do their jobs better.

These dialogue experiences lubricate the flow of organizational information, improve productivity and morale, and advance communication and collaborative relationships. They do this by drawing everyone affected by a problem together; agreeing on ground rules for their behavior; encouraging listening on all sides to reduce personalization and hostility; raising awareness and understanding of complex policy issues to sharpen the identification and understanding of problems; and building consensus by honestly discussing polarizing events and beliefs, openly exploring ideas without predetermining outcomes, and valuing everyone's contribution.

There is a fine art to facilitating dialogue and making it feel safe for employees to take risks, honestly communicate what is important to them, and listen empathetically, even to those with whom they disagree. Linking leaders facilitate dialogues, make connections between participants, and expand conceptual frameworks so learning can take place. These dialogues, or collaborative conversations, are the soul of self-managing teams and democratic organizations. They are arenas in which values are surfaced, problems are solved, insights are gained, and new ideas are tested. They are the method by which individuals and organizations learn.

Chapter Fifteen

Integrate Strategically, and Change the Way We Change

What moves us to accept a new paradigm, finally?
Experimental data alone can never fully establish the
truth of a new paradigm, for the paradigm itself orders
and makes sense of the data. Are we not moved to embrace
a paradigm when it somehow resonates with the richness
of what we already implicitly know? In this sense, is it not
perhaps our intuitive sense of the implicate order of things
that actually validates a new paradigm and encourages
us to adopt it?
JOHN WELWOOD, *Ken Wilber*

Individuals, organizations, and societies are constantly changing, yet we rarely stop to consider how we change or whether what we are changing actually improves our lives. Organizations seldom examine the long-term consequences of the changes they initiate. Rarely do they pay conscious attention to the subtleties of the change process, calculate its effect on individuals, relationships, and society, or develop the practical skills required by successful change agents. As a result, change often results in unnecessary conflicts, resistance, damage to relationships, and injured morale.

As Adam Urbanski, vice president of the American Federation of Teachers, points out, "Change is mandatory; improvement is optional." Hierarchical organizations change all the time, often in ways that undermine their effectiveness and take them in the wrong direction. Change for the sake of change is no virtue, yet managers often seek to make their mark by initiating changes that result only in confusion and alienation.

As organizations shift from management to self-management, hierarchy to heterarchy, and autocracy to democracy, they are required to transform what they do, why they do it, the processes they use to do it, and the relationships they engage in while doing it. To succeed, they are also required to change the way they change and integrate their values, structures, systems, processes, and relationships strategically and synergistically.

Mismanaging Change

Every significant change triggers powerful emotions, including loss of the known, fear of the unknown, anxiety about failure, anger at those who resist or push too hard, denial, disillusionment, and uncertainty over the consequences of what is being created. It also triggers euphoria, excitement, anticipation, joy, love, and fulfillment. Many people's change experiences, especially in hierarchical, bureaucratic, autocratic organizations in which change is managed from above with little input from below, follow the pattern shown in Figure 15.1.

When employees experience change in these ways, apathy, cynicism, distrust, and resistance appear rational, and commonly used expressions such as "this too shall pass" make perfect sense. But when organizations change the way they change by making the process democratic, collaborative, and self-managing, everyone feels more honest, open, and interconnected, and conflicts and resistance dwindle.

Management as a system seeks to control the way change takes place within it, and hierarchical, bureaucratic, autocratic organizations typically manage the change process to make sure that fresh ideas are consistent with fundamental managerial principles. This allows the system to become self-reinforcing, making it difficult to alter even a small part without placing the entire complex at risk.

The key change assumptions of hierarchical organizations are that change needs to be controlled from the top down, that this can be done without seriously reducing its effectiveness, and that change automatically means progress and improvement. Yet the

Figure 15.1. Stages in the Mismanagement of Change.

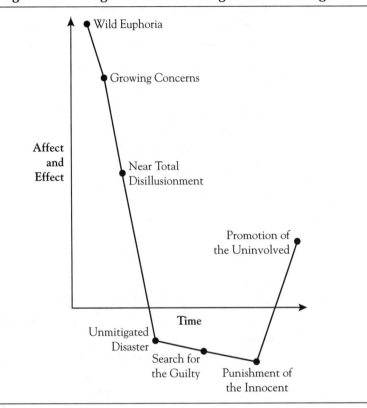

top is removed from both the problems that prompted the change and the process of implementation, and for these reasons can easily get it wrong. Top-down change nearly always means reduced participation, creativity, and commitment, and for this reason frequently moves the organization backward.

Hierarchy encourages the assumption that someone above is in charge of the change process, making sure that values, ethics, and integrity are translated into action; that important public interests are being met; employees are being treated justly and fairly; resources are not being wasted; and the environment is being protected from destruction. What hierarchically managed change actually means is that *no one is in charge*. Why? Because managing

change from above encourages those at the bottom to avoid taking personal responsibility for what is being changed. Employees
then resist necessary and important changes, become cynical and
apathetic about improvement, and communicate unclearly and ineffectively about what they need. This encourages their managers
to think bureaucratically and inhumanely about things that are
deeply human, apply simple solutions to complex problems, and
behave timidly and autocratically when boldness is needed or ego-
centrically when humility is essential. They see critics as enemies
and dismiss their concerns, manipulate change to advance careers
or placate superiors, fear taking risks, become defensive about honest feedback, and avoid conflicts that are essential for learning,
growth, and transformation.

When change is managed, hierarchy, bureaucracy, and autocracy are reinforced, and self-management, collaboration, and democracy are weakened. This is partly because managerial processes
encode and reinforce managerial content, and partly because managing change encourages nonmanagers to opt out. While everyone
wants to change others, no one wants to *be* changed by them.

By contrast, collaborative, democratic, self-managed change
wakes people up and challenges them to surrender their illusions.
What is changed is *who they are* and how they live their lives, which
gives them the right to participate in managing it themselves. The
challenge is not only to change organizations in ways that make
them more collaborative, democratic, and self-managing, but simultaneously to change the way change takes place, so the process
reinforces the results and increases the organization's ability to
adapt to changing conditions. As Charles Darwin wrote, "It is not
the strongest of the species that survive, nor the most intelligent,
but the one most responsive to change."

The Possibilities of Democratic Change

Every change presents us with choices, and every choice has consequences—internally and externally; for ourselves and for others;
in content, process, and relationships; in what is possible and what
is not. To some extent, all change is time-bound and irreversible,
bringing outcomes that cannot be foreseen. We pass on to future

generations not only the consequences of what we change but what we *fail* to change, the processes we use, and those we fail to use.

Collaboration, democracy, and self-management are not changes that can be imposed on organizations from without. They are movements toward more advanced forms of organization that make management increasingly unnecessary. Organizational democracy is a form of power sharing. When employees regulate themselves, even in unimportant ways, they learn something about their capacity for more radical self-regulation and undermine the assumptions on which hierarchy is based.

Rather than oppose increased collaboration, democracy, and self-management simply because they are insufficient, restricted, perfunctory, or others profit by them, employees need to push for fuller, deeper, more consequential involvement. As small changes accumulate, management appears less inevitable, and arguments of employee inexperience and the need for managerial control collapse. Hierarchy becomes increasingly inefficient, bureaucracy is understood as a limit on participation, and autocracy obstructs the synergies that are sparked by strategic integration.

Strategic Integration

Collaboration, democracy, and self-management are prerequisites for evolution to higher levels of organizational development based on synergy, community, and strategic integration. Through these processes, it becomes possible to build creative, motivated, high-performance, self-managing teams that harmonize and orchestrate a wide range of organizational skills, strategies, systems, processes, and relationships to produce synergistic results.

Creating fully democratic, collaborative, self-managing organizations requires more than fragmented, step-by-step, tactical reforms. It requires integrated, holistic, strategic transformations that increase diversity, complexity, synergy, and interconnectedness and challenge everyone to operate at their highest levels of effectiveness. In the process, employees need to become owners of the organizations they are changing and of the processes by which they are changed.

Hierarchical organizational systems are insular and defensive, walling themselves off from internal and external criticisms to preserve the status quo and promote an image of success and self-confidence. Yet in the process, they also wall themselves off from customers, clients, citizens, employees, external competitors, internal departments, other professions, and disciplines. Democratic organizations need to dismantle these walls and integrate an increasing variety of strategic, resource, and relational possibilities. Enormous opportunities for growth and learning then arise.

Strategic integration reduces internal boundaries. It encourages employees to work freely across traditional organizational separations, link isolated departments, and cascade changes in one area to produce changes in others. It supports employees in eliminating external boundaries and linking directly with customers, community, environment, and society; producing goods and services that meet unique human needs; and developing shared values to guide the organization. In these ways, strategic integration creates a third dimension of organizational freedom by adding depth to vertical and horizontal relationships.

This added dimension of organizational freedom also transforms the way we change by making the entire process more strategic and integrated, and therefore more collaborative, democratic, and self-managing. The freedom permitted by organizational depth turns every employee into a leader and the change process into an exercise in democracy. Beyond this lies a fourth dimension of synergy and community, which uniquely require collaboration, democracy, and self-management, as integration cuts across traditional organizational lines.

For example, the strategic integration of technology, finance, and management skills can rapidly transform organizational functions, roles, and partnerships, and the context in which they arise. It can create value by offering new ways of doing business and allowing diverse departments, divisions, and business functions to understand each other better and collaborate more effectively. It can build rich information infrastructures, leading to greater organizational flexibility and responsiveness, production planning, data for performance assessment, opportunities for internal partnerships, and recognition of the human side of technological change. It can create entirely new products and services and dramatically increase customer satisfaction. It can give employees instantaneous access to critical organizational data, allow them to communicate with everyone in the organization, and change their personal information and benefit allocations on-line.

The strategic integration of self-management with technology and finance takes place only at the highest of three distinct levels of skill that define the practice of each of these specializations:

1. Basic knowledge, literacy, and competency
2. Creating goals and objectives, strategic planning, and complex problem solving
3. Synergistic integration, shared values, and holistic design

To operate as owners, employees require basic knowledge, literacy, and competency in self-management, including human resources, finance, and technology, and it is possible to function at this first level of skill without a great deal of information or assistance from others. After developing a general understanding in any of these areas, it becomes possible to set goals and use that information strategically to solve higher-order problems. But strategic application and complex problem solving require perspective and judgment, which depend on information and assistance from people across the organization. After developing their capacity for strategic thinking, it becomes possible to introduce strategic integration, leading by values and holistic design, which blend these separate capabilities into a single strategic whole. This step uniquely requires collaboration, democracy, and self-management, as illustrated in Figure 15.2.

Strategic integration means creatively connecting skills across the organization at all levels and improving efficiency, productivity, quality, and customer service consistent with shared values. It means merging values, ethics, and integrity with living, evolving webs of association; ubiquitous, linking leadership; innovative self-managing teams; streamlined, open, collaborative processes; and complex self-correcting systems. It means changing the way we change.

Strategic integration encourages employees at all organizational levels to collaboratively redefine their boundaries, eliminate interfaces and overlaps, search for potential synergies, and create partnerships and alliances. It supports teams in reaching consensus

Figure 15.2. Three Stages of Strategic Integration.

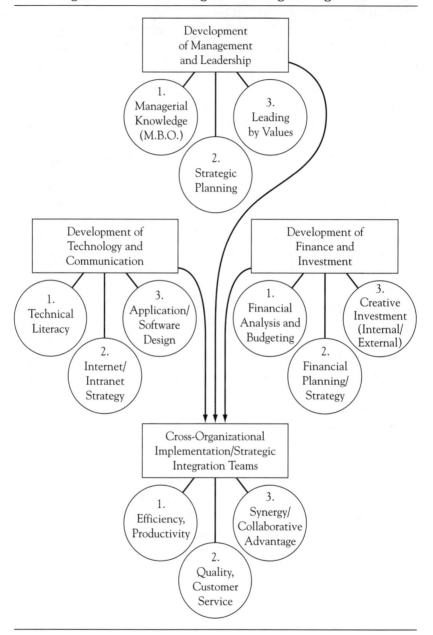

on processes, negotiating handoffs and expectations, defining roles and responsibilities, aligning on strategies, and delivering on results. It guides organizations in shaping a culture of values and respect for differences, raising performance measures, eliminating inefficient, unproductive processes, and improving systems for feedback, conflict resolution, and organizational learning. Figure 15.3 displays some of the potential outcomes of strategic integration that derive from combining self-management with technology and finance.

Guidelines for Democratic Change

If we want to increase organizational democracy, we cannot impose it by fiat but must build democratic principles into the ways it is achieved. These changes cannot be mandated or controlled from above but must be discussed, designed, forged, and led from above, below, and sideways through ubiquitous, linking leadership.

To create organizational democracy, the change process has to be congruent with the values that guide the system, and the deeper the change is, the more these values prove useful. Democratic change subtly depends on leaders' intentions, unity among followers, clarity of vision, handling of diversity, honesty of feedback, and other elements that cannot be managed. The more revolutionary the change, the more it must be led and the less it can be managed.

The change process is automatically democratized by involving employees in defining their shared values; strategically planning their futures; opening communications regarding goals, process, and relationships; inviting feedback, coaching, and mentoring; evaluating and assessing progress; and challenging assumptions about what is possible and acceptable.

Research regarding the change experiences of large corporations, e-commerce start-ups, universities, schools, nonprofit organizations, community groups, and government agencies reveal the following lessons in planning the change process:

- Change always generates feelings of loss, insecurity, and fear, which need to be aired and overcome.
- People resist change because they do not feel a need for it or have not been listened to or had their objections answered.

Figure 15.3. Possible Outcomes of Strategic Integration.

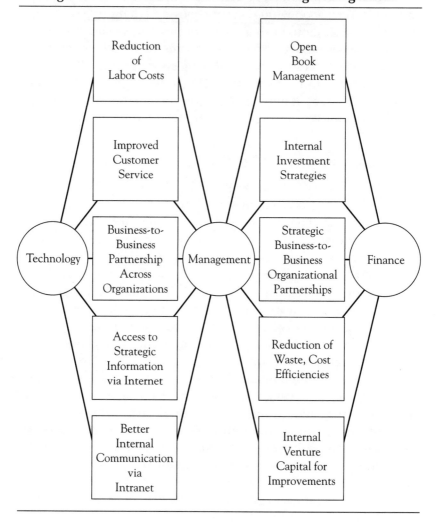

- No one wants to "be" changed, but everyone wants to learn, grow, and become more effective.
- People resist when they do not know where change is headed or when goals have not been collaboratively or clearly identified.
- In every change, there is a period of transition in which nothing is clear and no one is satisfied.
- Vision, courage, persistence, teamwork, and leadership are required to get through periods of transition.
- Change often means shifting the way things are done on a small scale and minutely targeting specific human behaviors.
- For change to last, reinforcing cultures and systems must also be changed.
- Change efforts need to be coordinated among diverse constituencies where local variability is the rule.
- Full involvement and the ability to make choices fuel the change process, causing most pilot projects to succeed and most models to fail.
- Changing part of a system changes the system as a whole.
- The effects of change last long after the change is over and need to be addressed as much as the change itself.
- Change takes place more smoothly when feedback, evaluation, and self-correction are built into the process.

All change holistically affects the system in which it occurs, much like a wave or ripple on a pond. Even a small change in a period of crisis can produce an enormous impact because chaos multiplies sensitivity and unpredictability, making few outcomes predictable. At the same time, change is an attribute of power, and power is measured in strength and cohesion. Thus, there is a strong relationship between democratic change processes and the ability to coalesce the forces that will support it and reduce those that oppose it or favor the status quo. The broader the coalition supporting the change and the greater the internal cohesion, the more powerful will be the effect, making the top priority for change agents the building of broad, deep coalitions with clear, unified visions. Yet the broader the coalition, the more difficult it is to create the internal cohesion required for the change to succeed.

Advice for Democratic Change Agents

Those who seek to expand organizational democracy need to make their means as well as their ends transparent, human, understandable, and personal. They need to make the change congruent with ethics, values, history, logic, and self-interest. They need to be willing to face criticism and hostility, and to beware of the twin narcotics of power and praise. As Jean Cocteau wrote of those seeking change, "The instinct of nearly all societies is to lock up anybody who is truly free. First, society begins by trying to beat you up. If this fails, they try to poison you. If this fails, they finish by loading honors on your head."

Democratic change agents also have a special obligation to avoid making unnecessary enemies. They can do so by combining opposition to the old system with unconditional acceptance of those who are stuck in it, and looking for ways of changing not only the content but the processes that encode and recreate it. They can do so by supporting diversity and unity, independence and collective action, individuality and community, difference of opinion and consensus; by establishing links with people outside the organization; and by creating an integrated way of changing.

By accepting people wherever they are in relation to the old system, looking for ways of helping them move forward, and not judging them for where they were or how far they moved, democratic change agents can travel further, faster, and more fully than autocratic change managers. Democratic change agents create a sense of community and mutual acceptance that situates the change in an open, hospitable environment. They progress from simple to complex changes and from small, acceptable reforms to revolutionary transformations.

Democratic change agents also have a special obligation to protect themselves from the arrogance and narcotic of power that emanate from the change process, as well as from false leadership, attitudes of self-righteousness and entitlement, and the corruption of task-oriented sacrifice in the name of expediency and results. They need to recall that leadership is a relationship with those who follow and that a good leader is one who catches up quickly with the "followers" once they begin to move. They need to be able to lighten the process, sing and dance, and enjoy the process of change. Here is some advice for democratic change agents, drawn from our book *Thank God It's Monday!*

- *Walk your talk.* Be consistent. Practice what you preach, and let them see you do it when it counts. If you cannot, let them hear you acknowledge it, learn from it, and try to do better next time.
- *Don't drink the water.* Do not let the negativity that infects the organization get you down. Do not get trapped in self-defeating, apathetic, cynical cultures produced by the old paradigm, whose purpose is to discourage participation in change.
- *Fix systems rather than people.* Rather than focusing on changing people, change the systems that shape how they behave and relate to one another. Both problems and solutions have systemic roots, and the change process is easier when you concentrate on the ways a system rewards negative behaviors rather than the personalities of people who have been trapped by that system.
- *Changing yourself automatically changes others.* You are also part of the system. If you change, everyone else has to change as well. They will need to reexamine how they relate to you and how they deal with one another when they are around you. Changing some of the ways an organization operates results in changing the system as a whole.
- *There is no such thing as neutral observation.* Just looking at a problem initiates the process of changing it. If you observe a problem or system long enough, you call attention to it, and the solutions start to arise.
- *Look with peripheral vision; use a floodlight as well as a spotlight.* Look at all aspects of the situation. What is directly in front of you may not be the entire story. Use a floodlight to observe the surrounding area and a spotlight to zero in on specifics. Change needs to be global and systemic, but it also needs to reach the smallest level to be successful. Often, the smallest details make or break a change effort.
- *Float like a butterfly; sting like a bee.* Be open and flexible yet focused and hard hitting. Stay on your toes so you do not get knocked over by problems. Be deeply honest about what is not working, but do not blame others or get stuck on a single solution.
- *Search for preventative opportunities.* It is easier to prevent a problem than to solve it repeatedly. Head off conflict with communication

and conciliation before it is needed. Design systems to prevent problems you know you are going to face or that send a warning sign that something is not right.

• *Go slow to go fast.* Use consensus, and make sure everyone is included and feels heard. Do not try to force decisions when it gets difficult. Stop and recognize you are stuck. Look at the interests of each side, and improve ideas or proposals before moving forward. Take a little longer to make it right.

• *Think of conflict as an opportunity for growth, improvement, and learning.* Do not suppress conflicts, but look for what can be learned from them. Define the new paradigm to which the conflict is pointing. Try to take issues to a deeper level and see conflict as an indication that you need to improve the way things are working or the level of skill you bring to solving problems.

• *Change "me versus them" into "us versus it."* Be hard on the problem and soft on the people. Shift the focus from personalities and people to problem solving and growth. See others not as enemies but as allies, and they will be more likely to respond with support than self-defense or counterattack.

• *Do not stand between an addict and their substance.* A frontal assault does not always work as well as an end run, particularly if you are dealing with someone who is addicted to problems, power, status, or job security. Model a different way of approaching problems by seeing them as challenges and opportunities. Do not fight battles over false issues or coerce people into doing it your way. The best strategy is to be honest about what you think is really happening, and let each person decide on the right response for himself or herself.

• *Be optimistic in your heart and realistic in your head.* Be open to your heart's message and your mind's logic. Hope for success, and recognize that it might not happen. Look for the intrinsic potential in each human being, but do not ignore their weaknesses. Use your heart to affirm and accept and your mind to understand and strategize.

• *Let go. Give up your expectations.* If you expect change to take place in a predictable way or for others to adopt your personal ideas or solutions, you may be disappointed. Allow the results of the change process to instruct you. The greater the openness, the greater the potential for change.

- *Different strokes for different folks.* You cannot mandate what matters to people. The same solutions do not work for everyone. Allow room for diversity, and see differences as a source of strength.
- *Change always takes longer than planned.* Double the planning time, and do not expect to make the target date. Renegotiate deadlines as you progress. Change takes whatever time it actually requires. How long it takes is based not on how soon you would like it to be completed, but how soon all the real requirements come into place.
- *Learn from each other.* Change efforts need to be coordinated, and diverse constituencies need to be united to succeed. Your greatest teachers should not be change gurus but other people.
- *Do not dominate the process; leave room for others.* You do not need to control the process or solve all the problems yourself. The best solutions are those that people create for themselves, because it is a way of owning them. Full involvement and the ability to choose between alternatives fuel the change process and develop leaders. Remember that leadership *adores* a vacuum.
- *There are no magic wands.* Most of what actually happens in change is discovered as it unfolds. The chaos in complicated change makes it inherently unpredictable. There are no formulas or blueprints or guarantees. Following someone else's blueprint leads you in a different direction from your own.
- *Do not be afraid of failure or success.* Do not let your self-doubts or fear of the unknown get in your way. Allow yourself to be successful by trying to make what you want actually happen. Let your fears dissolve by starting with small steps. In other words, *just do it!*

From Change Agents to Organizational Revolutionaries

In the October 2000 issue of *Fast Company,* former Secretary of Labor Robert Reich, critiquing traditional change management, called for redefining *change agents* as *change insurgents:*

> Change today happens suddenly, unexpectedly, unpredictably. It occurs in companies the way that we see it occur in biological systems or in technological breakthroughs: Change is sudden, non-linear, and constant. Its amplitude and direction can't be forecast. . . .

Companies that can't change in this new environment can't play in this new economy. Companies that can't change the way that they think about change won't be able to change the way that they compete. And hiring change agents, who used to carry the banner for change inside large companies, is no longer the right way to think about or to practice change.

Change today demands the change insurgent.

In order to integrate strategically across traditional organizational lines and change the way we change, it is necessary to move beyond even change insurgency, which implies a focus on power, to a revolutionary transformation in the nature of organizational power itself. This requires employees to shift from being change agents, or even change insurgents, to being organizational revolutionaries who seek to transform the way they bring about the changes they desire.

Changing the way we change requires the dismantling of organizational hierarchy, bureaucracy, and autocracy and using collaboration, democracy, and self-management to increase participation, motivation, unity, and responsibility. In the same way, changing the way we change means transforming, dismantling, and redistributing organizational power.

Organizational democracy requires that innovation, improvement, and adaptation take place throughout the organization. And just as leadership needs to be ubiquitous in self-managing organizations, so do the roles of change agent, change insurgent, and organizational revolutionary. All employees need to participate in revolutionizing the way they work and transforming the system that failed to see the need for change or responded to it hierarchically, bureaucratically, or autocratically. In order to do so, it is important to understand the deeper consequences of organizational democracy, collaboration, and self-management.

Chapter Sixteen

The Consequences of Organizational Democracy

The future business of businesses that have a future will be about subtle differences, not wholesale conformity; about diversity, not homogeneity; about breaking rules, not about enforcing them; about pushing the envelope, not about punching the clock; about invitation, not protection; about doing it first, not doing it "right"; about making it better, not making it perfect; about telling the truth, not about spinning bigger lies; about turning people on, not "packaging" them; and perhaps above all, about building convivial communities and knowledge ecologies, not leveraging demographic sectors.
CHRISTOPHER LOCKE, *The Cluetrain Manifesto*

Having contemplated the end of management, dissected its defects, and recommended practical ways of making organizations more collaborative, democratic, and self-managing, we acknowledge that we are describing fundamental, revolutionary transformations in the nature of organizations: what they are, how they function, and how they change.

In doing so, we want to move beyond the use of analytical reductionism as in other chapters, where we scrutinized problems with management or identified possible solutions. We recognize that we have separated, disengaged, detached, distinguished, and divided what are actually organic wholes in order to clarify, categorize, and recommend precise changes. We now want to consider not the superficial structures, systems, and strategies of organizations, but their zeitgeist—their spirits, souls, and quintessence—and the likely consequences of changing them.

The Consequences of Democratic Change

Perhaps the greatest consequence of organizational democracy lies not in the workplace but in the impact it is likely to have on society and politics. It is clear that without organizational democracy, there can be no fully effective system of political and social democracy, just as without political and social democracy, there can be no fully effective organizational democracy. Undemocratic management in organizations and undemocratic processes in politics and society are mutually reinforcing. They lead everywhere to corruption, abuse of power, internal opposition, inequality, bureaucratic rules, inefficiency, dishonesty, dependency, self-aggrandizement, irresponsibility, inflexibility, alienation, conflict, and waste.

Since the birth of Athenian democracy, we have known that the best form of government is self-government. If we believe people are entitled and capable of making decisions regarding their political futures and electing their political leaders, how can we deny them the right to make decisions regarding their economic futures and electing their organizational leaders? If we believe that all people are created equal and entitled to life, liberty, and the pursuit of happiness, how do we justify second-class citizenship and managerial tyranny in the workplace? If we believe in political government of, by, and for the people, must we not also accept organizational government of, by, and for the people?

It took centuries in the United States to extend citizenship to those who did not own property, to African Americans, and to women. Yet we still have not integrated the top ranks of organizations, eliminated the glass ceiling, or equalized pay for equal work. The democratization of organizations promises to provide a higher quality of work life for all employees; create a more integrated, egalitarian, democratic society; and realize the promise that was made in Athens nearly twenty-five hundred years ago.

Organizations and Social Responsibility

The full implementation of collaboration, democracy, and self-management will have consequences that go far beyond productive efficiency, agility, and constructive social values. When the paradigm of work changes, so must organizational design, and when these change, so must responsibility for societal outcomes and organizational values. These values include recognizing the primacy of human needs over economic gain, transforming organizations into collaborative associations, and placing social contribution and environmental responsibility on a higher level than competitive advantage.

Operating from a context of values, ethics, and integrity means making individuals, teams, and organizations responsible for the social, political, ecological, and ethical environments in which they work. Managed organizations with hierarchical, bureaucratic, autocratic structures were designed to insulate management from social responsibility. But responsibility is *always* personal and nondelegable, and when an organization, society, or nation assumes responsibility, individuals are let off the hook, and no one is held responsible.

Encouraging a larger sense of responsibility for the whole of society, rather than simply looking out for one's own organization, team, family, or self, can produce dramatic results that affect the entire infrastructure in which organizations operate. For example, in the United States, socially responsible work was legislated in response to the devastating impact of the Great Depression, and the Works Progress Administration (WPA) created during the Roosevelt administration compiled an extraordinary record of achievement, recorded in the *New York Times Magazine* in August 1996:

> In its eight-year existence, according to official records, the W.P.A. built or improved 651,000 miles of roads, 953 airports, 124,000 bridges and viaducts, 1,178,00 culverts, 8,000 parks, 18,000 playgrounds and athletic fields and 2,000 swimming pools. It constructed 40,000 buildings (including 8,000 schools) and repaired 85,000 more. Much of New York City—including LaGuardia Airport, F.D.R. Drive, plus hundreds of parks and libraries—was built by the W.P.A.

To measure the true impact of this work, we have to consider not only the structures that were built but the new work processes that were invented, the relationships that were forged, the skills that were developed, the organizational advantages that followed, and the lives of employees and families who were rescued from despair and improved through meaningful work. We have to include the satisfaction of having made a contribution to society, the positive effects on the lives of entire communities, the futures of millions of children, and the improved quality of all our lives today. Their work was a gift—not only to the present but to the future. It was an investment in unborn generations.

Some groups, such as Corporations for Social Responsibility, have contributed substantially to the well-being of their communities and encouraged employees in supporting social programs, but participation is thin, local, and limited. Why have so many organizations abdicated responsibility for socially responsible work to nonprofits and the federal government? Why has the federal government abdicated its responsibility for improving the quality of civil society?

The answer, we believe, is partly that social and environmental responsibility are seen by many organizations as running counter to immediate financial gain and competitive advantage. And as political novelist Upton Sinclair remarked, "It is difficult to get a man to understand something when his salary depends upon his not understanding it." The primary barrier to expanded organizational responsibility, we believe, is the drive for economic dominance and competitive advantage that is part of the adversarial managerial paradigm. This barrier reaches devastating social and ecological proportions in the form of globalization.

Values, Globalization, and the Limits of Economic Self-Interest

Globalization is a process of economic expansion dedicated to the elimination of virtually all barriers to competitive economic exchange, whether they are social, cultural, environmental, ethical, legal, financial, or political. Every nation's products, services, resources, artifacts, and ideas increasingly are being forced to compete in the world market. Success in this competition is measured by profitability, which is the ratio of monetary returns to costs of production.

The costs of production for any product or service include not only wages but taxes and the economic, social, political, cultural, and organizational systems that keep them competitive. The fact of competition is being used to encourage nations and corporations to reduce wage guarantees, cut social supports, and destroy the environment in order to maximize productivity. Human rights, living wages, safe working conditions, and environmental protections are seen as unnecessary costs that reduce global competitiveness.

The primary values that emerge from this process are those that support a race for the bottom and economic domination. These translate practically into an unchecked drive to increase output, slash wages and environmental expenditures, and jettison social programs that fail to result in increased profitability. Human values, social needs, economic sustainability, environmental protection, craftsmanship, and cultural traditions become secondary to the maximization of economic advantage and the generation of profits.

These problems result not from international economic development and investment but from unchecked competition based on private profit. What we call globalization is actually the domination of the world economy by multinational corporations from the Northern Hemisphere, especially the United States, in order to transfer wealth from the poor to the rich, both domestically and internationally. Globalization diminishes responsibility for the damage it causes to individuals, cultures, and the sustainability of life on the planet.

To counteract this destructive force, we face a critical need at a global level to create new forms of economic organization that are simultaneously values based, productively efficient, and able to produce high-quality, competitive products without destroying the environment, degrading human life, or disfiguring indigenous cultures. Without values, our very successes will be transformed into failures, our growth into destruction, and our progress into barbarism.

Creating sustainable forms of economic development means determining when and where economic growth will stop and when it will be restrained from overrunning and defeating human and environmental values. Without such limits on economic expansion, there will be no end to greed. There will never be enough. The ecological imperative of our time is to decide what is *not* for sale.

Ultimately, this comes down to a question of values, which are primarily a question of limits, defined partly by what one will not do. But ethics and values also have a positive side, which consists less in having what we want and more in being who we want to be. The focus of competitive economics is on *having* and *doing;* the focus of values such as collaboration, democracy, self-management, and environmental sustainability is on *being.* Each is important, but in globalization, only the former is used to measure success.

There are four significant ways of limiting unregulated economic expansion and globalization in relation to environmental impact: first, by completely exhausting the environment and depleting natural resources; second, by shifting political direction through international protest and deepening understanding; third, by response to a global economic crisis; and fourth, by creating socially acceptable limits to environmental degradation and exploitation based on values. In essence, a clearly articulated, publicly maintained sense of ecological and social values is the only stopping place short of environmental or social catastrophe.

To understand the unforeseeability of environmental catastrophe, consider the following mathematical example drawn from science writer K. C. Cole's *The Butterfly and the Teacup.* Assume a bottle with two bacteria inside it, which double in population every minute. By the end of one hour, they completely fill the bottle. How much warning will the bacteria have that their expansion is about to end and they will reach their limit of a full bottle? The answer is none, or at most one minute, because with one minute remaining, the bottle is still only half full. Even if they move to a second bottle, it will fill up in just one more minute. This is not to assert that human populations double or that Malthus was correct, but that with regard to the environment, we could be a minute short of filling our first bottle without a second one in sight.

The Consequences of Organizational Democracy

If we are going to halt environmentally destructive growth and unregulated globalization, we need to agree to limit economic expansion. In order to do so, some yet-to-be-imagined form of transnational democracy will be required. Among the main obstacles to creating this democracy are the hierarchical, bureaucratic, autocratic, global corporations that benefit financially from unregulated competition and that use their immense transnational resources to command national governments, curb environmental protections, and block democratic change. Every increase in organizational democracy reduces the strength of these obstacles.

Over the past several hundred years, capitalism has made human labor power efficient beyond anyone's wildest expectations. At the same time, it has created a system of management that encourages adversarial labor-management relations, competition, organizational isolation, and divisions between owners, managers, employees, and society. As productivity has increased, the accumulation of wealth has become more dependent not only on technology but on collaboration, ubiquitous leadership, and self-management—in other words, on organizational democracy.

Thus, a significant shift has taken place as the production and distribution of goods and services has been internationalized, and colossal transnational corporations have come to dominate national economies and the lives of indigenous people. Many of these conglomerates have annual sales larger than the gross national products of all but a few of the world's countries. As the world market and international production have grown beyond the capacity of individual owners to supervise, control by shareholders has become increasingly passive and oriented to achieving a return on investment, and organizational administration has been left in the hands of managers.

At the same time, as industrial technology has developed, ownership has not only become increasingly separated from management, it has become increasingly *superfluous*. Ownership has long ceased being productive or adding any value to products and services other than investment and operating capital. Owners have effectively been stripped of the ability to direct the organizations they economically own but do not practically control.

In a similar way, management is becoming increasingly expendable. A combination of independent decentralized services, technological innovation, collaborative relationships, self-regulatory processes, and self-managing teams has proven highly successful in solving operational problems and making management increasingly unnecessary. Historically, control over the economy and political power first passed from owners to bureaucratic managers and administrators, effectively disenfranchising employees and the public. A second transition is now taking place in which control over economics and politics is being further democratized and passed directly to teams of employees and linking leaders who perform the work and whose lives are directly affected by these decisions.

Indeed, there are sound financial reasons for doing so. Dramatic increases in technological productivity have spawned an oversized population of unproductive middle managers who live off the surpluses created by other people's productive labor and whose salaries result in nothing that has tangible economic value. As competition in the world market increases and margins of profitability fall, the effort to reduce production costs escalates. These efforts include process mapping, quality circles, and transferring managerial functions to self-managing teams.

Each of these shifts reflects the increasing obsolescence of hierarchical forms of organization and evolution in the direction of collaboration, democracy, and self-management. Under democratic forms of organization, management and labor become universal and general, followed by ownership. Just as political democracy makes every citizen a ruler by inviting people to participate in political discourse and expanding the base of political decision making, self-management makes every employee an owner by including employees in economic decision making.

When we choose our work and decide how it is to be done, we come to see it as an end in itself and gain access to the most powerful motivational device ever invented: love, made tangible through chosen work. Our deepest motivation comes from the heart yet is also based in common sense. Although organizations do not have hearts *or* common sense, the people who work in them do, and increasingly it is their choices that matter.

As we create organizations where people listen to their hearts and follow their common sense, we reaffirm two essential truths: that work is both a manifestation and a means of happiness and love and that we create ourselves through work by contributing to others and to society. Finally, it is love not simply of self but of self in relationship with others and the desire to express this love through work that ends management and gives rise to organizational democracy.

We close not with logic or argument but with poetry, which always says it better. As Sigmund Freud wrote, "Everywhere I go I find a poet has been there before me." We leave the final words to Marge Piercy:

I want to be with people who submerge
in the task, who go into the fields to harvest
and work in a row and pass the bags along,
who are not parlor generals and field deserters
but move in a common rhythm
when the food must come in or the fire be put out.
The work of the world is common as mud.
Botched, it smears the hands, crumbles to dust.
But the thing worth doing, well done
has a shape that satisfies, clean and evident.
Greek amphoras for wine or oil,
Hopi vases that held corn, are put in museums
but you know they were made to be used.
The pitcher cries for water to carry
and a person for work that is real.

Acknowledgments

We want to acknowledge our own webs of association: the countless colleagues who inspire us with their commitment to living the transformations we only describe. We acknowledge our teacher, mentor, and friend, Heinz von Foerster, whose clear, impeccable integrity, discerning mind, and joyous wit have enlightened and sustained us. We thank our dear friend Warren Bennis, whose warmth, creativity, and empowering ideas have helped us craft and hone our thinking about leadership and democracy set forth in this book. Our special thanks also go to Peggy Dulany, whose vision of bridging leadership and commitment to fostering international partnership have led to many of the ideas expressed in this book.

We thank the many outstanding organizational leaders and original thinkers with whom we have had the pleasure of working and whose ideas have contributed to this book, including our brothers who are also partners in our work, Steve Goldsmith and Bill Cloke, Sidney Rittenberg, George Rusznak, Tom Gerrity, Joan Dunlop, Ken Anbender, Michael Johnston, Steve Heffernan, Lance Dublin, Josy Callagher, Ann Overton, Allan Cohen, Adam Urbanski, Ellen Dempsey, Eileen Brown, Blenda Wilson, Lewis Fair, Ron O'Conner, Marsha Shiff, Jerry Cooper, Jerry Scro, and our friend Dick Beckhard, who recently died.

We are grateful to our friends and colleagues working in countries in the Southern Hemisphere who inspire us with their courage and creativity in bringing new solutions to problems we have not yet conquered, including Roberto Mizrahi, Wanda Engel Advan, Gustavo Esteva, Fernando Remirez de Estenoz, Mariela Columbié, Angel Luis Protoundo, Ariel Ricardo, Enrique Oltuski, Arturo Rodriguez, Loly Hernández, Aurora Fernandez, Oneida Alvarez, Roberto Puyada, Oscar Oramas, Maria Antonia Fernández, Fernando Vecino, Rudolfo Alarćon, Marcus Portal, Jesus Perez Oton, Rudolfo Martinez,

Antonio Romillo, Sithembiso Nyoni, and Rose Mazula, to name only a few.

Our thanks also to our agent, Michael Cohn, whose belief in our work has been sustaining. Our editor, Susan Williams, and our copyeditor, Beverly Miller, have enabled our voice to be heard, as have our faithful indexer, Carolyn Thibault, and our insightful proofreader, Miriam Goldsmith. We also thank Solange Raro and Grace Silva, whose loyalty, commitment, and support make all the difference. Finally, we want to acknowledge Elka, Nick, Shetu, Tinku, Soraya, Sam, Kristen, and Glen, who teach us to value democracy, manage ourselves, be leaders in our lives, and take responsibility for ourselves and the world around us.

The Authors

Kenneth Cloke is director of the Center for Dispute Resolution. He is a mediator, arbitrator, consultant, and trainer, specializing in resolving complex multiparty conflicts. He is a nationally recognized leader in the field of conflict resolution. His consulting and training practice includes organizational change, leadership, communication, conflict resolution, negotiation, team building, and strategic planning. He is the author of many journal articles and books, including *Mediation: Revenge and the Magic of Forgiveness* and *Mediating Dangerously: The Frontiers of Conflict Resolution.* He is coauthor with Joan Goldsmith of *Thank God It's Monday! Fourteen Values We Need to Humanize The Way We Work, Resolving Conflicts at Work: A Complete Guide for Everyone on the Job,* and *Resolving Personal and Organizational Disputes: Stories of Transformation and Forgiveness.* He received a B.A. from the University of California at Berkeley; a J.D. from the University of California's Boalt Law School; a Ph.D. from the University of California at Los Angeles (UCLA); and an L.L.M. from UCLA Law School; and has done postdoctoral work at Yale Law School. He is a graduate of the National Judicial College in Reno, Nevada. His university teaching includes law, mediation, history, and other social sciences at a number of colleges and universities.

Joan Goldsmith is an organizational consultant and educator, specializing in leadership development, organizational change, conflict resolution, team building, and information systems. From 1985 to 1990 as a principal with CSC Index, she directed Index China, developing business bridges between the United States and China, and assisted Fortune 100 clients in business reengineering, change management, and human resource development. In addition to being coauthor with Kenneth Cloke of the previously mentioned books, she is coauthor with Warren Bennis of *Learning to Lead: A Workbook on Becoming a Leader.* She is founder of a national program for women in leadership development, "Women Leaders: Creating Ourselves at the Crossroads." She has been a family therapist and serves on the boards of directors of three national organizations. She is an associate of the Synergos Institute, which builds collaborative partnerships to end poverty in the Southern Hemisphere, and has been an adviser in organizational development and school reform to school districts in major cities. She is cofounder of Cambridge College and a former member of the faculties of Harvard University, UCLA, and Antioch University. She holds a doctorate in humane letters.

Index